44930

SKELETONS IN OUR CLOSET

Skeletons in Our Closet

Revealing Our Past through Bioarchaeology

CLARK SPENCER LARSEN

PRINCETON UNIVERSITY PRESS

PRINCETON AND OXFORD

Library of Congress Cataloging-in-Publication Data

Larsen, Clark Spencer.
Skeletons in our closet : revealing our past through
bioarchaeology / Clark Spencer Larsen.
p.   cm.
Includes bibliographical references and index.
ISBN 0-691-00490-0 (alk. paper)
1. Human remains (Archaeology). 2. Human skeleton—Analysis.
3. Population—History. 4. Human geography. I. Title.
CC77.B8 L375 2000
930.1—dc21   99-053724

This book has been composed in Janson

The paper used in this publication meets
the minimum requirements of
ANSI/NISO Z39.48-1992 (R1997)
(*Permanence of Paper*)

www.pup.princeton.edu

Printed in the United States of America

10 9 8 7 6 5 4 3 2

TO R. CLARK MALLAM
(1940–1986)

who helped me get started

CONTENTS

PREFACE

I HAVE always been interested in just about anything ancient, especially people—their activities, the difficulty of their lifestyles, what they ate, how they lived, and what their health was like. As a child, I was a frequent visitor with my family to the Homestead National Monument—the site of the first 160-acre land claim following passage of legislation signed by President Lincoln in 1862—located a few miles outside my hometown of Beatrice, Nebraska. Surrounded by seemingly endless cornfields in the rolling and nearly treeless terrain of the southeastern part of the state, Beatrice has few draws, but the "Homestead" has a wonderful little museum containing all types of pioneer and Indian artifacts. From my many visits to the museum, I channeled my interest in old things into archaeology, a branch of the field of anthropology; I wanted to become an anthropologist.[1]

While I was in high school, I met archaeologist Clark Mallam, who was about to start teaching at Luther College in Decorah, Iowa. Clark had grown up in Wymore, a small town just down the road from Beatrice, and he knew a great deal about local history and archaeology. He offered me some advice: Get myself onto an archaeological field project. He suggested that I contact Carl Jones, staff archaeologist for the Nebraska State Historical Society in Lincoln. I wrote to Carl, who sent me an application and an accompanying letter saying that he was hiring a crew to work for the summer at the site of an early frontier fort—Fort Atkinson—located on the Missouri River, north of Omaha. During its occupation in the 1820s, this was the most remote American military outpost on the western frontier, and served as the largest United States garrison at the time. I completed and returned the application, and much to my delight, Carl hired me. Soon after my graduation from high school in June 1970, I joined the other members of the crew in Lincoln for the trip to the site.

After setting up camp on a high bluff overlooking the Missouri River valley, our crew began work, mostly digging in the floors and foundations of the military barracks located along the perimeter of the fort palisade. The work that summer turned out to be tough stuff—the physical labor was backbreaking, the hot and humid weather was unrelenting, and our discoveries were unexciting (to the other members of the crew, anyway), consisting mostly of old nails, bottle fragments, and bricks. The tedium of the work was inconsequential to me, however—I was doing archaeology.

One event stood out that summer that was to help direct my future interest in ancient bones. Halfway through the eight-week field season, on an especially miserably hot day in mid-July, a crew member working next to me unearthed some old bones with his trowel in an area located adjacent to the foundation to the fort barracks. Carl carefully examined the find, identifying the bones as part of a human skull. He pointed out subtle features that indicated the age, sex, and race of the individual; the skull was from a young adult female, probably of European ancestry. Carl speculated that the woman had been either a spouse of one of the officers or, perhaps, one of the many laundresses who lived and worked at the fort. Whoever she was, I was transfixed by the presence of these remains that were staring up at me. Here were the bones of someone who had once been alive, and whose skeleton—at least part of it, anyway—had ended up inside the walls of the fort. What were her remains doing there in the first place? Her location within the fort itself was puzzling to us, especially because the official cemetery for soldiers and other persons was located well outside the fort. Moreover, why were only parts of her skull present, and not the rest of her skeleton? Was there more to learn about this person besides her age, sex, and race? Did she die of some disease, perhaps one of the cholera epidemics that passed through the fort periodically? How did her lifestyle differ from my lifestyle as a twentieth-century American? Because I was then merely a young student, I did not yet have the tools to investigate these questions further, but my imagination had been ignited.

My work at Fort Atkinson and the discovery of human remains there fostered my growing fascination with archaeology, and it kindled my interest in physical anthropology, the branch of anthropology that includes the study of ancient bones and teeth. I knew that people made a living from doing archaeology, but I began to wonder if I could do both archaeology and physical anthropology, combining two branches of anthropology.

With the completion of my first field experience at Fort Atkinson, I enrolled as an anthropology major at Kansas State University. In my freshman year, my professor and mentor, Patricia O'Brien, suggested that I take a course in human osteology from William M. Bass. Bass, one of the leaders in the field, was then on leave from the University of Kansas and was a visiting professor at Kansas State before beginning his new appointment as head of the anthropology department at the University of Tennessee. I signed up for the course, and within a few short months, I learned a great deal about basic bone and tooth identification, how to age and sex skeletons, and some of the fundamentals of the field that would later become known as bioarchaeology. Moreover, a project in his class led to my first scientific publication, co-authored with a classmate.[2]

Bass must have been pleased with what I had accomplished in his osteology course. He secured a place for me on an archaeological field project for the upcoming summer excavating skeletons near Mobridge, South Dakota, working under the direction of two prominent Smithsonian Institution scientists, Douglas H. Ubelaker and T. Dale Stewart. I could not believe my good fortune. Studying with Bass in the classroom and digging with Ubelaker and Stewart in the field, all within a period of a few months, were too good to be true. These three individuals—Bass, Ubelaker, and Stewart—were among the most knowledgeable physical anthropologists in the world about the excavation and study of archaeological human skeletal remains. By the time I returned from the field for the fall term, my interest in studying human bones and teeth was firmly entrenched. Little did I realize, at age nineteen, the importance of these early formative experiences, setting the stage not just for my interests that would eventually lead to a doctoral dissertation at the University of Michigan, but also for the course of my entire life.

WHAT THE BOOK IS ABOUT

This book is *not* about how anthropologists go about the business of determining age, sex, race, facial reconstruction, or other aspects of human identification, those areas of study that typically come under the purview of forensic anthropology.[3] Rather, I present in the following pages a nontechnical and personal account of what we have learned about the lives and lifestyles of earlier peoples—our ancestors—from their bones and teeth. I convey in this book a new approach to reconstructing human life in past cultures and past times, a multidisciplinary approach that combines several branches of anthropology—archaeology, biological anthropology, and sociocultural anthropology—and other scientific disciplines (such as molecular genetics, biology, physics, engineering, and chemistry). The most important lesson that I have learned from studying the skeletal remains of thousands of people from around the world is the dynamic nature of our biology and the awesome adaptability of our species. Reflecting this adaptability, I explore in this book the demands and consequences of different lifestyles and critical adaptive shifts in past human beings, resulting in who we are today. In a nutshell, the biology of our past has played an enormous role in shaping the biology of modern human life.

NOTES

1. American anthropology is traditionally divided into four subfields or branches—archaeology, physical (or biological) anthropology, cultural (or social) anthropology, and linguistic anthropology. This book deals with a combination of archaeology and physical anthropology.

2. K. Hart and C. S. Larsen (1972) Skeletal remains from the Utlaut site. *Missouri Archaeologist* 34:67–75.

3. Some excellent technical books on forensic anthropology and human oste-ology include: Shipman et al.'s and White's books provide good overviews of bone biology. Hillson's book gives an important overview of human teeth and how they are studied by anthropologists. Gerasimov's book, one of my all-time favorites, deals with facial reconstruction and identification from human skulls. My book listed in the references below is a technical treatment of bioarchaeol-ogy. Popular accounts of forensic anthropology are presented by Joyce and Stover, Maples and Browning, and Ubelaker and Scammell. Bass's and White's books are thorough overviews of human osteology.

REFERENCES

Bass, W. M., (1995) *Human Osteology: A Laboratory and Field Manual*, 4th edition. Columbia: Missouri Archaeological Society.

Gerasimov, M. M. (1971) *The Face Finder*. London: Hutchinson & Co.

Hillson, S. (1996) *Dental Anthropology*. Cambridge: Cambridge University Press.

Joyce, C., and Stover, E. (1991) *Witnesses from the Grave: The Science of Identi-fying Human Remains*. London: Bloomsbury Publishing.

Larsen, C. S. (1997) *Bioarchaeology: Interpreting Behavior from the Human Skele-ton*. Cambridge: Cambridge University Press.

Maples, W. R. and Browning, M. (1994) *Dead Men Do Tell Tales*. New York: Doubleday.

Shipman, P., Walker, A., and Bichell, D. (1985) *The Human Skeleton*. Cam-bridge: Harvard University Press.

Ubelaker, D. H. (1989) *Human Skeletal Remains: Excavation, Analysis, Interpre-tation*, 2nd edition. Washington: Taraxacum.

Ubelaker, D. H. and Scammell, H. (1992) *Bones: A Forensic Detective's Casebook*. New York: Edward Burlingame Books.

White, T. D. (1991) *Human Osteology*. San Diego: Academic Press.

ACKNOWLEDGMENTS

MANY agencies, colleagues, and friends were instrumental in all that entered into the writing of this book. First and foremost, I owe a huge debt of gratitude to my research collaborators, especially Dale Hutchinson, Mark Griffin, Katherine Russell, Margaret Schoeninger, Mark Teaford, Chris Ruff, Scott Simpson, Nik van der Merwe, Joe Ezzo, Michael Schultz, Rika Kaestle, and David Smith. I also thank my students, past and present, who were active in the research in so many ways: Becky Shavit, Dale Hutchinson, Shawn Philips, Matt Williamson, Leslie Sering, Mark Griffin, Anastasia Papathanasiou, Katherine Russell, Inne Choi, Joanna Lambert, Dawn Harn, Hong Huynh, Elizabeth Moore, Marianne Reeves, Liz Monahan, Ann Kakaliouras, Tiffiny Tung, and Celeste Gagnon. I collaborated with archaeologists on several key field projects discussed in the book: in the Stillwater Marsh, Nevada, with Bob Kelly; on St. Catherines Island, Georgia, with Dave Thomas; on Amelia Island, Florida, with Ken Hardin, Jerry Milanich, and Becky Saunders; at Mission San Luis de Apalachee in Tallahassee, Florida, with Bonnie McEwan; and at the Cross Homestead site in Illinois with Joe Craig. These collaborations have been ideal in every way.

Most of my research has been funded by the National Science Foundation over the last decade and a half. I thank the Edward John Noble and the St. Catherines Island Foundations for support of fieldwork on St. Catherines Island, Georgia, and especially the interest shown by Mr. and Mrs. Frank Y. Larkin in my work over the years. On St. Catherines Island, former superintendent John Toby Woods Jr. and current superintendent Royce Hayes gave logistical support. I gratefully acknowledge all of their help over the years, especially in facilitating fieldwork in one of the most beautiful places in the world. I thank Dr. and Mrs. George Dorion for their generous support of the fieldwork on Amelia Island, Florida. Anan Raymond and the United States Fish and Wildlife Service were enormously helpful in doing bioarchaeological fieldwork in western Nevada. The American Museum of Natural History, the University of Florida, the Florida Bureau of Archaeological Research, and the National Endowment for the Humanities also supported fieldwork and research.

From the start of my professional career, it was clear to me that research and teaching have a very special symbiotic relationship—each informs the other in many ways, and I cannot imagine doing one without the other. I acknowledge my home academic institutions and especially the hundreds of undergraduate and graduate students that I have had the privilege of teaching over the years, in chronological order, at Southeastern Massachusetts University (now University of Massachusetts-Dartmouth), Northern Illinois University, Purdue University, and the University of North Carolina, Chapel Hill. I finished writing the book manuscript while on temporary academic leave from the University of North Carolina and teaching at the University of California, Berkeley. Some of these institutions went to great lengths to see that I had laboratory space in which to do my work. At S.M.U., the administration converted what had once been the president's office into a laboratory, and Purdue University converted a classroom into a bioarchaeology lab at a time when classroom-to-laboratory conversions were prohibited, due to a shortage of classrooms on campus.

The critical evaluation of drafts of the manuscript by a number of readers greatly improved the content and clarity of the book. I am grateful to reviewers George Armelagos and Mary Powell for their many helpful suggestions and comments. Pat Lambert, Steve Churchill, Phil Walker, Bruce Winterhalder, Catherine Lutz, and Tiffiny Tung read the manuscript in its entirety, telling me what worked and what didn't. Brian Billman, Doug Ubelaker, and Joe Craig offered valuable comments on parts of the book. Chris Brest prepared the line drawings, and Tracy Baldwin designed the jacket cover.

The successful writing and production of a book is made possible only through a highly supportive press and a dedicated editor. I thank Princeton University Press and its former science editor, Jack Repcheck, for his encouragement along the way and his critical reading of the book manuscript at its various stages. Completion of the work was done with the able guidance and advice of current science editor Kristin Gager.

My wife, Christine, and son, Spencer, have shown enormous patience with me at the dinner table, on family vacations, and in other settings where I probably should have spent less time talking about bones and teeth.

Thank you all.

Chapel Hill, North Carolina
17 July 1999

SKELETONS IN OUR CLOSET

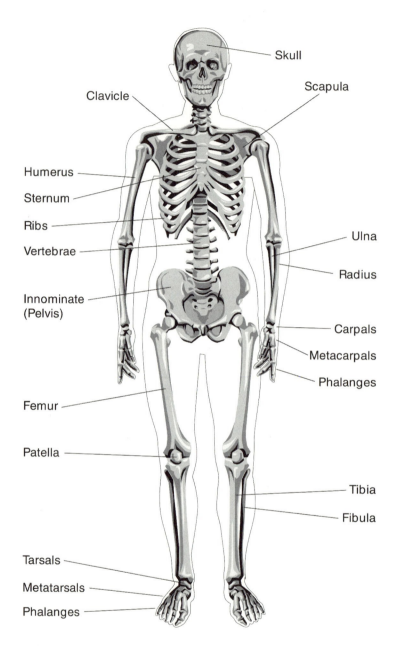

The human skeleton.

INTRODUCTION

*Tales from the Dead: What Bones Tell Us about
Our Past, and Why We Should Know*

IF ONLY the dead could talk. If they could talk, just imagine what
they could tell us about their lives, the foods they ate, the diseases
they experienced, and the stresses they encountered. In fact, from
the point of view of someone like me who studies bones and teeth,
the dead do talk in a way. Specifically, bones and teeth bear the
physical signs of a person's diet, disease, stress, and lifestyle—the
skeleton is a "voice" of the past.

In this book, I share with you some of the exciting break-
throughs in the emerging field of science called bioarchaeology,
the study of human biological remains from archaeological settings.[1] Bioarchaeology explores the lives and lifestyles of human
beings in the past. During a person's life, his or her skeleton is
sensitive to the environment, from well before birth through the
years of infancy, childhood, and adulthood. Our environment includes the foods we eat, the illnesses we experience, and the physical activities to which we expose our bodies. The ancient skeletons
studied by bioarchaeologists serve as a kind of a memory of the
environment. Each skeleton tells a unique and highly individualis-
tic story about the life of the person it represents. By studying the
individual stories, we are able to look at ancient skeletons as
though they were alive today, representing members of function-
ing, living populations.

Bioarchaeology is a multidisciplinary science. In recent years,
the field has developed methods for addressing important issues

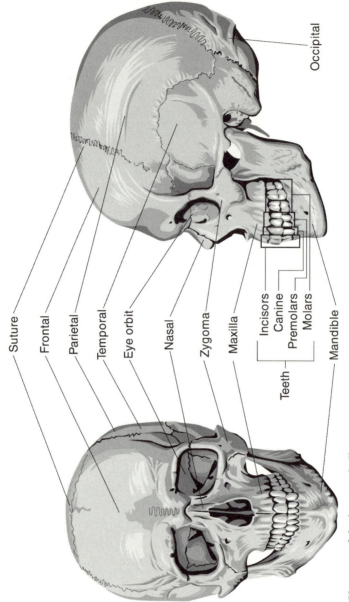

Suture

Frontal

Parietal

Temporal

Eye orbit

Nasal

Zygoma

Maxilla

Incisors

Canine

Premolars

Molars

Teeth

Mandible

Occipital

Close-up of the human skull.

about the human past, in part by drawing from methods worked out in other disciplines, such as chemistry, geology, physics, and biology, and within the subdisciplines of anthropology. The reader will see the strong influence of these various fields throughout this book—for example, we apply the study of stable isotopes in bone tissue to reconstruct diet, we use new and developing technology involving imaging methods from scanning electron microscopy and computed axial tomography (CAT or CT scans) to identify tooth use and bone shape, we analyze microscopic sections of bones and teeth to diagnose ancient diseases, and we extract ancient DNA from bone samples to help us identify population history. Importantly, bioarchaeologists seek to find out the cultural context of the populations they study in order to understand the broad implications of behavior on the skeletons they study. In a typical large bioarchaeological research project being undertaken today, it is no longer possible for one person to do all the work that is necessary for a comprehensive study of large samples of ancient skeletons. Simply, single individuals do not have the background and technical expertise for addressing complex issues relating to human biology in the past. The collaboration between scientists facilitates sharing of different knowledge bases and exchanging ideas that contribute to a broader and more informed perspective on the complexities associated with the study of the remote past. Thus, many of the projects I discuss—my own included—involve teams of scientists, with each member of the team bringing an area of expertise to the table that collectively helps to address an issue or problem.

How the Book Is Organized

The form and content of the book reflect personal interests that I have chosen to focus on in my own scientific career. I study adaptive transitions in recent human evolution, focusing on the Western Hemisphere, and viewing the transitions that took place in the Americas in a global perspective over the last ten thousand years. The evolution of our species is one of dynamic change, and the last ten thousand years are no exception. This book traces changes in our biology, especially relating to health and lifestyle, over this time frame.

For most of human history, people have been hunter-gatherers—what some anthropologists call foragers—depending exclusively on collecting wild plants and hunting animals for food. Many believe that foragers in prehistoric times had a difficult existence, barely able to eke out enough food to stay alive, and constantly moving from place to place in search of scarce resources. In the 1960s and 1970s, anthropologists began to think that perhaps prehistoric foragers had easier lives, with plenty to eat and living a leisurely lifestyle. Which of the two perspectives is the correct one? Through the study of ancient disease, biological stress, bone structure, and activity from bones and teeth, bioarchaeology allows us to assess whether past foragers had a difficult or an easy existence, or something between these two extremes.

One of the best settings in which to look at the health and quality of life of past hunter-gatherers is in the American Great Basin, a vast region encompassing a large chunk of the western United States. Anthropologists, archaeologists, and others have studied both prehistoric archaeology and the ethnographic present for quite some time. The wealth of information about native peoples—their behavior, culture, and society—provides a rich context for bioarchaeological study. Chapter 1 presents an overview of the history and archaeology of the Great Basin, building a backdrop for the study of ancient skeletons from a place called Stillwater in the western margin of the Great Basin. The findings from the study of these skeletons are discussed in chapter 2. The work done by my research collaborators and me indicate that life as a hunter-gatherer—at least in this setting—was a mixed picture, reflecting both the good times and the bad. Namely, the skeletons tell us that people worked extremely hard to acquire food and other resources, they experienced occasional food shortages and nutritional deprivation, but essentially, their health was reasonably good.

Beginning sometime at or slightly before about ten thousand years ago, when climates became essentially modern following the Ice Age (what geologists call the Pleistocene epoch), people began to domesticate plants and animals. Domestication took place independently in at least seven places worldwide, in Asia, Africa, and the Americas. The earliest center was in far western Asia, in a region called the Levant or Fertile Crescent. Over the next five to six thousand years, agriculture took on an increasingly important role in human survival and adaptation, and the idea and its consequences spread rapidly throughout Europe, Asia, and Africa. By the time Europeans arrived in the Americas, agriculture had spread throughout much of South America and North America, forming an essential part of adaptation. The invention and spread of agriculture comprised a major turning point in our history, setting the stage for urbanization and the rise of civilization, writing, complex societies, population explosion, and all the various characteristics that we associate with our modern world.

By most accounts, both scientific and popular, this turning point was a major improvement in the human condition, leading to what we think of as modern, good, and wholesome. Bioarchaeology is now in the process of rewriting these long-held conclusions about the so-called agricultural revolution. Indeed, as discussed from the perspective of my research in the American Southeast and the research of other bioarchaeologists working elsewhere in the world, we are learning that just the opposite occurred in our health and quality of life (chapters 3 and 4). Surely, agriculture laid the foundation for the major world civilizations, both in the past and in the present, but new insights provided by bioarchaeological study of ancient skeletons from around the globe is showing that there was a health cost to the shift from foraging to farming.

Foragers studied by bioarchaeologists had a health profile much like the Stillwater foragers—their health was generally good. After the shift to farming, quality of life declined—and greatly so in many regions of the globe. Bioarchaeology shows that the last ten thousand years have seen periods of pestilence, deprivation, and decline on an unprecedented level. People have had more infections, poorer health, more growth disruption, and more stress. We have developed problems with our teeth, such as increases in decay and crowding. Teeth have become poorly aligned and impacted to the point where chewing of food is often difficult. The changes in the foods we eat and how they are prepared have resulted in changes in our teeth and faces that are some of the most extreme in the history of our species. The biological changes that we see in humans in the last ten thousand years indicate that agriculture is one of the defining characteristics of our species, along with bipedalism and speech. The adoption of agriculture was a threshold point in the history of our health, and it set the stage for modern patterns of disease, especially the array of various chronic diseases that afflict our species.

The explosion in human population size during the Middle Ages—which was fueled, at least in part, by the invention of agriculture millennia before—may have been a catalyst for the spread of people across the Atlantic into the Americas and elsewhere following the "discovery" of the New World. Whatever the cause, the spread of Europeans around the world beginning soon after Columbus's landfall in the Americas represents another major transition in the history of the biology of our species. This population movement resulted in the exchange of diseases, foods, and cultures on a global scale, the likes of which had never been experienced before.

The study of the skeletons of the people contacted by Europeans in the centuries following the arrival of Columbus reveals a profound and long-lasting impact. The establishment of what historian Alfred Crosby has called the "Neo-Europes"—areas of the world that Europeans reframed into a European mold—resulted in widespread changes in the health and lifestyles of native, non-European peoples throughout the world. Heretofore, the impact of colonization on native peoples was known mostly from written sources, written by Europeans. Native voices were unheard. Skeletons offer a new and unique source of information that is only now being tapped, offering new perspectives about this important period of human history.

I have had a long-standing interest in the bioarchaeology of the contact period in North America, and especially in the American Southeast, where in the 1600s the Spanish crown established dozens of mission outposts among native groups, well before similar events occurred in other regions of northern New Spain, such as

Texas and California. In chapter 5, we look at this period of human colonization, discussing the context and setting for doing bioarchaeology of contact and understanding some of the profound health and lifestyle changes that took place in native populations, some of the earliest to be contacted by Europeans north of Mexico. Chapter 6 presents results of the study of contact-era skeletons from the perspective of a large, multidisciplinary research team I directed over the last couple of decades. We look specifically at what has been learned about the biology of the contact period from the study of the descendants of the Indians who underwent the transition from foraging to farming in the Georgia Bight, in the region called La Florida by imperial Spain. This long-term investigation reveals that the impact of European contact was complex, involving issues relating to dietary change, labor exploitation, harassment by the Spanish military, and social disruption. These factors and their consequences are far more complex than the singular focus on European-introduced epidemic disease and demographic collapse that is so (overly) emphasized by historians.

Our study reveals that a range of factors, and not any single cause, fueled the demographic changes in native populations during the first decades and centuries following the arrival of Columbus in 1492. Importantly, there were reductions in health and quality of life for native groups, but many survived and adapted to new challenges brought into motion by the arrival of Europeans. Native Americans remain a vital part of the social, cultural, and biological landscapes of the Western Hemisphere.

The impact of colonization was a two-way affair. As with native populations being contacted, the colonists experienced health and lifestyle changes as a result of settling new lands and adapting to unfamiliar terrain and the associated plants and animals. From the very beginning, the stresses of colonization were heavy. In the English colony of Jamestown, for example, mortality was truly horrific—of the 6,000 colonists who made the passage across the Atlantic Ocean to Virginia from England during the period of 1607 to 1625, only 1,200 survived beyond 1625. In chapters 7 and 8, I discuss what we have learned from the study of skeletons of Europeans and Euroamericans who first settled areas of North America previously inhabited exclusively by Native Americans. The settlement of the Chesapeake Bay region of Maryland and Virginia in the 1600s and, later, central Illinois in the early 1800s—both regions considered to be the extreme edge of the North American frontier during the periods of their settlement—represented hardship for most people involved. The life experiences of these colonists are displayed in vivid detail in their bones and teeth. Reflecting the hardships described in early accounts, the bones and teeth of these individuals bear the impressions of disease and heavy workloads—life was tough going for the early colonists. The study of their skeletons allows us to look at the details of changes in health, diet, and workload that have not been possible from historical records alone.

Most of the book focuses on a series of key transitions in the recent history of our species, especially in view of the outcome of these transitions for our health and well-being during the last ten thousand years. In the concluding chapter, I reflect back and take a look at motivations for making these transitions, especially what may have caused humans to make the shift from a way of life based on hunting wild animals and collecting wild plants to one based on plant and animal domestication. Although there were certainly benefits for humankind, this book provides a perspective on the accompanying costs.

In the final analysis, human remains from archaeological sites are important because they put otherwise missing faces on the past. Archaeological interpretations of artifacts, animal and plant remains, house structures, settlement patterns, and the like provide important images of life and living in the ancient past, but in imprecise terms. For example, it is possible to draw inferences about behavioral differences between men and women in the archaeological past, but in point of fact, it is not possible to distinguish sex in the archaeological record without skeletons. Only skeletons can provide that key information. These skeletons tell us that the last ten thousand years of our history have been a period of incredible change, especially involving health costs, new diseases, the spread of disease, major changes in diet and nutrition, and huge alterations in workloads and activities. Bioarchaeology opens a new window onto the past. In the following pages, we open that window wide and take a look inside the storehouse of information that bones and teeth provide about our past. We have much to learn from the dead.

Notes

1. The science that is concerned with learning about the past from the perspective of skeletons has been variously called osteology, osteoarchaeology, human zooarchaeology, archaeological skeletal biology, biological archaeology, osteobiographic analysis, and human skeletal analysis. All of these descriptors more or less adequately capture the content and focus of the field generally. Bioarchaeology was the term first used at a conference in 1976 by Jane Buikstra in reference to her study of prehistoric populations in the lower Illinois Valley of North America. It expresses the breadth and scope of the field and its emphasis on *biological* perspectives of the human past. Bioarchaeology includes the study of all past biological human remains. I have chosen to focus just on bones and teeth, which form most of the record of past human biology. A great deal of information is also available from the study of other types of remains, bodies partially or completely preserved by natural or intentional means, such as the bog bodies of northern Europe, the "Ice Man" from the Tyrolean Alps, and mummies in the American West, Japan, Greenland, Egypt, and elsewhere.

References

Crosby, A. W. (1986) *Ecological Imperialism: The Biological Expansion of Europe, 900–1900.* Cambridge: Cambridge University Press.

Larsen, C. S. (1997) *Bioarchaeology: Interpreting Behavior from the Human Skeleton.* Cambridge: Cambridge University Press.

Murphy, C. (1998) Jamestown revisited. *Preservation* 50(4):40–51.

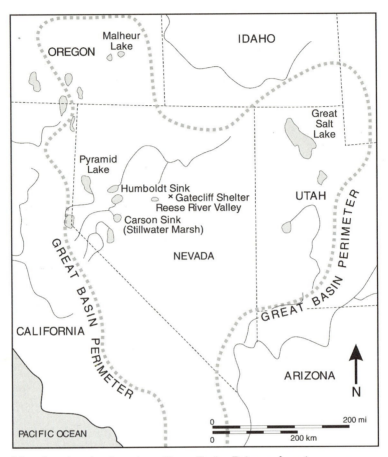

Map showing the American Great Basin. Primary locations mentioned in text include the Carson Sink (Stillwater Marsh), Malheur Lake, Great Salt Lake, Reese River Valley, and Gatecliff Shelter. Adapted from Larsen and Kelly 1995; reproduced with permission of the American Museum of Natural History.

1

The Lives and Lifestyles of Ancient Hunter-Gatherers: "Poor, nasty, brutish and short" in the American Great Basin?

FOR ALL but the last ten thousand years or so, our species has depended solely on wild plants and animals for food. In some regions of the world, this lifestyle continued until very recent times. In the American Great Basin, a vast region encompassing much of the western United States—including most of Nevada and parts of Utah, California, Oregon, Idaho, and Wyoming—native peoples have always lived exclusively on wild plants and animals, at least until relatively recent times. The study of the skeletal remains of these natives—viewed in the context of environment and culture—offers us insight into the quality of life that is associated with hunting and gathering. In this chapter, we look at what the study of skeletons of early hunter-gatherers can tell us about our past.

I began thinking about ancient foragers long before I began to look at archaeological skeletons from the Great Basin. In the summer of 1973, I was fortunate to participate in the National Science Foundation's Undergraduate Research Participation (URP) program, having been selected to work with David Hurst Thomas of the American Museum of Natural History on archaeological excavations that he was directing at Gatecliff Shelter, Nevada. Gatecliff is a deeply stratified archaeological site located in the desert of central Nevada, the heart of the American Great Basin. In fact, it is one of the most deeply stratified sites in the Western Hemisphere. I was thrilled to be able to gain experience in an area of the world that I knew nothing about, and at such an important archaeological site. The summer before, I had worked with Smithsonian Institution physical anthropologist Douglas Ubelaker as an URP summer intern in his excavations of skeletons from a late prehistoric ossuary in southern Maryland and in follow-up laboratory analysis. Although I could have continued to work solely on bones, I decided that it was more important at this early stage of my education to see a wide range of archaeological settings, especially before making decisions about how I would focus my graduate studies that would be coming up in a couple of years. Prehistoric Indians used Gatecliff mostly as a living site, and it contained none of their skeletal remains. However, I knew that my experience doing archaeology at the site would give me new and valuable perspective on the ancient past. I was not to be disappointed. Although arduous—the desert is not an especially hospitable place, and the labor was intensive at times—the work in Nevada that summer was terribly interesting and exciting.

Thomas was keenly interested in the prehistoric settlement systems and lifestyles of the Great Basin Shoshone Indians. His work showed that the prehistoric Shoshoneans who lived in the Reese River valley of central Nevada moved about the landscape according to the season of the year and availability of wild foods. The seasonal round involved harvesting nuts from forests of piñon pine (*Pinus monophylla*) trees in the mountains in the autumn. Piñon pine nuts were a highly nutritious food staple for Great Basin Indians; these nuts are high in fat, carbohydrates, and protein, and they sustained the local populations through the long winter months. During the winter, people moved very little from their upland homes. Once Indian rice grass (*Oryzopsis hymenoides*) ripened in the summer, small bands of foragers moved out of their mountain communities onto the valley floors for the summer harvest. Because the food sources on the valley floors were scattered in isolated patches, the summer camps moved frequently from one location to another. The eminent cultural anthropologist Julian

Steward identified this pattern of resource exploitation and seasonal mobility in Indians living in the area in the 1930s. Forty years later, Thomas's innovative research confirmed the pattern, and he suggested that this way of life had lasted for hundreds, if not thousands, of years.

In working with Thomas at Gatecliff, I began to ponder the questions and issues raised by archaeologists interested in human adaptation. I asked myself, could the study of skeletal remains of these ancient populations inform our understanding of prehistoric lifestyles in the Great Basin? Thomas's research was compelling, but wouldn't it also be important to increase the comprehensiveness of the research and tie in the special knowledge gained by the study of ancient skeletons? As a lowly undergraduate working with a team of seasoned archaeologists, I kept these thoughts to myself until such time that I could contribute substantively to the ongoing discussion of prehistoric Great Basin lifestyles.

From my training in physical anthropology, I began to think a lot about variation in lifestyles and adaptation in prehistoric Great Basin (and other) people. Thomas's work suggested that the prehistoric Shoshone were highly mobile foragers, taking advantage of a wealth of nondomesticated plant and animal resources in different ecological settings. Archaeologist Robert Heizer and his students at the University of California at Berkeley had been studying prehistoric Indians from farther to the west in the Great Basin, having excavated such famous sites as Lovelock Cave and surrounding sites in the Humboldt Sink. Contrary to Thomas's model of Great Basin adaptation, Heizer contended that native peoples relied on resources associated with permanent and semipermanent Pleistocene-remnant lakes of western Nevada (the lakes had long since disappeared in the central Great Basin). He believed that these populations lived fairly good lives, with plenty of plants and animals that lived along the margins of these lakes and associated wetlands. In contrast to the settlement pattern in central Nevada, native peoples in the Humboldt Sink region were apparently sedentary, with little individual or group movement— the lakes and their shores offered just about all anyone would need for a productive, if not healthy, existence.

After defending my doctoral dissertation at the University of Michigan in the summer of 1980, Thomas invited me to fly out to Nevada from Ann Arbor to see new excavations that he was conducting at a key western Great Basin site known as Hidden Cave, located almost within view of Heizer's research area in the Humboldt Sink. Overlooking the wide expanse of the Carson Sink, the site provides some tantalizing clues about Great Basin adaptation and lifestyle. Along with skeletal remains found by the earlier archaeologists excavating in the cave, Thomas's crews had found several dozen fragmentary bones and teeth that he wanted me to study.

Hidden Cave: Hints at Health and Lifestyle

Hidden Cave had apparently functioned for storage of tools and other essentials—a so-called cache site—used by a group of native peoples known in historic times as the Toedökadö (translated, "Cattail eaters"), a local band of Northern Paiute Indians. The presence of the skeletal remains in the cave was puzzling, especially since they didn't appear to be from a formal burial context—all the skeletal elements were separate and disarticulated. Regardless of the context of the human remains, the discovery of bones and teeth refueled my earlier interest in addressing issues relating to prehistoric biocultural adaptation in the Great Basin. For the remainder of the summer, I studied the bones and teeth from Hidden Cave.

In particular, I looked at three indicators in teeth and bones that are highly informative about the quality of life: hypoplasias, porotic hyperostosis, and infection. Hypoplasias are grooves, lines, or pits in the teeth that reflect periods of time when, due to either poor nutrition or disease (or some combination thereof), the outer covering of the tooth—the enamel—stops or slows in its growth. The cells that normally create the enamel—called ameloblasts—fail, and the hypoplasia caused by arrested growth results. The teeth that I looked at from Hidden Cave had only a moderate number of hypoplasias.

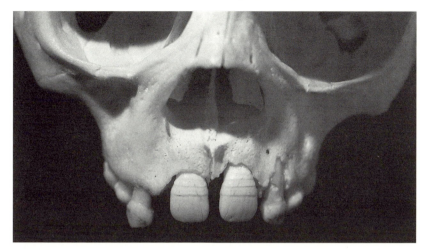

Maxillary teeth with enamel hypoplasias (horizontal grooves) on incompletely erupted permanent central incisors. Hypoplasias reflect periods of physiological stress and poor growth. Photograph by Barry Stark; from Larsen 1994, and reproduced with permission of Academic Press, Inc.

I next looked at the skull fragments for evidence of iron deficiency anemia; if this had been present in the population, it would be represented by bone pathology called porotic hyperostosis or cribra orbitalia. These pathological conditions are areas of porous bone in the flat bones of the skull, such as the parietals (porotic hyperostosis) or in the eye orbits (cribra orbitalia). They are created when red blood cell production increases, causing the bone to become porous. The increase in red blood cell production occurs when iron, an element required for the production of red blood cells, is deficient. Red blood cells, among their other functions, are absolutely necessary for transport of oxygen to the various body tissues. Without it, the tissues—and the person—are unable to function properly. Iron depletion occurs either as a result of some deficiency in diet, or chronic diarrhea, blood loss, or in many settings, parasitic infection. A number of parasites—such as hookworm—bleed the human host, resulting in loss of essential iron stores. None of the skull fragments I looked at had pathology reflecting iron deficiency.

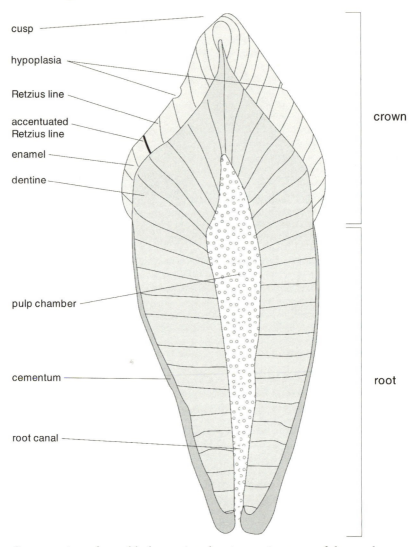

Cross-section of mandibular canine showing major parts of the tooth with enamel hypoplasia.

Last, I examined the bone fragments from Hidden Cave for presence of periosteal reactions. These reactions are abnormal growths on the periosteum, the outer surface of bones. Bioarchaeologists and paleopathologists are usually not able to provide a specific diagnosis—what caused the infection—but most are

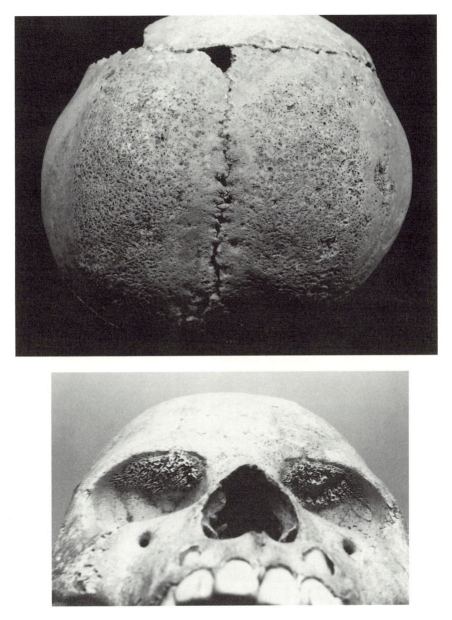

Porotic hyperostosis (top) and cribra orbitalia (bottom) in juvenile skulls. These conditions can be caused by iron deficiency anemia. Photographs taken by Mark C. Griffin; bottom photograph from Larsen 1994, and reproduced with permission of John Wiley and Sons, Inc.

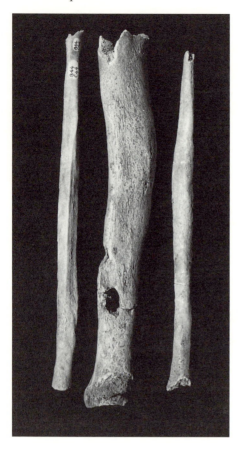

Adult tibia (middle) and left and
right fibulae with periosteal
reaction and inflammation,
probably due to infection.
The large hole in the tibia
is caused by drainage of pus.
Photograph by Mark C. Griffin.

caused by bacterial infections originating from the surrounding
soft tissue. Usually, the tibia (lower leg bone) is involved because
so little soft tissue separates the skin from the bone. Thus, if there
is a cut or abrasion to the skin of the lower leg and an infection
involving the skin and soft tissue ensues, the infection can then
readily pass to the bone.

Periosteal reactions are commonly found in skeletal samples
representing populations living in dense, crowded living situations
where sanitary conditions may have been poor. My survey of the
bone fragments—especially tibia fragments—showed no evidence
of periosteal reactions. Thus, based on this limited sample, infection did not seem to be a problem for these early hunter-gatherers.

What *was* striking about the skulls and teeth of the Hidden Cave
people was the sheer size of the faces and jaws, the very large areas

of muscle attachment for the chewing muscles, and the high degree of tooth wear and large numbers of chipped teeth. This pattern suggested to me that the masticatory complex was adapted for heavy chewing.[1] Lots of chewing demands big jaws, and heavy chewing of gritty, hard foods results in chipping and wear of teeth. Similarly, the postcranial bones, the area of the skeleton below the neck, were large and had big muscle attachment sites, indicating that these people must have led a highly active lifestyle. These were remains of people who didn't hang out around lake margins enjoying a sedentary lifestyle, which seemed to contradict Heizer's hypothesis about Great Basin adaptations and was more in line with Thomas's ideas. Based on this limited sample, I reached the tentative conclusion that the people I studied from Hidden Cave were healthy, but ate tough foods, and were physically active.

Independent of my work, Thomas came to a similar conclusion regarding the activity of these populations: He hypothesized that these people were highly mobile (the *limnomobile* hypothesis), in contrast to Heizer's *limnosedentary* hypothesis, which argued that wetland resources could provide sufficient food and other resources for a hunter-gatherer population. The limnomobile hypothesis argued that, although these wetlands offered plenty to eat and formed a kind of a "hub" of activity in the western Basin, fluctuations in food and other essential resources would have required travel to other areas—sometimes involving great distances. This is not just a local debate of concern only to Great Basin archaeologists. Rather, the debate is couched within the larger problem of the role of the environment in hunter-gatherer adaptations and how archaeologists go about documenting mobility and lifestyle in earlier societies. Unfortunately, I couldn't say much at the time—my work was based just on the tiny collection from Hidden Cave and it could provide only some very preliminary conclusions.

MORE SKELETONS AND MORE DEAD ENDS

Over the course of the year following the summer's research at Hidden Cave, I learned just about all there was to know about the bioarchaeology of the western Great Basin—what skeletons had been found, from where, and by whom. I also found the locations of existing collections of skeletons from sites in the Great Basin. From published and unpublished reports and by word of mouth from various archaeologists, I learned that there were many Great Basin remains in the collections at the Lowie (now Phoebe Hearst) Museum of Anthropology at Berkeley and at the Las Vegas campus of the University of Nevada. With a small grant from the American Museum of Natural History, I traveled to Berkeley and Las Vegas, aspiring to study skeletons in order to address unresolved issues about prehistoric native lifestyles in the Great Basin.

After spending about two months collecting data, I developed a fuller picture of the health, lifestyle, and activity levels for native peoples living in the prehistoric western Great Basin. Indeed, this study confirmed my earlier suspicions about health and activity in prehistoric Indians in this region. Based on my documentation of the skeletons, like the Hidden Cave material I had studied earlier, it became clear to me that health of these people was reasonably good, at least as can be determined from the absence of hypoplasias, porotic hyperostosis, and periosteal reactions.

On the other hand, the skeletons had an abundance of a pathological condition called osteoarthritis, something I was not able to identify in the Hidden Cave sample owing to the highly fragmentary nature of that collection. Osteoarthritis is highly revealing about lifestyle and workload. Although the disorder is somewhat influenced by climate, genetics, and other factors, workload and physical activity—what bioarchaeologists call the mechanical environment—best explain the presence of osteoarthritis. The bone surfaces of the joints of the skeleton (for example, the elbow or knee) are covered with a thin layer of a highly lubricated substance called hyaline cartilage. This lubrication facilitates ease of motion in the joints by greatly reducing the friction between the two (or more) bones making up articular joints. Early in adulthood, if not before, this cartilage begins to erode slowly. Simultaneously, along the margins of the joint, tiny spicules of bone begin to develop. If the erosion of the joint surface is severe enough, the bones making up the joint begin to rub against each other, and the surfaces become polished. Called eburnation (from the Latin *eburnea*, or

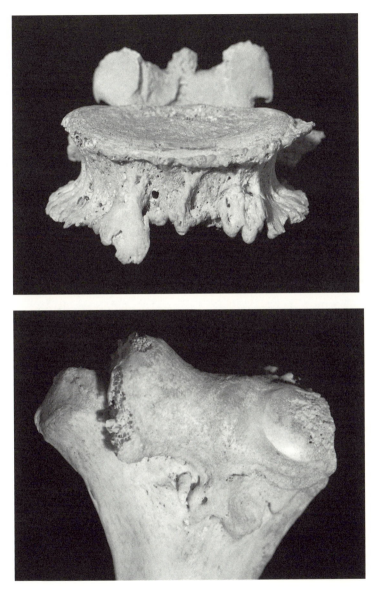

Top: Marginal lipping (osteophytes) on adult lumbar vertebra. Bottom: Eburnation on articular surface of humerus in the elbow joint. These are the classic symptoms of osteoarthritis in the skeleton. Photographs by Barry Stark; from Larsen 1987, and reproduced with permission of Academic Press, Inc.

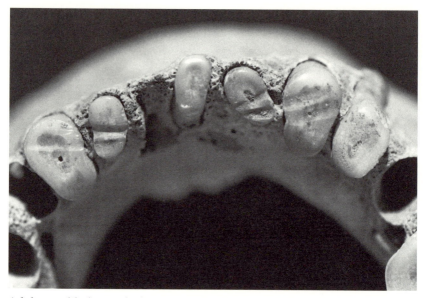

Adult mandibular teeth showing occlusal grooves (Humboldt Lake Basin, Nevada). Grooves are caused by pulling some material across the surfaces of the lower front teeth, such as plant material or animal sinew. From Larsen 1985; reproduced with permission of John Wiley & Sons, Inc.

ivory), this polishing reflects severe wear and tear on the joint. Similarly, bony spicules can develop into large projections of skeletal tissue, sometimes causing joints to immobilize and fuse together (in the vertebrae, for example). Bioarchaeologists and paleopathologists have learned that lifestyle is the essential determinant of osteoarthritis—both in severity and in frequency—in human populations. In situations involving minimal physical activity (such as in sedentary modern Americans), the disorder is relatively rare, whereas in situations of high physical activity, the disorder can be quite prevalent.

The presence of so much osteoarthritis led me to conclude that the Great Basin people I studied had been physically active in life. Moreover, the bones were large and showed markings indicating large muscles. The teeth were highly worn, and in some of the adult males, the front teeth—the incisors and canines—had grooves worn into the chewing surfaces. This unique tooth wear pattern indicated to me that these people—especially men—were using their teeth for more than just chewing food; they were also using their teeth as tools, perhaps for preparing plant fibers for construction of mats, baskets, and other material culture that ethnographers have identified in Great Basin Indians.

These were all interesting clues about the lives and lifestyles of prehistoric Great Basin people, but frankly, I was still at an impasse about building a solid bioarchaeological picture. Most of the skeletons I studied that summer were undocumented: There were almost no field notes associated with excavated remains, places of origin were largely unknown, there were no dates on the remains, and the majority of the bones were collected by amateur archaeologists with no formal training in fieldwork. In other words, I had lots of bones, but there was little contextual information I could use in the formal analysis that I had hoped to complete, making for frustrating work.

When I returned to campus in the fall to teach, I decided to put the project on hold indefinitely—or so I thought at the time. As things stood, the skeletons I had studied simply were inappropriate for the kind of scientific investigation that I was interested in doing.

Disaster at Stillwater and the Outcome

A couple of years passed, and just as I was about to give up on doing serious work in this fascinating area of desert-west North America, there was a completely unforeseen development that would dramatically alter our understanding about the prehistoric Indians living in this setting centuries before the intrusion of Euroamericans. In 1985, the melting of record snowfalls in the Sierra Nevada mountains to the west had produced massive flooding throughout the wetland areas of the western Great Basin, including the Humboldt and Carson sinks. Extensive erosion due to water, wind, and ice literally scraped the top foot or so from the surface of the Carson Sink landscape, particularly in the area known as the Stillwater Marsh, an ecologically rich region covering some 150 square miles of the eastern Carson Sink. This erosion opened up a window on prehistoric land use patterns, exposing numerous archaeological sites and hundreds of human skeletons. A new chapter was about to be written on forager societies in this region of the world.

From the start, the archaeological community was completely unprepared for the extent of burial activity by prehistoric peoples living in the region. Before the floods, the region was known mostly from its caves and rock shelters. Following the floods, however, a whole new perspective on prehistoric native peoples was exposed. Many of the remains were isolated bones and teeth, but many were also partially or mostly undisturbed burials.

On the surface, the region looked like an archaeological disaster area. With sites, artifacts, and skeletons exposed to the harsh desert environment of the Great Basin, continued destruction of invaluable cultural and biological resources seemed inevitable. To add to the problem, unscrupulous nonprofessional collectors were beginning to visit the newly exposed sites and remove artifacts and bones for their personal collections. Something had to be done on a massive scale to protect the area from future destruction. Consequently, archaeologists Amy Dansie and Donald Tuohy of the Nevada State Museum and Anan Raymond of the United States Fish and Wildlife Service undertook a survey, excavation, and recovery of artifacts and bones from the newly exposed archaeological sites. Parts of the hundreds of skeletons scattered about the surface of the Carson Desert were carefully collected and taken to the Nevada State Museum for preliminary assessment and study by Sheilagh Brooks, a physical anthropologist at the University of Nevada, Las Vegas.

The fortuitous exposure of skeletal remains in the Carson Sink represented an important opportunity to address issues being debated by archaeologists regarding lifestyle and adaptation. The archaeological materials, including various living sites, storage and house pits, plant and animal remains, and human remains, offered a remarkable data source on the human ecology and behavior in the region. Importantly, the study of the Stillwater skeletons was also key to addressing the broader issue of adaptive efficiency or "affluence" of hunter-gatherers. In his highly influential textbook published in the 1960s, archaeologist Robert Braidwood of the University of Chicago characterized forager lifestyles as "a savage's existence, and a very tough one . . . following animals just to kill them to eat, or moving from one berry patch to another."[2] About the same time, Richard Lee of the University of Toronto and Irven DeVore of Harvard University organized a conference in which various cultural anthropologists having firsthand experience with living foragers around the world reported on their findings relating to health, activity, diet, and other factors specific to hunting and gathering societies.

Collectively, these various anthropologists found that foragers may not have had it all that bad. This assessment was confirmed by Lee in his research among the Ju/'hoansi (!Kung). In contrast to Braidwood's perspective, a different pattern characterizing foragers began to emerge—life appeared to be leisurely and bountiful for them. From this point on, anthropologists began to study modern hunter-gatherers from diverse settings worldwide. Far from being able to easily characterize forager lifestyles, this later work has shown that they are remarkably diverse: Some appear well off, others are highly stressed, and many lie somewhere between these two extremes. The bioarchaeological work in the Stillwater Marsh could potentially add a new and important contribution to the discussion about forager lifestyles.

The Stillwater Project

Soon after Dansie, Tuohy, and Brooks completed their formal reports on their work in the Stillwater Marsh, archaeologist Robert Kelly approached the Nevada State Museum, the United States Fish and Wildlife Service (which oversaw the protection and control of the region), and the Fallon Paiute-Shoshone Tribe about the possibility of conducting more fieldwork. He proposed an additional archaeological survey, excavation of threatened human remains and sites, and a study of existing bioarchaeological col-

lections that would tie into his long-term study of prehistoric foragers in the Carson Sink. For his doctoral dissertation, Kelly had
completed a large survey of the Carson Sink before the floods, and
he had learned a great deal about prehistoric lifestyles in the region. Most of the survey was based on surface sites, and the new
alterations of the landscape offered a chance to investigate the region more fully. As students, Kelly and I had worked together for
a number of years on Dave Thomas's archaeological projects in
the Great Basin and elsewhere, and on many occasions we had
discussed how human remains could potentially broaden the understanding of prehistoric lifestyles and adaptations. We agreed
that here was a project worth collaborating on.

Kelly and I received the necessary approvals from various state,
federal, and tribal authorities to do the work we were proposing.
We were ecstatic. Here was a chance to study a large, well-documented series of skeletons—this was unprecedented in the Great
Basin. In the summer of 1987, my wife and I spent part of our
honeymoon (I have a *very* understanding spouse) collecting data
on skeletons excavated by Dansie and Tuohy and then housed at
the Nevada State Museum research and collections facility outside
of Carson City.[3] With funding from the National Science Foundation and our home institutions (at the time, I was at Northern
Illinois University, and Kelly was at the University of Louisville),
we completed a survey of the Stillwater Marsh, locating additional
burials and archaeological sites. In agreement with the Fallon Paiute-Shoshone Tribe, only threatened burials—those with more
than 50 percent of the skeleton already exposed by erosion—were
excavated by our crews. The cooperation between archaeologists
and Native Americans contributed to the success of the fieldwork,
serving as a model for future work. In the following summer, along
with physical anthropologists Dale Hutchinson and Christopher
Ruff, we returned to Nevada to complete our data collection. This
work resulted in a dream come true regarding the important place
of bioarchaeology in addressing issues that I had begun to think
about while an undergraduate student years earlier, digging at
Gatecliff Shelter.

Ancient DNA and Arrowheads: Who Were
the Stillwater People?

Bioarchaeological study of the Stillwater skeletons is somewhat complicated by both cultural and other factors that cloud the archaeological picture. For one, the skeletons are not from a tightly dated cemetery. Most skeletons are from isolated graves scattered throughout the marsh region. As such, we concluded that prehistoric peoples in the region did not bury their dead in formal cemetery areas, but rather, they interred their deceased in isolated areas of relatively high elevation (such as along crests of sand dunes). My guess is that, like many foragers, when someone died, the other members of the group buried the deceased wherever the group happened to be camped at the time. Some of the archaeological sites yielding human remains contained a relatively large number of skeletons—by Brooks's count, one site had nearly sixty individuals. But even at that locality, there were no clear associations among individual burials—they were not part of a cemetery, planned or otherwise. The burials were simple: The remains of the deceased were placed in an oval-shaped pit with the body in a kind of fetal posture, whereby the arms and legs were drawn up toward the torso.

Also problematic for our study was the determination of the length of time that the Stillwater Marsh was used for burial and the identification of the origin of the people. Regarding the length of time that the region was used for burial of the dead, the half-dozen or so radiocarbon dates associated with individual burials, the few diagnostic artifacts that can be assigned to a specific time period (such as arrowheads) that were found in direct association with skeletons, and relative dating of archaeological sites indicate that the region was most heavily trafficked by native groups during the Reveille phase (1300 B.C.–A.D. 700), and less so during the following Underdown phase (A.D. 700–1300).

Regarding the population history—who were the people we were studying—it is fully within the realm of possibility that people from the earlier periods may be different from the people from the later periods. Today, most of the native peoples living in the Great Basin are Numic speakers. In the 1940s and 1950s, social anthropologist Julian Steward and linguist Sidney Lamb suggested that Numic speakers originated in a southwestern Great Basin homeland in southeastern California and eventually spread throughout the Great Basin. Linguistic evidence suggests that the expansion and replacement of earlier groups took place at least one thousand years ago.

Analysis of ancient DNA offers important insight into population origins and the identification of the Stillwater people. DNA, or deoxyribonucleic acid, is the chemical found in cells of the body that presents the genetic code. The unraveling of this code provides all sorts of important information about genetic relationships among people, whom they derive from, evolutionary history, and geographic origins. The use of DNA has already been instrumental in identifying perpetrators of crimes and identities of deceased individuals. DNA analysis in bioarchaeology is still in its infancy, but promises to be a powerful tool for identification of population history. One of the first large-scale projects involved the analysis of ancient DNA extracted from the Stillwater bones. DNA was successively extracted from Stillwater skeletons by Frederika Kaestle of Yale University and coworkers Joseph Lorenz of the Analytical Genetic Testing Center and David Glenn Smith from the University of California, Davis. Their analysis indicates that if Numic people did move into the region, they likely did not replace populations living there.[4] Rather, this new molecular genetic information from the DNA analysis suggests that there may have been admixture between Numic and pre-Numic peoples; the genes identifying both groups of people are present in the Stillwater bones.

Thus, many generations of people possibly representing different genetic groups were likely buried in the Stillwater Marsh. It is entirely possible that the human remains from Stillwater that my collaborators and I have studied are not representative of a population or series of populations that we could use to address issues relating to bioarchaeology and human adaptation. However, research by both Sheilagh Brooks and my team of bioarchaeologists found a homogeneity of skeletal measurements, cranial shape, tooth wear patterns, and other data in the Stillwater series. This homogeneity suggests that the series can be regarded as a biological unit of study amenable to the kinds of questions raised here and the types of data analyses outlined in the introduction to this book.

The bioarchaeology of the Stillwater skeletons provides an independent means for evaluating and understanding behavioral patterns, land use, and adaptive efficiency in the western Great Basin. In the next chapter, I will address a series of questions fundamental to our understanding of the lives of ancient foragers in this and other regions of the world: What were the health and activity like in prehistoric western Great Basin foragers? Were the lifestyle and adaptive pattern of these foragers consistent with the Hobbesian portrayal of "poor, nasty, brutish, and short"? Or, was it more along the lines of the consensus that emerged among many anthropologists that far from being nutritionally deprived and subject to excessive workloads, foragers had adequate nutrition and were not subject to huge amounts of work—was life for hunter-gatherers bountiful, leisurely, and productive in this setting? Or, was it somewhere between these extremes? Closer to questions regarding native peoples in the Stillwater Marsh region of the Great Basin, were these populations tied to the marsh, living a sedentary and affluent lifestyle, or did they move about the landscape, extracting resources from both marsh and uplands settings, eating just enough to get by?

NOTES

1. Mastication, or chewing, is one of the important "activities" of the skull that is discussed throughout the book. The masticatory complex refers to the area of skull anatomy involved in chewing, namely the muscles that are responsible for making the chewing motion, the bones that anchor the muscles, and the teeth coming into direct contact with the food. The muscles of the masticatory complex move the lower jaw, the mandible, in order to bring the teeth together in a chewing motion. Five different muscles are included in the chewing motion: temporalis, masseter, lateral pterygoid, medial pterygoid, and digastric. The two major muscles that account for most of the chewing

power are the temporalis muscle and the masseter muscle. The temporalis is a large fan-shaped muscle that attaches on the side of the head and on the upper part of the mandible. The masseter attaches to the zygomas (cheekbones) and the bottom and back of the mandible. When the muscle contracts, it pulls the mandible in an upward and forward direction. If you clench your jaw, and touch the side of your head and the back of your lower jaw, you can feel these muscles contracting. When the masticatory muscles relax, gravity allows the mandible to lower, and when the muscles contract, the mandible is brought up for chewing.

The skull bones that provide the attachment sites for the masticatory muscles are the mandible, zygoma and other facial bones, and the temporal and parietal bones on the sides of the skull.

The teeth come into direct contact with the food when it is being chewed. Human beings have two sets of teeth. The first set is the deciduous (or milk) teeth, and includes the front teeth (incisors and canines) and back teeth (molars). By age ten to twelve, most or all of the deciduous teeth have been replaced by the permanent (or adult) teeth. In addition to having incisors, canines, and molars, the adult dentition also has premolars, the teeth located between the canines and molars in the jaws.

2. Braidwood 1967, p. 113.

3. The skeletons are now protected in an underground concrete vault on the reservation of the Fallon Paiute-Shoshone Tribe near Fallon, Nevada.

4. The study of genetic material extracted from ancient skeletons and other tissues is beginning to advance our understanding of past population history in ways that were not envisioned a decade ago. With a technology called polymerase chain reaction (PCR), scientists can amplify tiny fragments of (DNA), reconstructing key components of the genes of people and other organisms long deceased. This is a powerful new tool for testing hypotheses about ancestor-descendant relationships in the past and present, such as the origins of prehistoric and living populations in the Great Basin—or anywhere, for that matter. Some very rare mutations indicate common ancestry in ancient populations. For Native American populations, the study of ancient DNA has resulted in the identification of four distinct founding lineages or haplogroups, which may represent four separate waves or migration of populations from Asia to the New World.

The DNA study undertaken by Frederika Kaestle and her coworkers is one of the first to successfully analyze genetic material from a sizable sample of archaeological skeletons. The DNA extraction techniques are currently being worked out in a number of laboratories around the world. Kaestle and her team removed the protein from small samples of ground-up bone, the DNA was extracted from the deproteinized bone through a series of chemical and mechanical processes, and then it was subjected to PCR amplification. For the Stillwater bone sample (n = 19), three of the four haplogroups identified in living Native American populations are represented by at least one individual each. The analysis reveals that some language groups can be eliminated as related (e.g., Zuñi, Yuman, Washo, Takic, Northern and Central Uto-Aztecan), and interestingly, the Stillwater series is statistically different from the far eastern Great Basin Fremont populations analyzed by physical anthropologist Dennis O'Rourke and coworkers (1999) at the University of Utah. Although the Stillwater molecular genetic study does not prove or disprove the Numic expansion hypothesis, it does serve to eliminate specific relationships. The study represents a landmark in our understanding of Great Basin population history.

REFERENCES

Braidwood, R. J. *Prehistoric Men* (7th ed.). Glenview, Illinois: Scott Foresman and Company.

Heizer, R. F., and Napton, L. K. (1970) *Archaeology and the Prehistoric Great Basin Lacustrine Subsistence Regime as Seen from Lovelock Cave, Nevada*. Contributions of the University of California Archaeological Research Facility, No. 10.

Kaestle, F. A., Lorenz, J. G., and Smith, D. G. (1999) Molecular genetics and the Numic expansion: a molecular investigation of the prehistoric inhabitants of Stillwater Marsh. In B. E. Hemphill and C. S. Larsen, (eds.) *Prehistoric Lifeways in the Great Basin Wetlands: Bioarchaeological Reconstruction and Interpretation*. Salt Lake City: University of Utah Press.

Kelly, R. L. (1995) *The Foraging Spectrum: Diversity in Hunter-Gatherer Lifeways*. Washington, D. C.: Smithsonian Institution Press.

Larsen, C. S. (1985) Human remains from Hidden Cave. In D. H. Thomas, ed. *The Archaeology of Hidden Cave, Nevada*. Anthropological Papers of the American Museum of Natural History, vol. 61, part 1, pp. 179–182.

―――. (1985) Human remains from the Carson Sink. In D. H. Thomas, ed. *The Archaeology of Hidden Cave, Nevada*. Anthropological Papers of the American Museum of Natural History, vol. 61, part 1, pp. 395–404.

―――. (1997) *Bioarchaeology: Interpreting Behavior from the Human Skeleton*. Cambridge: Cambridge University Press.

Larsen, C. S., and Kelly, R. L., eds. (1995) *Bioarchaeology of the Stillwater Marsh: Prehistoric Human Adaptation in the Western Great Basin*. Anthropological Papers of the American Museum of Natural History, no. 77.

Lee, R. B., and DeVore, I., eds. (1968) *Man the Hunter*. Chicago: Aldine Publishing.

O'Rourke, D. H., Parr, R. L., and Carlyle, S. W. (1999) Molecular genetic variation in prehistoric inhabitants of the eastern Great Basin. In B. E. Hemphill and C. S. Larsen, eds. *Prehistoric Lifeways in the Great Basin Wetlands: Bioarchaeological Reconstruction and Interpretation*. Salt Lake City: University of Utah Press.

Thomas, D. H. (1973) An empirical test of Steward's model of Great Basin settlement patterns. *American Antiquity* 38:155–176.

————. (1979) Complexity among Great Basin Shoshoneans: the world's least affluent hunter-gatherers? In S. Koyama and D. H. Thomas, eds. *Affluent Foragers: Pacific Coasts East and West*. Senri Ethnological Series, no. 9, pp. 19–52. Osaka, Japan: National Museum of Ethnology.

————. (1983) *The Archaeology of Monitor Valley: 2. Gatecliff Shelter*. Anthropological Papers of the American Museum of Natural History, vol. 59, part 1.

————., ed. (1985) *The Archaeology of Hidden Cave, Nevada*. Anthropological Papers of the American Museum of Natural History, vol. 61, part 1.

Skeletons from Stillwater:
Good Times and Bad Times

THE STUDY of foragers, both ancient and modern, has a long tradition in the field of anthropology, but until recently, ancient skeletons were not seen as an important source of understanding about the lives and lifestyles of these people. In this chapter, we will take a look at the study of human remains recovered from the Stillwater Marsh of western Nevada. The bioarchaeology of this setting tells about what life was like for these ancient hunter-gatherers, especially with regard to the difficulties of the forager lifestyle in this region of North America.

Climate must have had a huge impact on the lives of prehistoric foragers living in the Great Basin. Because of the rain shadow effect of the Sierra Nevada mountains located about sixty miles west of Stillwater in California, virtually no rain or snow falls on the Carson Sink in Nevada. These mountains prevent weather systems from passing eastward to the Great Basin, thus severely limiting the amount of rain and snowfall. Therefore, virtually all water supplying the lakes and marshes in the western Great Basin is derived from the Carson and Humboldt rivers, which are fed exclusively by melting snow during the spring and summer from the Sierra Nevada mountains. Due to the high variability in the amount of snowfall from one year to the next in the Sierras, the amount of water in the Great Basin wetlands fluctuates dramatically. In years when the Stillwater Marsh is adequately supplied with water, the plants and animals that people like to eat are abundant. Some 160 species of waterbirds, including mallards (*Anas platyrhynchos*), cinnamon teal (*Anas cyanoptera*), and coots (*Fulica americana*), were hunted by native peoples. Fishing involved the capture of several species, but tui chub (*Gila bicolor obesus*) was especially important. Edible plants, such as bulrush (*Scirpus* sp.) and cattail (*Typha* sp.), provided essential nutrition from their seeds and roots.

As one moves away from the marsh into surrounding areas that look more like a typical desert, one finds fewer plants and animals. Still, the outlying desert contains some important grasses that do provide sustenance. The nearby uplands are also quite dry, and the terrain is rough and difficult to traverse. The uplands also contain various foods that are found throughout the Great Basin. Ethnographic and archaeological information indicates the importance of piñon pine seeds in a number of regions of the Great Basin. However, piñon may have been introduced to the Carson Sink region only within the last several hundred years, and may not have been important in prehistoric times (see below). Game animals hunted by native populations in the mountains included bighorn sheep (*Ovis canadensis nelsoni*) and antelope (*Antilocapra americana*); smaller mammals (e.g., rodents) were also hunted and trapped on a regular basis. Overall, then, the Great Basin people had access to various plants and animals. Unfortunately, access does not translate into what foods were actually eaten. Our job is to find out what was eaten, in order to understand nutrition, other aspects of health, and lifestyle.

STILLWATER DIET, HEALTH, AND QUALITY OF LIFE

Diet and Nutritional Adequacy

The reconstruction of the diet of the Stillwater people is important because it helps us to identify where people gathered or hunted their food—wetland marshes, uplands, or both settings. Moreover, dietary reconstruction can identify the nutritional adequacy of these resources, and provide strong inferences about the health and quality of life of these populations. Although plant and animal remains found in archaeological sites at Stillwater and elsewhere in the Great Basin provide valuable clues to dietary and nutritional history, there has been a major scientific breakthrough that has given us incredible insight into what people ate in the past. This breakthrough is the application of stable isotope analysis—a development that occurred in the field of geology—to the study of human bones and dietary reconstruction.

STABLE ISOTOPES IN BONE

As living organisms, the tissues of plants and animals are composed of various elements, such as carbon (C), nitrogen (N), hydrogen (H), and so forth. Each of these elements occurs in various forms called isotopes, which are identified on the basis of the number of neutrons in the nucleus of the atom. Carbon has three isotopes, one of which is unstable or radioactive—^{14}C used in dating—and the other two, ^{12}C and ^{13}C, are stable. Living plants use both of the stable forms of carbon, which they acquire from atmospheric carbon dioxide (CO_2) during photosynthesis.

Most plants eaten by humans and other animals use one of two photosynthesis types, either the C_3 (Calvin-Benson) or C_4 (Hatch-Slack). C_3 plants are found in temperate climates, and include such domesticated plants as wheat, barley, and rye, grains that have served as primary staples for much of the Old World—Europe, Asia, and Africa—for the last five to ten thousand years. Other C_3 plants include various trees, fruits, and tubers. C_4 plants are found mostly in tropical climates, and include the domesticated plants corn, millet, and sorghum. Corn is a New World plant, and millet and sorghum are Old World plants.

The distinction between C_3 and C_4 plants lies in how the plant uses carbon. Because carbon is used differently by C_3 and C_4 plants, the ratios of the stable isotopes—^{12}C to ^{13}C—that are measured in the laboratory are distinctive. C_3 plants have lower carbon stable isotope ratios than C_4 plants.[1] When humans eat these plants, the carbon is digested and passed onto the various body tissues, including bone, allowing bioarchaeologists to identify what kinds of plants were eaten and when they were adopted by earlier peoples. In North America, distinctive patterns of plant use based on isotopic analysis of bones have emerged. For example, in

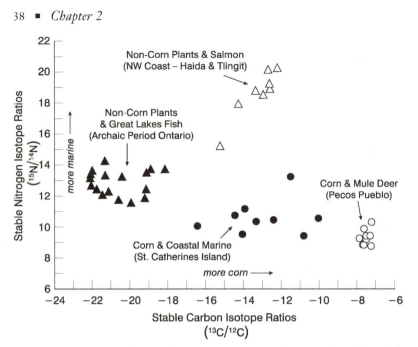

Examples of stable carbon and nitrogen isotope values resulting from different diets in North America. Each triangle or circle represents one person. The people from the northwest coast (Haida, Tlingit) had diets heavy in marine foods, the Southwest (Pecos Pueblo) on C_4 foods (corn), the Archaic period Ontario on C_3 foods (pre-corn), and the St. Catherines Island (historic mission Guale from Santa Catalina) on C_4 (corn), C_3 (various wild plants and animals), and marine foods. Higher nitrogen isotope values represent more marine food, and higher carbon isotope values represent more corn. Adapted from Schoeninger and Moore 1992; reproduced with permission of the authors and Plenum Publishing Corporation.

eastern North America, corn was the only major C_4 plant eaten by prehistoric and historic Indians. Stable carbon isotope ratios are low before about A.D. 900, but then become increasingly higher after that date. This pattern indicates that corn did not become a major part of diet until the end of the first millenium A.D., but became used across the region after that time.

In western North America, a range of C_3 and C_4 plants were eaten, thus making it difficult to identify food use patterns with any degree of certainty. In the American Great Basin, no domesticated plants were eaten (see below), but the wild plants were both C_3 and C_4.

Analysis of stable isotopes of nitrogen, ^{14}N and ^{15}N, has also proven highly informative about dietary patterns in North America and elsewhere around the world.[2] Like carbon, nitrogen is an essential element for plants. Some types of plants obtain nitrogen directly from the atmosphere, whereas others take it from the soil. The soil-based nitrogen derives from decayed vegetation. These differences in the way plants obtain and use nitrogen are expressed as differences in the values of the ratios of ^{14}N to ^{15}N. One of the major distinctions is between marine plants and terrestrial- (land-) based plants is that marine plants have higher stable nitrogen isotope ratios than terrestrial plants. For humans eating these different plants, like those of carbon, the stable nitrogen isotope ratios are passed from digestion to the tissues of the body. In coastal settings, based on analysis of stable nitrogen isotope ratios, it is now possible to identify how much of the diet was marine-based versus terrestrial-based. In purely terrestrial settings, such as the Great Basin, there exists a group of plants that derive their nitrogen directly from the atmosphere. In these plants, such as piñon pine, the stable nitrogen isotope ratio is close to zero (like air). Most plants in the region obtain nitrogen from soil, however. In these contexts, soil nitrogen has generally higher stable nitrogen isotope ratios, and so do the plants deriving their nitrogen from the soil. Theoretically, then, bioarchaeologists should be able to identify what types of plants are eaten, based on the stable isotope ratios of carbon and nitrogen.

The University of Wisconsin at Madison has one of the premier archaeological stable isotope laboratories in the world. Founded and directed by physical anthropologist Margaret Schoeninger, this laboratory has analyzed thousands of plants, animal bones, and human bones from diverse global settings. Margaret and I had been graduate students together at the University of Michigan in the 1970s. As we both developed our careers, I watched her put together one of the most impressive bone chemistry research programs anywhere. Bob Kelly and I invited her to join the Stillwater project, and she subsequently analyzed stable carbon and nitrogen isotopes from human skeletons. Importantly, she also analyzed archaeological and recent plants and animals in order to address the issues of both what foods were eaten by Stillwater people and where they got these foods in this desert landscape.

Schoeninger's analysis of stable carbon and nitrogen isotope ratios reveals that prehistoric diets included a mixture of C_3 and C_4 foods, thus indicating that diet in this region was extraordinarily variable during the prehistoric period. The carbon isotope ratios derived from the analysis of the bone are fairly high, thus indicating that some individuals ate a significant amount of C_4 foods. Great Basin Indians were exclusively hunter-gatherers, and with the exception of populations living on the eastern side of the Great Salt Lake in the eastern basin, corn (a major C_4 food in prehistoric North America) was not grown and eaten in the region. Possibly, the C_4 foods documented by isotopic bone analysis were derived from upland settings outside the marsh region. Bones from two marsh animals recovered from Stillwater Marsh archaeological sites, rabbit (*Lepus* sp.) and diving duck (*Aythya* sp.), have high carbon isotope ratios, which suggests that they ate nonmarsh C_4 foods. These animals either migrated to the marsh from the uplands, or much more likely, they were hunted in the uplands by people and then brought down to the marsh for consumption at the home living site. The low carbon isotope values found in the human bones are from people that ate mostly C_3 foods collected in the marsh, such as cattail and bulrush.

Schoeninger's nitrogen isotopic analysis of the Stillwater human skeletons indicates fairly high values. The plant remains that she analyzed show a wide range of values for plants eaten by Great Basin Indians, from very high for cattail to low for bulrush, reflecting the differences in how these plants obtain nitrogen. This finding suggests a range of localities from where plants were extracted as food sources, involving both the marsh and mountains. Importantly, the very high nitrogen ratios in the Stillwater people argue against consumption of piñon pine nuts as a major component of diet because of the low values in this plant, approaching or at zero. This finding confirms earlier speculation by some archaeologists and others that piñon, although present in the mountains surrounding the Stillwater Marsh region today, was probably a latecomer, probably within the historic period (post-1820s). Had the plant been present prehistorically, it would have almost certainly been exploited, given the highly nutritious seeds that it produces on an annual basis.

In general, the carbon and nitrogen isotope analysis indicates that the diet of the majority of Stillwater individuals living in the region in prehistoric times depended on plants and animals similar to those present in the region today, with piñon being an important exception. This finding does not refute the model suggesting that people remained in the marsh year-round. However, neither does it contradict the limnomobile hypothesis that resources were also gathered from other settings surrounding the marsh. Moreover, the wide range of variation in both carbon and nitrogen isotope values indicates a great diversity of diet, which speaks to the availability and consumption of a wide range of foods in this Great Basin setting.

TEETH AND FOOD

Apparently, the diet did not include foods that produced dental decay. Of all teeth in the Stillwater series, only about 3 percent have evidence of tooth decay—what dentists call "dental caries." Dental caries (*caries* is Latin for "decay") or cavities is one of the most significant diseases to affect humankind. Dental caries is a disease process characterized by progressive destruction of teeth by acids produced by bacterial fermentation of carbohydrates, especially sugar. The bacteria in the mouth secrete glucosyltransferase, an enzyme that causes the production of sticky chemical compounds called glucans, which form the "glue" that causes plaque on the teeth to hold together and to cement the caries-causing bacteria to the teeth. The acid produced by the bacteria literally dissolves the tooth enamel, producing the cavities, which range in size from barely visible discolorations to massive holes. Few simple carbohydrates—i.e., sugars—were eaten by Great Basin people, which is reflected in the low caries frequency at Stillwater.

Our study of the Stillwater teeth shows that tooth loss did occur, but it was most likely due to excessive tooth wear, not carbohydrate consumption. Oral health in this area of the world was remarkably good.

HEALTH AT STILLWATER

Iron Status and Bone Pathology

Porotic hyperostosis and cribra orbitalia, markers of iron deficiency anemia discussed above, are very infrequent in the Stillwater people—only four individuals (out of fifty-four) had any indication of the porous skull bones that are characteristic of this condition. Such low prevalence suggests that iron status was normal during the years of growth and development for most people. Michael Schultz of the University of Göttingen has found that other possible causes of porotic hyperostosis and cribra orbitalia are scurvy (vitamin C deficiency), rickets (vitamin D deficiency), and infection. Regardless of the cause, the evidence from this bone pathology suggests that iron status was fairly good in this setting.

Growth Stress

ENAMEL DEFECTS

In order to systematically assess growth arrest from the hundreds of teeth from Stillwater, bioarchaeologist Dale Hutchinson of East Carolina University and I examined incisors and canines for enamel hypoplasias. We found that nearly two-thirds of individuals displayed at least one hypoplasia in their teeth. Comparison with a wide range of other populations studied by bioarchaeologists indicates that physiological stress, as represented by dental growth disruption, was not rampant, but on the other hand, neither was it infrequent in the Stillwater Marsh. The prevalence is moderately high and even exceeds more stressed late prehistoric populations in eastern North America from the Mississippian period (post-A.D. 1000). As mentioned above, a variety of causes have been identified with enamel hypoplasia, including various nutritional disorders, disease, or other factors predisposing individuals to physiological disruption. For example, low socioeconomic status and poor nutrition associated with it may contribute to low birth weight or other factors that lead to physiological disruption. Laboratory studies have linked enamel hypoplasia to diabetes, fever, and parasitic infection. In environmentally disadvantaged populations, the defects have been found to be present where both malnutrition and infectious disease are present. Malnutrition and infection are highly synergistic—the two conditions acting together have a far more devastating impact on health of a person than when either is acting alone.

As with living populations, attempts at linking dental defects with a particular cause in archaeological skeletons has been unsuccessful, and this would seem to be the case with the Stillwater series as well. Indeed, due to the nonspecific nature of enamel hypoplasia, we would be hard-pressed to identify a single factor that we could say was responsible for growth disruption in the Carson Sink. For the Stillwater setting, we can eliminate some causes, however. For example, there are some genetic conditions that have been linked to enamel defects, but these conditions are usually profound and life-threatening. In a traditional group of hunter-gatherers, the survival of a person with a genetic disease much beyond birth or infancy would be highly unlikely.

Alternatively, localized trauma to the face and jaws can also cause enamel defects, but evidence for these kinds of injuries has not been found in the Stillwater series. Some of the Stillwater adults display healed nasal fractures—probably resulting from interpersonal conflict. But, the trauma to the nasal areas of these people probably occurred well after they had reached adulthood, and therefore would not have caused enamel defects. Thus, Dale and I ruled out genetic factors or localized trauma as a cause for dental growth disruption at Stillwater.

Two other possibilities—infectious disease and malnutrition—stand out for explaining the presence of physiological stress and dental defects in this and in most other archaeological settings. A

wide range of infectious diseases has been tied to enamel hypoplasias. During periods of infection, the body's immune system is
activated at the expense of growth and development of body tissues, resulting in slowing of the growth of teeth and bones. Infectious disease, however, seems unlikely as a major concern for these
Great Basin populations, for a couple of reasons. First, skeletal
infection, and by inference, infectious disease, is rare in this population. Only 16 percent of the Stillwater people have a periosteal
reaction, and most of these are localized in one place on a person's
skeleton, usually the tibia, the major bone of the lower leg. Only
one individual, an adult male, has widespread infection involving
most of the skeleton. Second, infectious disease is usually—
although not always—associated with dense, crowded living conditions, where the circumstances promote the spread of microbes
from one person to the next. The Great Basin populations in this
desert setting were small, highly dispersed about the landscape,
and mobile (see below), an adaptation that would not promote the
spread of infection.

It is possible that individuals with enamel hypoplasias experienced parasitic infections potentially contributing to growth disruption. Parasitic infection is systemic, leading to a range of
chronic problems for the individual. Parasites have been identified
in archaeological human feces—called *coprolites* by archaeologists—found in a number of cave sites in the Great Basin, such as
Lovelock Cave in the nearby Humboldt Sink. Some of the parasites are lethal (e.g., thorny-headed worm, *Acanthocephala*),
whereas others are relatively harmless (e.g., pinworm, *Enterobius
vermicularis*). Karl Reinhard, a specialist in coprolite analysis at
the University of Nebraska, believes that some parasitic infections
were commonplace in the Great Basin. Thus, parasitic infection
may have been a factor contributing to growth disruption.

A number of epidemiological studies of living traditional societies with protein-energy malnutrition are beginning to show the
strong influence of nutrition on enamel development. In their
study of two groups from Tezonteopan, Mexico, one group eating
the typical local protein-poor diet and the other receiving a sup-

plemented diet, physical anthropologist Alan Goodman and his colleagues at Hampshire College have found a higher number of enamel defects in the unsupplemented group. Their important investigation shows that even mild to moderate undernutrition can result in enamel defects in the growing child.

Because infectious disease was probably rare in the Great Basin—populations were simply too small and too dispersed to have been able to support communicable pathogens—nutritional deficiencies were probably a more common cause of growth disruption at Stillwater. In the desert setting of the Carson Sink, the availability of edible plants and animals is determined by annual precipitation levels, which amounts to only about four inches of rainfall per year. In years involving high snowfall in the Sierra Nevada Mountains, the rivers feeding the Stillwater Marsh are full, thus resulting in a well-watered landscape and an abundance of plants and animals that people could eat. However, the amount of snowfall in the Sierras—and, hence, water to the wetlands— is highly variable (as any skier will tell you). For many years, there can be little snowfall, resulting in severe water shortages and shrinkage of lakes and marshes in the western Great Basin. These dry episodes can continue for several consecutive years, resulting in disappearance of edible plants, loss of waterbirds, and reduction of other food sources. The relative availability of water and its impact on plant and animal communities in the region was underscored by ethnographer Margaret Wheat, who commented, "In the Great Basin the marshes . . . were intermittent affairs, always at the mercy of dry cycles and shifting dunes and channels. In a half a dozen years a marsh could change into a dust bowl."[3]

Could these episodes of environmental stress lead to food shortages and nutritional stress? Of course. In ruling out other causes— with the possible exception of parasitic infection—we believe that growth disruption observed in the Stillwater teeth was due in large part to food shortages brought about by periods of drought. I emphasize that the growth disruption was not widespread in the Stillwater people, but it did have a significant presence.

PHYSICAL ACTIVITY, WORKLOAD, AND MOBILITY:
MAKING A LIVING IN THE GREAT BASIN

Osteoarthritis

Osteoarthritis is an important indicator of physical activity in human beings, and the Stillwater series is no exception. Osteoarthritis in the Stillwater skeletons is ubiquitous. Virtually every adult skeleton has it (77 percent); every person over the age of thirty has osteoarthritis in at least one joint. This is in sharp contrast to modern Americans, where few individuals under age 30 have osteoarthritis. Slightly more Stillwater males have osteoarthritis than do Stillwater females. The prevalence by articular joint shows a pattern that is typical of a highly mechanically stressed population. Namely, the hand joints are least affected (13 percent), and the lumbar spine is most affected (67 percent). The elbow is also high on the list (50 percent) of affected joints.

The pattern of distribution of osteoarthritis in the skeletons of adult females and males is generally similar, but with some important differences. Females show very little osteoarthritis in the ankle and foot joints, whereas almost half the males have osteoarthritis in these joints. The differences suggest some important behavioral differences along gender lines in these prehistoric people. The ankle and foot joints are especially prone to mechanical stress during walking, running, or any other ambulatory behavior. And, if this ambulatory activity occurs in the mountains in rough terrain, the stresses can be even more severe. The high frequency of ankle and foot osteoarthritis in males tells me that Stillwater men were doing a lot more moving around the landscape than women, and plausibly in rough terrain—men were more active travelers than women. We believe that this greater travel reflects frequent forays into the mountains or elsewhere for hunting.

The Stillwater osteoarthritis is some of the most severe that I have seen in looking at skeletons from throughout North America or, for that matter, worldwide. Individuals with the disorder all show marginal lipping of the articular joints, and some have joints with severe degeneration, including eburnation. The eburnation—expressed as pronounced polishing of the joint surface—occurs when the articular cartilage has all but disappeared due to excessive mechanical loading. For example, one of the Stillwater adult females who was over forty years of age has extremely polished surfaces on the ends of the humerus and radius in the elbow joint where these two bones articulate. All the margins of her joints have extensive marginal lipping. This pattern, along with the fact that the osteoarthritis is found mostly on weight-bearing joints, indicates that the degenerative changes that we observed in the Stillwater series are due to an excessive mechanical environment, suggesting that this population led a rigorous and demanding lifestyle.

What are some of the activities that could cause osteoarthritis in this setting? Ethnographers Julian Steward and Margaret Wheat documented and recorded a range of behaviors that certainly would explain these levels of osteoarthritis, including carrying heavy loads, cutting animal hides, seed grinding and pounding with mortars and pestles, stone tool production, and the use of the bow and arrow. Given the ubiquity of osteoarthritis in the sample, it is not possible to say exactly what behaviors these people engaged in that would cause the mechanical stresses. That said, it is still quite clear that this population was extraordinarily active, and my hunch is that this activity involved travel over difficult terrain, away from the marsh.

Biomechanics and Activity: The Shapes of Bones

My immediate impression of the Hidden Cave bones was that the people represented by them were physically active, and extraordinarily so. In the early 1980s, I had just completed a study on osteoarthritis patterns in hunter-gatherers and later, agriculturalists from the Georgia coast of eastern North America, showing changes over time that suggested clear alterations in workload and activity (see chapter 3). I then began a collaborative study with Chris Ruff, a physical anthropologist at Johns Hopkins University, looking at biomechanics and bone structure in order to provide more detailed information on activity patterns that might help better explain the changes I was seeing in the American Southeast. The work there was proving enormously informative about human activity. The application of this analytical approach to the Stillwater skeletons was obvious, especially given the debate about the degree of mobility in the region in native populations in the prehistoric past. If patterns of activity and mobility could be identified by studying the skeletons, then we would know much more about prehistoric lives and lifestyles, settling (or at least better informing) the debates that heretofore had been addressed by archaeologists exclusively.

BEAMS AND BONES

Biomechanical analysis places a more revealing light on the issue of mobility and activity in Stillwater Marsh prehistoric Indians than either osteoarthritis or simple measurement of bones. When I first saw the Stillwater long bones, I was struck by their profound size and robusticity. That is, the bones are large, and have heavy markings where the muscles attach. This is one of the most robust modern human samples that Chris and I have encountered in our research collaborations over the years. In order to investigate the functional and behavioral meaning of the massive degree of robusticity in the Stillwater skeletons, we use the biomechanical model based on engineering principles—called beam theory—in our analysis. This is a powerful tool for inferring past behaviors, and certainly informative about patterns of activity here in the Great Basin or elsewhere.

From the perspective of a civil or mechanical engineer, long bones—such as the femur and humerus—can be modeled as hollow beams. Just like building materials that go into the construction of a skyscraper or a bridge, the ability of these hollow beams to resist mechanical forces—that is, their ability to resist breaking under mechanical loading—can be accurately measured. The ability of the bone to resist these mechanical loads is called the "strength" of the bone.

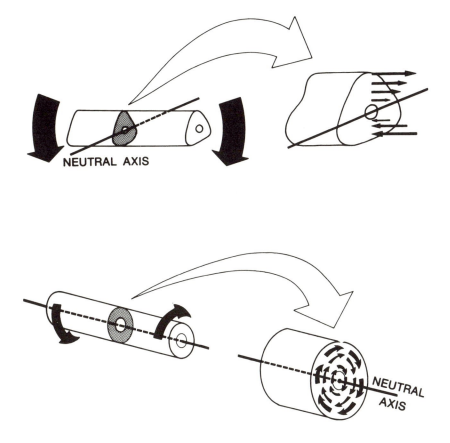

NEUTRAL AXIS

NEUTRAL AXIS

Cross section of schematic long bones showing *bending* (top) and *torsion* (bottom). The arrows in the cross sections show stress distribution around the neutral plane and axis, respectively. The heavier arrows indicate greater magnitude of force (and greater strength) around the periphery of the bone and the lighter arrows indicate lesser magnitude of force (and lesser strength) closer to the neutral plane or axis. Adapted from Nordin and Frankel 1980; reproduced with permission of authors and Williams & Watkins.

Engineers have learned that in bending and torsion (twisting) of a hollow beam, the magnitude of mechanical stresses is directly proportional to the distance from a central or "neutral" axis of the bone. The central axis is an imaginary line or plane running along the long axis of the bone. Mathematically, the combined stresses from bending and torsion at this central axis are equal to zero, and the further one gets from this axis, the greater the magnitude of mechanical stress. This means that when viewing the cross sections of a group of bones—such as in the midshaft regions of a number of femurs from an archaeological site—the ones with the strongest cross sections are those in which the bone material is placed farthest from the central axis. In effect, the farther that bone tissue is placed from the central axis running along the midline of the bone, the greater the strength and the better that bone is able to withstand the forces of bending or torsion.

A good analogy illustrating the principles of bone strength and resistance to mechanical forces is bending a ruler. If you bend the ruler along its flat surface, the ruler deforms with little effort on your part. However, try to bend the ruler against the narrow edges, and there is little or no give. The ruler, then, is a structure that efficiently resists bending in one plane; this plane has much greater strength—in the biomechanical sense—than in any other plane, because the material that the manufacturer used to construct the ruler is placed far from the central axis. A long bone from a human skeleton is structured so as to be able to resist bending (and torsion) from virtually any direction. If the tubular structure is perfectly round in cross section, then the strength of the structure will be equal in any cross-sectional plane.

The strength of long bones is measured by mathematical formulas developed by mechanical engineers to measure the strength of beams and other building materials. We bioarchaeologists have borrowed the formulas for the analysis of ancient skeletons. Beam analysis involves the measurement of cross-sectional geometric properties taken at specific cross sections measured perpendicular to the long axis of the bone. These properties measure the strength of the bone section. Unlike building materials, strength

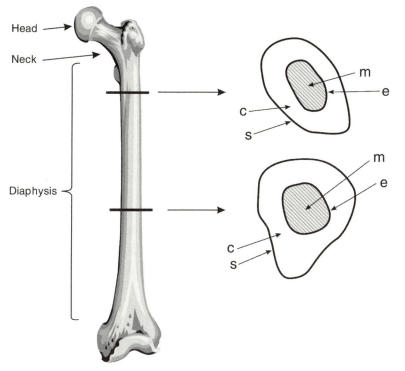

Two cross sections of a femur showing the subperiosteal surface (s), endosteal surface (e), cortical bone (c), and medullary cavity (m).

of bone develops through a lifelong process of remodeling. Geometric properties that measure bone strength include two groups of measurements, called "areas" and "second moments of area." The former represents the amount of bone in a cross section, and the latter measures the distribution of bone mass and the ability of bone in the cross section to resist bending and torsional forces, called "I" and "J" values, respectively. The properties can only be determined by viewing the complete cross sections of the bones, because both the outer surface (subperiosteal) and inner surface (endosteal) must be visible. This can be done by either cutting the bone or by noninvasive approaches, such as by computed axial tomographic (CAT or CT) scans. The images are then projected onto a screen, and the subperiosteal and endosteal surfaces traced with a digitizer hooked up to a desktop computer. With computer software, the areas and second moments are then calculated automatically.

The premise of bone changes in response to mechanical forces is an outgrowth of work done in the late 1800s by the eminent German anatomist and orthopedic surgeon, Julius Wolff. He observed that during life—from infancy through adulthood—bone tissue is added in areas of the skeleton where it is needed, and is taken away where it is not needed. Such an overwhelming amount of experimental and other research has accumulated in support of Wolff's conclusions that the phenomenon is identified simply as Wolff's Law.

After reaching the conclusion that biomechanical analysis would be very important if we were going to draw substantive conclusions about behavior in these ancient populations, Ruff and I sought and received permission from the Veterans Administration Hospital in Reno to do computed tomography of the long bones, femora and humeri. Our agreement with various governmental and tribal authorities did not allow cutting the bones, so CT was our only alternative for assessing bone strength of the Stillwater skeletons. The CT technician at the VA hospital was more than slightly amused to see these bones being passed through his CT scanner, but once we explained what we were doing and what we would learn, he was only too happy to help.

MOBILITY AND BONE STRENGTH

Because the Stillwater skeletons could not be partitioned by time period with any degree of certainty, we decided that once the bone scans were completed and analyzed, comparison with other samples we studied using the same methods would provide a context from which to interpret bone structure and infer behavior from a more global perspective. Bone areas measuring amount of bone and second moments of area measuring distribution and strength of bone were measured and analyzed.

Earlier, Ruff had analyzed the ratio of bending strength of the femur measured in the front to back (anterior-posterior) direc-

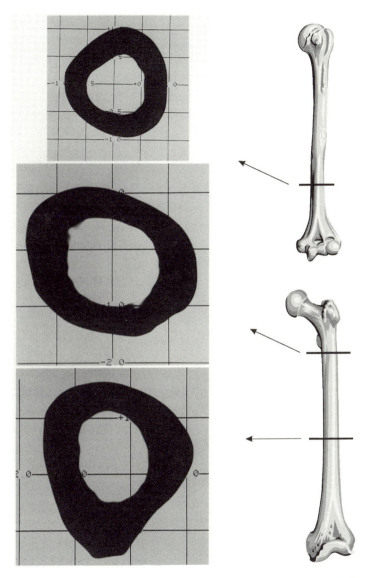

Computed axial tomographic (CT) scan images of humerus shaft (top), upper femur shaft (middle), and midshaft femur diaphysis (bottom) from an archaeological skeleton from the Stillwater Marsh region of Nevada. Adapted from Larsen et al. 1995; reproduced with permission of the American Museum of Natural History.

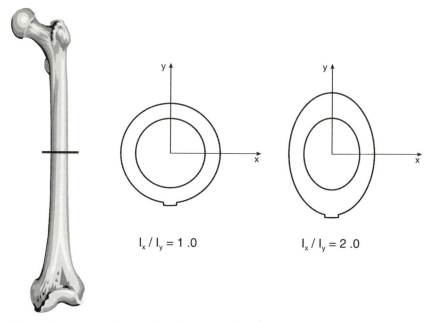

$I_x / I_y = 1.0$ $I_x / I_y = 2.0$

Schematic cross sections of two femur midshafts. The top of each section is the front of the bone, and the bottom of each section is the back of the bone. I_x measures the bending strength in the front-to-back direction relative to the x-axis, and I_y measures the bending strength in the side-to-side direction relative to the y-axis. In the left section, bending strength is approximately equal in both planes and represents a person who is sedentary (I_x/I_y = 1.0). In the right section, bending strength from front to back is greater than from side to side and represents a person who is mobile, such as that involving long-distance travel on a frequent basis (I_x/I_y = 2.0). Adapted from Ruff 1987; reproduced with permission of author and Academic Press, Ltd.

tion—called I_x—to bending strength in the side-to-side (medial-lateral) direction—called I_y, in a range of ancient and modern humans. He has found that this ratio of I_x/I_y is an excellent indicator of mobility, and especially amount of long-distance traveling a person has done. People with I_x/I_y values close to the value of 1 have roughly the same bending strength in both planes because of low mobility—the femur simply isn't stressed more in one plane than the other. Therefore, as the bone grows and remodels during childhood and afterward, it does so evenly in both the front-to-back and the side-to-side directions, producing a rounded cross section. In contrast, people who are physically active and doing a lot of walking and running tend to bend the bone more in the front-to-back direction, due to increased mechanical demand during these activities. Ruff's work demonstrated that sedentary industrial populations (like Americans) have the lowest ratios (close to 1.0) and mobile prehistoric foragers have the highest ratios (greater than 1.0); the ratios for prehistoric farmers lie between the two extremes.

BONE MASS, NUTRITION, STRENGTH, AND GENDER

Analysis of the cross sections in the Stillwater femora and humeri indicates that bone areas, a measure of bone mass, are on the low end of the range for human populations from across North America. However, second moments of area measuring outward distribution of bone, the primary indicator of bone strength, are quite high, especially in males, compared to other modern human populations. The mobility ratio I_x/I_y in the Stillwater series shows that the males are on the very high end of the range, whereas the females are relatively low compared to other populations.

Collectively, these cross-sectional geometric values are highly informative about behavior and health in the Stillwater group. In particular, two findings stand out in our analysis. First, there is a low amount of bone mass in the Stillwater people. The most important factor—aside from age—that determines the amount of bone mass in adults is nutritional quality. Human populations with low nutritional status have generally low bone mass. Thus, poor nutrition is likely an important factor in the biocultural framework of the western Great Basin, and is consistent with the above-discussed observations on and interpretation of enamel defects in this group. Years of food shortages during droughts were likely a key factor in determining these indicators of physiological stress in the Stillwater population.

Despite the relatively low bone mass, bone strength is quite high in the Stillwater group, particularly in the femur. Clearly, these people were subjecting their legs to very heavy physical activity, compared to other populations. Findings based on our analysis of the upper limb (humerus bone) are considerably different from those based on the lower limb. Namely, bone strength in the arm is not different in comparison with the other populations. The mobility index, I_x/I_y, suggests that the heavy use of the legs is due to high levels of mobility, namely long-distance travel, especially in adult males and less so in adult females. This underscores the important observation that the long bones are not just large in comparison with other archaeological series; rather, the shapes are modified over the lifetimes of the Stillwater people such that they reflect highly active and mobile behaviors.

These findings cannot be accounted for by foraging in the wetland marshes alone. If movement were restricted to the marsh, then the patterns presented here would be found in both males and females equally. It is clear that these patterns are different—males were more active and more mobile than females. To take this conclusion one step further, I think that their settlement pattern involved a great deal of mobility. The stable isotope data suggest that resources were indeed extracted from the marsh region for at least part of the year, but the biomechanical findings strongly suggest that travel over difficult terrain in the surrounding uplands was an important part of their adaptation, especially in males. This conclusion is consistent with the few early accounts by explorers, military, and other early visitors to the region, namely that native groups were observed to travel long distances—upwards of 60 miles—to collect and transport foods that were hunted and gathered. These findings argue for a position lying somewhere between Heizer's limnosedentary and Thomas's limnomobile hypotheses, but closer to the latter. The population overall was active and highly mobile, primarily the adult males.

This pattern infers then that like many living hunter-gatherer groups worldwide, men in the prehistoric Great Basin were responsible for acquiring resources involving travel such as hunting large animals, and women were more involved in plant collection and activities such as cooking, child care, and maintenance of the household and living setting. The marsh likely served as a settlement hub, but residential and logistical (food acquisition) movements away from the marsh were important for the adaptation to be successful.

Comparing Regions: The Big Picture in the Great Basin

As it turned out, the record levels of winter precipitation that hit the western Great Basin in the mid-1980s were to have an impact on other areas of the Great Basin, with a similar outcome for bioarchaeology. To the north, in the Malheur Lake wetlands of Oregon, and to the east, on the shores of the Great Salt Lake region of Utah, record snowfalls occasioned unprecedented levels of erosion of their respective landscapes, resulting in exposure of many archaeological sites and human remains. In the Malheur Lake region, Brian Hemphill of Vanderbilt University and Greg Nelson of the University of Oregon have studied the skeletal remains, and likewise, Carol Loveland, Jason Bright, Joan Coltrain, and Thomas Stafford have studied human remains from the Great Salt Lake wetlands, producing important findings on human adaptation in these settings. Their work serves as an important comparative base for interpreting patterns of health and activity from this vast region of the western United States.

Bioarchaeology in the Malheur Lake and Great Salt Lake wetlands shows some important parallels in health and activity, yet with some significant differences from Stillwater. The physiological stress levels, as represented by enamel defects, are virtually identical in comparison of the Malheur and Stillwater groups. In contrast, however, the Malheur group has many more infectious lesions than Stillwater—nearly half of the Malheur group (43 percent) has at least one bone with periosteal reactions, in contrast to the 16 percent observed in the Stillwater group. Most of the Malheur lesions are associated with a single late prehistoric site in which population may have been more concentrated around a tightly circumscribed area. In the Great Salt Lake sample, only two individuals in the series of fifty skeletons have periosteal reactions. Thus, with the exception of one site in the Malheur wet-lands, infection in the Great Basin is low. Porotic hyperostosis and cribra orbitalia across all three groups are also low, indicating normal iron status (or adequacy of vitamins C and D) throughout the region.

Especially striking in comparing the three regions is the wide-spread nature of osteoarthritis. All populations display high fre-quencies of osteoarthritis, which reflects the mechanically de-manding lifestyles of the Great Basin populations in general. There are some interesting differences, however, including more bilateral osteoarthritis of paired joints (for example, elbow and knee) in Stillwater than at Malheur. In sharp contrast to the Still-water group, where only two individuals showed unilateral osteo-arthritis of paired joints—especially the elbow—half of the Mal-heur group had osteoarthritis on one side. This indicates that the Malheur people were using just one arm, probably for some type of throwing activity (e.g., spear throwing). Across all three regions, there is a common pattern of joint involvement, with especially high frequencies in the lumbar spine and elbow for males, and males generally have more osteoarthritis than females. Thus, looking at osteoarthritis prevalence and pattern, the lifestyles ap-pear to be similar across the Great Basin, but with some variances suggesting more localized differences in activity (e.g., difference in bilateral involvement between Malheur and Stillwater). These differences are to be expected given the variation in cultural be-havior that almost certainly was present in regions separated by wide geographic distance.

Ruff's comparisons of long bone cross-sectional geometry in the three groups also indicate strong similarities in the size and struc-ture of long bones across the Great Basin. In fact, second moment of area values for the three groups confirm our suspicions that these populations pursued a similar lifestyle involving similar be-haviors and mechanical demands. Some differences are present in the bone cross sections, especially in comparing Stillwater with the Malheur and Great Salt Lake groups. The Stillwater group shows a tendency for lower values of bone mass, suggesting lower nutritional health than in the other two groups. The Malheur mobility index (femur I_x/I_y) is low, which suggests that the Malheur group engaged in less long-distance travel and mobility than either of the two other samples. This is consistent with the finding of higher frequency of periosteal reactions in the late prehistoric Malheur group. That is, we should see a higher frequency of infection in a population that was large and sedentary, where sanitation and health would be reduced in comparison with a small, dispersed population. In all regions, males have significantly larger mobility indices than females, suggesting the common pattern of men traveling over longer distances than women.

Dietary patterns, as identified by carbon isotope ratios, show significant difference in comparison of Stillwater and the Great Salt Lake populations (data are not available for Malheur). This variation reflects strong differences in foodways between the two regions: The Stillwater population relied on a combination of C_3 and C_4 wild plants and animals, whereas at least some of the Great Salt Lake people consumed C_3 and C_4 wild plants and animals in combination with corn, a major C_4 plant domesticate. In the Great Salt Lake series, the isotope ratio variation indicates a marked change in diet after about A.D. 1150. Before A.D. 1150, native people from the Fremont culture consumed corn in the Great Salt Lake region, which is indicated by high carbon isotope ratios. These values may have also been due at least in part to consumption of wild C_4 plants and bison grazing on C_4 grasses. After that date, the values become lower, reflecting the shift to a more foraging-based C_3 diet. Like the Stillwater series, these variable isotope values make clear that diets in the Great Salt Lake area were highly variable. The major difference lies in the use of corn in the far eastern Great Basin, a pattern that is shared with adjacent Southwestern groups (e.g., the Anasazi). The drop-off in C_4 consumption after A.D. 1150 shows that at least one set of resource options available before A.D. 1150 was eliminated after that date. Environmental reconstructions indicate that this change was tied to a shift from summer-to winter-dominated rainfall, which limited farming in some regions and altogether eliminated it in others.

Like the Stillwater series, dental caries in the Great Salt Lake was quite low (3.5 percent). These values demonstrate the overall good oral health of foragers in the Great Basin generally.

In summary, the study of Great Basin skeletons reveals three basic findings about health and activity. First, the prehistoric people living in the region were generally healthy. Of course, there likely were off years when water and food shortages owing to climatic fluctuations presented challenges to health and well-being. But the combination of wetlands and uplands resources suggests some measure of adaptive success. Second, native diets were diverse and generally nutritious. Our analysis of bone mass suggests some problems in nutrition, but the overall pattern—at least compared with other prehistoric North Americans that I will talk about in upcoming chapters—shows a generally healthy nutritional environment. Finally, Great Basin populations had to work hard for the foods they acquired.

Like so much of science, data in bioarchaeological research that are needed to address a particular problem or set of problems may not be readily available or easily acquired. This certainly was the case for my own work in the Great Basin—I had to wait a decade and a half before an appropriate skeletal series became available for addressing issues about the human condition that were being considered in various circles of anthropology, particularly by archaeologists. And, like so much of science, the data were made available by an act of nature, followed by a lot of hard work. Had the Sierra Nevada Mountains not been blanketed by record snows in the mid-1980s, we simply would not have had the new and exciting picture of past peoples living in the Great Basin that was presented in this chapter. This natural event was to have an enormous impact on what we now know about Great Basin foragers. It was also a fortuitous event that competent bioarchaeologists and archaeologists were in the right place and at the right time for studying and interpreting skeletons from other regions of the Great Basin. What appeared to be a catastrophe to us when first viewing the damage on these desert landscapes turned out to be one of the most important developments in the history of anthropology of the American Desert West.

The bioarchaeological picture presented here of a group of prehistoric foragers from the Great Basin provides an important backdrop for understanding the causes and consequences of the shift from foraging to farming that took place worldwide during the Holocene epoch. With the exception of the people living on the eastern fringe of the Great Basin in Utah, prehistoric Indians never adopted the agricultural lifestyle in the Great Basin. Nevertheless, what we learned in this specific region helps inform our understanding of the dynamics of a hunter-gatherer lifestyle in comparison with the very different patterns observed in farmers, especially in health and activity. In the next chapter, I will consider the biological outcome of the transition from foraging to farming in regions of the world where this major dietary change took place, using my own research in the American Southeast as a test case.

NOTES

1. Isotope ratios are expressed using the Greek delta symbol (δ) as parts per thousand (‰; read as parts "per mil" from the Latin for thousand, *mille*) difference from an accepted reference standard. The reference standard for stable carbon isotopes is Pee Dee Belemnite (PDB), a carbonate rock from South Carolina. The δ values for stable isotope ratios for carbon are mostly negative, and are calculated by the formula:

$$\delta^{13}C = \{[(^{13}C/^{12}C)_{sample} - (^{13}C/^{12}C)_{PDB}] \div (^{13}C/^{12}C)_{PDB}\} \times 1000‰$$

C_3 plants have $\delta^{13}C$ values that average around −26‰, C_4 plants have higher (less negative) $\delta^{13}C$ values that average about −12‰, and CAM plants (only rarely consumed by humans) have $\delta^{13}C$ values that occur across the range of C_3 and C_4 plants, but usually fall somewhere between the ranges for C_3 and C_4 plants. The actual carbon isotope values are measured from bone samples, usually the collagen (organic) component, with an instrument called a mass spectrometer. Once the values for ^{12}C and ^{13}C are determined, then they are plugged into the above formula for determining the stable isotope ratio, the $\delta^{13}C$ value.

Field and laboratory studies involving controlled feeding experiments of different kinds of plants to animals demonstrate that stable carbon isotope ratios in an animal's tissues—including bone—reflect the ratios of the diet. Thus, animals (including humans) that eat mostly C_3-based foods have lower (more negative) $\delta^{13}C$ values than animals consuming C_4-based foods. In essence, then, the values are transferred up the different trophic levels—the food chain—to humans.

Recognizing the potential for identifying the history of use of corn by ancient people, J. C. Vogel and Nikolaas van der Merwe determined $\delta^{13}C$ values in a series of archaeological skeletons from New York state. Their study produced compelling results about dietary history and the use of corn in prehistory. Contrary to an opinion held by many archaeologists that corn became an important crop in North America early in the first millennium A.D., their study indicated that corn dependence actually occurred late in prehistory, occurring only during the final centuries prior to European contact. This research opened a floodgate of studies on carbon isotopes in a wide range of archaeological settings, especially in North America. Today, hundreds of skeletons in eastern North America and elsewhere have been analyzed for stable carbon isotope ratios, presenting clear indications of when, where, and at what rate corn became important in native diets (see figure on page 38 for a graphic depiction of how the values differ according to the kind of diet eaten).

2. The two different kinds of plants produce different values of ratios of stable nitrogen isotope ratios relative to the standard of atmospheric nitrogen known as ambient inhalable reservoir (AIR). These stable isotope ratios are determined by the formula:

$$\delta^{15}N = \{[(^{15}N/^{14}N)_{sample} - (^{15}N/^{14}N)_{AIR}] \div (^{15}N/^{14}N)_{AIR}\} \times 1000\%o$$

In general, the isotope ratios for terrestrial (land-based) plants are lower than for marine plants by about 4‰. These differences are passed up the food chain to marine and terrestrial animals, so that marine animals have higher values than terrestrial animals, and similarly, humans consuming marine plants and animals have higher values than humans consuming terrestrial plants and animals. The $\delta^{15}N$ stable isotope values are always positive.

3. Wheat 1967, p. 3.

References

Bridges, P. S. (1995) Skeletal biology and behavior in ancient humans. *Evolutionary Anthropology* 4:112–120.

Bright, J. R., and Loveland, C. J. (1999) A biological perspective on prehistoric human adaptation in the Great Salt Lake wetlands. In B. E. Hemphill and C. S. Larsen, eds. *Prehistoric Lifeways in the Great Basin Wetlands: Bioarchaeological Reconstruction and Interpretation.* Salt Lake City: University of Utah Press.

Coltrain, J. B., and Stafford, T. W., Jr. (1999) Stable carbon isotopes and Salt Lake wetlands diet: toward an understanding of the Great Basin Formative. In B. E. Hemphill and C. S. Larsen, eds. *Prehistoric Lifeways in the*

Great Basin Wetlands: Bioarchaeological Reconstruction and Interpretation. Salt Lake City, Utah: University of Utah Press.

Goodman, A. H., Martinez, C., and Chavez, A. (1991) Nutritional supplementation and the development of linear enamel hypoplasias in children from Tezonteopan, Mexico. *American Journal of Clinical Nutrition* 53:773–781.

Goodman, A. H., Pelto, G. H., Allen, L. H., and Chavez, A. (1992) Socioeconomic and anthropometric correlates of linear enamel hypoplasia in children from Solis, Mexico. In A. H. Goodman and L. L. Capasso, eds. *Recent Contributions to the Study of Enamel Developmental Defects. Journal of Paleopathology, Monographic Publications*, no. 2, pp. 373–380.

Goodman, A. H., and Rose, J. C. (1991) Dental enamel hypoplasias as indicators of nutritional stress. In M. A. Kelley and C. S. Larsen, eds. *Advances in Dental Anthropology*. New York: Wiley-Liss, pp. 279–293.

Hemphill, B. E. (1999) Wear and tear: osteoarthritis as an indicator of mobility among Great Basin hunter-gatherers. In B. E. Hemphill and C. S. Larsen, eds. *Understanding Prehistoric Lifeways in the Great Basin Wetlands: Bioarchaeological Reconstruction and Interpretation*. Salt Lake City: University of Utah Press.

Hemphill, B. E., and Larsen, C. S., eds. (1999) *Understanding Prehistoric Lifeways in the Great Basin Wetlands: Bioarchaeological Reconstruction and Interpretation*. Salt Lake City: University of Utah Press.

Hutchinson, D. L., and Larsen, C. S. (1995) Physiological stress in the prehistoric Stillwater Marsh: evidence of enamel defects. In C. S. Larsen and R. L. Kelly, eds. *Bioarchaeology of the Stillwater Marsh: Prehistoric Human Adaptation in the Western Great Basin*. Anthropological Papers of the American Museum of Natural History, no. 77, pp. 81–95.

Larsen, C. S. (1997) *Bioarchaeology: Interpreting Behavior from the Human Skeleton*. Cambridge: Cambridge University Press.

Larsen, C. S., and Hutchinson, D. L. (1999) Osteopathology of Carson Desert foragers: reconstructing prehistoric lifeways in the western Great Basin. In B. E. Hemphill and C. S. Larsen, eds. *Prehistoric Lifeways in the Great Basin Wetlands: Bioarchaeological Reconstruction and Interpretation*. Salt Lake City: University of Utah Press.

Larsen, C. S., and Kelly, R. L., eds. (1995) *Bioarchaeology of the Stillwater Marsh: Prehistoric Human Adaptation in the Western Great Basin*. Anthropological Papers of the American Museum of Natural History, no. 77.

Larsen, C. S., Kelly, R. L., Ruff, C. B., Schoeninger, M. J., and Hutchinson, D. L. (1996) Biobehavioral adaptations in the western Great Basin. In E. J. Reitz, L. A. Newson, and S. J. Scudder, eds. *Case Studies in Environmental Archaeology*. New York: Plenum Press, pp. 149–174.

Larsen, C. S., Ruff, C. B., and Kelly, R. L. (1995) Structural analysis of the Stillwater postcranial human remains: behavioral implications of articular joint pathology and long bone diaphyseal morphology. In C. S. Larsen and R. L. Kelly, eds. *Bioarchaeology of the Stillwater Marsh: Prehistoric Human Adaptation in the Western Great Basin*. Anthropological Papers of the American Museum of Natural History, no. 77, pp. 107–133.

Nelson, G. C. (1999) Environmental fluctuation physiological stress in the northern Great Basin. In B. E. Hemphill and C. S. Larsen, eds. *Prehistoric Lifeways in the Great Basin Wetlands: Bioarchaeological Reconstruction and Interpretation*. Salt Lake City: University of Utah Press.

O'Rourke, D. H., Parr, R. L., and Carlyle, S. W. (1999) Molecular genetic variation in prehistoric inhabitants of the eastern Great Basin. In B. E. Hemphill and C. S. Larsen, eds. *Prehistoric Lifeways in the Great Basin Wetlands: Bioarchaeological Reconstruction and Interpretation*. Salt Lake City: University of Utah Press.

Ruff, C. B. (1987) Sexual dimorphism in human lower limb bone structure: relationship to subsistence strategy and sexual division of labor. *Journal of Human Evolution* 16:391–416.

———. (1992) Biomechanical analyses of archaeological human skeletal samples. In S. R. Saunders and M. A. Katzenberg, eds. *Skeletal Biology of Past Peoples: Research Methods*. New York: Wiley-Liss, pp. 37–58.

———. (1999) Skeletal structure and behavioral patterns of prehistoric Great Basin populations. In B. E. Hemphill and C. S. Larsen, eds. *Prehistoric Lifeways in the Great Basin Wetlands: Bioarchaeological Reconstruction and Interpretation*. Salt Lake City: University of Utah Press.

Schoeninger, M. J. (1995) Stable isotope studies in human evolution. *Evolutionary Anthropology* 4:83–98.

———. (1995) Dietary reconstruction in the prehistoric Carson Desert: stable carbon and nitrogen isotopic analysis. In C. S. Larsen and R. L. Kelly, eds. *Bioarchaeology of the Stillwater Marsh: Prehistoric Human Adaptation in the Western Great Basin*. Anthropological Papers of the American Museum of Natural History, no. 77, pp. 96–106.

Schultz, M. (1993) Initial stages of systematic bone disease. In G. Grupe and A. N. Garland, eds. *Histology of Ancient Human Bone: Methods and Diagnosis*. Berlin: Springer-Verlag, pp. 185–203.

Wheat, M. M. (1967) *Survival Arts of the Primitive Paiutes*. Reno: University of Nevada Press.

From Foraging to Farming:
A Regional Perspective

I AM WILLING to bet that the most fundamental change in humans—at least with regard to the evolution of *Homo sapiens*—occurred when we changed from being hunter-gatherers to being farmers. For most of the history of our species, all human beings depended exclusively on wild plants and animals for food. Soon after the close of the Ice Age and the appearance of modern climates, people began shifting to a wholly new form of adaptation involving the production of domesticated plants and animals. Today, all of our food is from domesticated sources—it is grown and harvested by human beings. This change from food collection to food production set the stage for the rise of civilization, urban centers, complex social organization, writing, art, and just about everything else we associate with modern living. By this measure, most conclude that the shift from foraging to farming represented an improvement in the human condition. In fact, though, bioarchaeology is showing that there was a health cost associated with the change—humans began to experience more illness, a poorer quality of life, and, in many settings, more work.

In this chapter, we move across the North American continent from the Great Basin to the Atlantic coast. In this new setting, we explore the outcome of the shift from foraging to farming along the southeastern U.S. Atlantic coast during the final few centuries before the arrival of Europeans in the mid-1500s. Unlike the Great Basin, where agriculture was not adopted in most places, agriculture spread rapidly in the American East, including the area

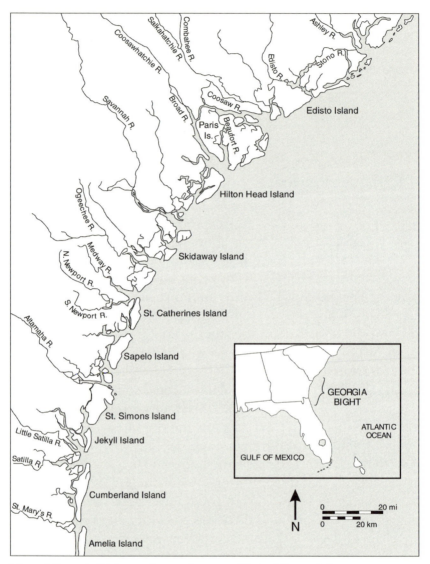

Map of Georgia Bight on the southeastern United States Atlantic coast, showing location of St. Catherines Island and other major localities. Adapted from Thomas 1987; reproduced with permission of author and the American Museum of Natural History.

discussed in this chapter. We will explore what we have learned about the impact of this adaptive shift on people living in this region. This serves as a starting point for understanding the event on a worldwide scale, which will be discussed in the next chapter.

While I was an undergraduate at Kansas State University, I developed a keen interest in the evolutionary history of humans, especially in a period of time that had received little attention—the Holocene epoch. The Holocene, the last ten thousand years, was surprisingly untouched; most physical anthropologists who study the past are much more interested in earlier humans and their ancestors, those who lived long before the beginning of the Holocene. When I returned for classes following fieldwork in the Great Basin at end of the summer of 1974, I had to decide where I wanted to go to graduate school. I especially wanted to pick a place of study where I could study human evolution. Patricia O'Brien, my advisor at Kansas State, told me that if I wished to pursue a career in physical anthropology and study evolution, the University of Michigan was the best place to go. As is true today, Michigan had an extraordinarily strong program in human evolution and skeletal biology, it had a superb faculty of physical anthropologists and archaeologists, it was among the best graduate anthropology programs in the United States, and the university was a premier academic institution. I applied to its program with high hopes of moving to Ann Arbor.

In the spring of my senior year, I got the letter from Michigan's Department of Anthropology that I had been hoping for: I was in—the department would be expecting to see me at the end of August. Within months of arriving on campus, another important event happened that was to steer much of the future course of my research interests and career in bioarchaeology. Dave Thomas, with whom I had been working at Gatecliff Shelter in Nevada the previous two summers, called me from his office at New York's American Museum of Natural History to say that he was starting a long-term archaeological field program on St. Catherines Island, Georgia. As he laid it out to me, this program would involve years, if not decades, of fieldwork and research. Generous funding from the Edward John Noble Foundation, the owners of this beautiful barrier island, would make it possible to excavate a series of prehistoric burial mounds and undertake extensive archaeological surveys. Dave asked me if I would be interested in serving as the project physical anthropologist (the term "bioarchaeologist" had not yet been invented), responsible for the study of all the skeletal remains recovered in the excavations. As he described the island's fascinating ecological setting, its exotic archaeology, and his proposed project, my thoughts immediately turned to a hot topic in anthropology—the shift from foraging to farming. I fantasized (science almost always starts with some kind of fantasy) that St. Catherines Island could serve as a natural laboratory for testing hypotheses about the human biology of this important adaptive shift that had taken place worldwide beginning about ten thousand years ago.

By the time Dave called me, I had read publications by a handful of physical anthropologists, such as those by George Armelagos and his collaborators working in Sudanese Nubia, Lawrence Angel in Greece, John Lallo and Jerome Rose in central Illinois, and Jane Buikstra and her collaborators in western Illinois. Their work focused mostly on pieces of the puzzle—such as the change in diet and its impact on dental growth and development. Overall, what I was gathering from these studies was that there were some fundamental biological changes that accompanied the shift from foraging-to-farming in ancient times. Admittedly, this wasn't much to go on, but I had a nagging suspicion that the foraging-to-farming transition had entailed a worldwide decline in health and dramatic changes in activity reflecting alterations in behavior and workload.

My suspicion about changes in human health ran completely counter to what I had been taught about the differences between prehistoric hunter-gatherers and farmers. I had been taught that hunter-gatherers had a very arduous existence, whereas agriculture was the basis of "civilization" and all things "civilized." After all, weren't hunter-gatherers the untamed savages, and farmers the civilized folk, spoken about by nineteenth-century anthropologist Lewis Henry Morgan in his classic book, *Ancient Societies*? The popular and often-cited archaeology textbook, *Prehistoric Men*, by the eminent Near Eastern archaeologist Robert Braidwood, said that foragers had always had it bad; once agriculture came along following the end of the Ice Age, opportunities opened up for all things good, including cities, art, society, leisure, medicine, good health and nutrition, and so forth. My perception of health in prehistoric farmers was inconsistent with this scenario. Here was a problem worth examining on St. Catherines Island and the region generally.

Although I was a typical naïve first-year graduate student, I did have the good sense to recognize the wonderful opportunity being handed to me—not to mention a great doctoral dissertation project—to look at the human biological record of the foraging-to-farming transition. I told Thomas to count me in; my agenda for dissertation research was set. So, before the close of an especially long Michigan winter, I was on a plane to subtropical coastal Georgia to begin working with Thomas's field crews on St. Catherines Island.

For the remainder of the 1970s, while completing my coursework and other degree requirements for a Ph.D., I helped direct the excavations of a number of burial mounds on St. Catherines Island, taking the skeletons back to my lab at Michigan for study as we completed each of many field seasons. The skeletal samples and burial archaeology turned out to be extraordinarily interesting. Some of the burial mounds were among the earliest to be found in this area of the American Southeast, dating to the first millennium B.C. However, the skeletons were of variable degrees of preservation—some of them consisted merely of bone dust and tooth fragments—and they dated mostly to before the twelfth century A.D., the time during which I thought that corn was adopted by prehistoric native populations living on the island and in the region generally. In order to broaden my samples and capture the subsistence and adaptive regimes involving both foraging and agricultural lifestyles on the prehistoric Georgia coast, I tracked down and studied other skeletons in the collections of the University of Georgia in Athens. These additional materials extended my study to include the entire region occupied by the tribe known as Guale (pronounced "walley") at the time of European contact in the sixteenth century. I then spent a year at the Smithsonian Institution recording and analyzing data from its enormous collection—numbering in the hundreds of individuals—of Georgia coastal archaeological skeletons that had been excavated by work relief crews during the Great Depression of the 1930s. With the completion of my research, I had an unprecedented data set dealing with changes in health and activity from the American Southeast.

THE SHIFT FROM FORAGING TO FARMING: A HUGE DEVELOPMENT

Why was I making such a big deal about the foraging-to-farming transition in this or any other region of the world? To my mind, the answer to this question was as obvious as it was simple: This issue is important because the shift from foraging to farming was one of the most comprehensive adaptive shifts to take place in the evolution of our genus, *Homo*. More than ten thousand years ago, all human beings and their ancestors ate wild plants and animals, exclusively. Within only a few thousand years, plant domestication was invented independently in at least seven places in the world— such as wheat and barley in the Middle East, rice in central China, and corn, beans, and squash in North America. The practice of plant cultivation then spread rapidly from these centers of domestication, so that today more than 99 percent of the world's population is dependent on agriculture to one extent or another.

For most of the world's population today, some two-thirds of calorie and protein intake is from cereal grains (wheat, barley, corn, rice, and others). Rice alone provides half of the food for some 1.7 billion people and more than one-fifth of the calories consumed by all humans. This is truly an amazing development when one considers the fact that our genus has been around for two to three million years and we have been agricultural for only ten thousand of those years. The first appearance and spread of agriculture is only an eyeblink in the evolutionary history of humans.

Finally, the adoption of agriculture involved a focus on cereal grains. No earlier hominid ate grains to this degree, and certainly no other living primate consumes the amount of cereal grain that humans have eaten in the last ten thousand years. The comprehensive nature of the dietary shift, the speed of the transition from foraging to farming, and the uniqueness of the dietary focus on cereal grains make this an important matter for investigation. Indeed, I would argue that agriculture is a defining characteristic of our species today, up there with bipedalism and speech.

Other transitions in our ancient past may have been equally (or even more) profound. There is some evidence to suggest that the earliest hominids living millions of years ago, human ancestors called *Australopithecus*, were opportunistic gatherers and scavengers, eating plants and small animals, and scavenging carcasses of large animals killed by carnivores. Pat Shipman of Pennsylvania State University has documented ancient animal bones that have carnivore tooth marks overlain by stone-tool cutmarks made by hominids as they removed meat from the carcass. This is clear proof of scavenging behavior in early human ancestors.

At some later point in our evolution, people shifted from a scavenging-gathering lifestyle to one involving organized hunting of large game; scavenging was no more. If scavenging-gathering did evolve into a lifestyle focused on full-fledged hunting, then this represented a major transition having important implications for the evolution of human diet, social organization, cultural behavior, and other elements of behavior that we take for granted as being typically "human." Unfortunately, the evidence documenting this transition, which may well have occurred a half-million years ago or so, is awfully sparse. When it comes down to it, paleoanthropologists have precious few facts that convincingly document the shift from scavenging-gathering to hunting.

By the same token, there is a widespread consensus among anthropologists that once big-game hunting developed, we were on the road to full-blown humanness. The evidence for hunting is based largely on the associations during the Pleistocene epoch of stone tools and the remains of large animals. There is a strong likelihood that these earlier hominids—*Homo erectus*—hunted animals, which provided a great source of protein. However, based on their extensive work with the Hadza tribe of East Africa, archaeologist Jim O'Connell and behavioral ecologist Kristen Hawkes of the University of Utah make the case that hunting in these living peoples doesn't provide most of the nutrients required for day-to-day living, and the hunting basis of human diets is more than a little exaggerated. Thus, the outcome and significance of the shift to hunting is unclear. Even if the shift to hunting was well documented, it may not have been all that important.

An understanding of the outcome for humans of the foraging-to-farming shift is a completely different story in the broad picture of human dietary evolution. We now have a surfeit of scientific data to show where and when the transition to farming took place and, importantly, what the consequences were for humans, especially in the realm of health and activity. The reasons why the shift happened are murky, however. Ever since V. Gordon Child coined the term "Neolithic Revolution," in the early 1950s, archaeologists have attempted to develop a universal theory explaining the foraging-to-farming transition worldwide. Despite the fact that the origin of agriculture is at the top of the list of topics that archaeologists discuss, the efforts to produce a single explanation have been inconclusive. The development of a universal model has eluded archaeologists because the shift to agriculture was mainly locally or regionally driven, depending to a large extent on unique environmental, social, cultural, political, and other factors.

Foraging to Farming: The Outcome

The shift from foraging to farming can best be evaluated on the basis of its outcome for people in the past. Archaeologists assess the outcome in various ways, such as with regard to settlement patterns—where people lived and in what types of communities. For most areas of the world, settlement change involved a shift from a mobile, foraging subsistence strategy to a sedentary village economy based on one or more plant (and sometimes, animal) domesticates. Change in material culture reflecting the shift from foraging to farming is also significant. In the earliest agricultural sites, archaeologists have found the tools that were used to culti-vate and process domesticated plants for food, reflecting the im-portant dietary change. The identification of tools used in a forag-ing economy versus those used in a farming economy can be difficult, however, because many of the same tools used for har-vesting the wild ancestors of domesticated plants (wheat and bar-ley)—such as sharp flakes attached to a handle—were used to har-vest the domesticated versions of the plants later in time (e.g., in the Levant region of the Middle East).

For the New World, various domesticated plant species origi-nated from wild ancestors growing in Mexico beginning within a few thousand years after the close of the Ice Age about ten thou-sand years ago. In Mexico, some six thousand years separate the appearance of plant domesticates and full dependence on plants involving sedentism and village life. From this Mexican agricul-tural heartland, the idea of using plant domesticates as a basis for diet spread to the American Southwest and later into eastern North America, to the vast region east of the Mississippi River valley called the Eastern Woodlands. There is some evidence for independent plant domestication in eastern North America, such as with the *Cucurbita pepo* squash around five thousand years ago in Missouri. Corn, however, was introduced to the American Southwest and Eastern Woodlands, rather than being indepen-dently domesticated. Corn agriculture was picked up quickly by native populations in the Eastern Woodlands.

An important part of the outcome of the foraging-to-farming shift is what it did to the health, well-being, and biology of the people involved. In the following discussion, I will lead you through the bioarchaeological context for the shift from foraging to farming on the Georgia coast, and address the nature of diet—when corn became important, and the changes in human health and activity that my research team and I have discovered based on our study of skeletons from this region.

The Georgia Coast: A Natural Laboratory for Doing Bioarchaeology

The Georgia coast is at the apogee of the Georgia Bight, a large embayment extending from Cape Hatteras, North Carolina, to Cape Canaveral, Florida. In addition to its being prone to hurricanes, a dominant feature of this long stretch of Atlantic coast is a chain of barrier islands sharing similar Pleistocene and Holocene depositional and ecological histories. Lying between the outermost barrier islands and the mainland are various marsh islands. Sounds, salt marshes, and tidal creeks separate the barrier islands and marsh islands. The topography of the islands and adjacent mainland is characterized by very low relief with a diverse subtropical flora and fauna. Primary plant communities on the islands and adjacent mainland are maritime oak and pine forests. The area today is one of the most diverse and rich in marine and estuarine resources in the world, as it must have been in the past. In particular, the inshore zone is endowed with a tremendous variety of sea life, including numerous fishes, such as red drum (*Sciaenops ocellatus*) and species of Clupeidae—blueback herring (*Alosa aestivalis*), menhaden (*Brevoortia* sp.), and gizzard shad (*Dorosoma cependianum*). Shrimp (*Penaeus* spp.), present in vast numbers, were heavily exploited by prehistoric Indians, as were various estuarine molluscs, especially the American oyster (*Crassostrea virginica*) and hard clams (*Mercenaria* spp.). The remains of terrestrial species of plants (e.g., acorns from live oak, *Quercus virginiana*) and animals (e.g., white-tail deer, *Odocoileus virginianus*) are frequently found in prehistoric archaeological habitation sites, indicating the importance of these resources in native diets in the past.

Prehistoric native settlement change in the Georgia Bight involved a general increase in living site size and density, mainly during the late prehistoric periods called by archaeologists working in the region the Savannah (A.D. 1150–1300) and Irene (A.D. 1300–1550) periods. These periods are the local variants of the huge cultural florescence that took place throughout eastern North America during late prehistory called the Mississippian period. The change in patterns of living sites reflects a dramatic increase in population size and density and the declining mobility of people. Although the reasons for this decline in mobility are unclear, the settlement changes are associated with an increasing focus on agriculture, having to do especially with production and consumption of corn by native groups living in permanent or semipermanent villages. It is also during the Savannah and Irene periods that we begin to see increasing complexity of burial practices. For example, at the Irene Mound site—the primary Mississippian center located slightly upriver from the mouth of the Savannah River on the north Georgia coast—archaeologists have identified successive stages of mound construction and other sophisticated architecture emblematic of complex societies in the late prehistoric American Southeast. This pattern of settlement and cultural change is consistent with the appearance of chiefdoms and elaboration of social order and structure in later prehistory.

From the perspective of bioarchaeology, the large and generally well documented series of hundreds of skeletons that span the transition from foraging to farming makes this area of the world attractive for studying the lives and lifestyles of the native people who underwent this adaptive change.[1] The following discussion highlights what we have learned about changes in health and activity based on this important record of biological history.

Measuring Health from Skeletons: Nutrition, Stress, and Disease

DIETARY RECONSTRUCTION ON THE GEORGIA COAST:
WHEN DID CORN ENTER THE PICTURE AND
WHAT ARE THE IMPLICATIONS FOR HEALTH FOR
THE PEOPLE EATING IT?

Georgia Bight archaeological sites are silent about use of plants, domesticated or wild, by prehistoric Indians in their diets. Aside from the few burned corn kernels and cobs found by archaeologists at a few prehistoric living sites, corn is virtually nonexistent. Does this mean that people living on the prehistoric Georgia coast didn't eat corn? The general lack of direct ethnobotanical evidence for the use of plants, and corn in particular, has led some authorities to believe that corn was unimportant in the diets of late prehistoric Indians living in the region. When doing my dissertation research, I became convinced otherwise, especially when I began to consider the changes in settlement and the evidence of increasing social and political complexity, such as those at the Irene Mound site. Every other major Mississippian center in eastern North America had its economic base in corn production (among other things). I could think of no reason why the Georgia coast should be different from these other settings.

The answer to this fundamental question—To what extent was corn used by late prehistoric people living on the Georgia coast?—appeared to be just around the corner with the development of the new technique of dietary reconstruction based on the chemistry of human bone from archaeological sites, which was discussed in the last chapter. Just as I was finishing my dissertation research at the Smithsonian Institution, I received a request from archaeologist Nikolaas van der Merwe, then at the University of Cape Town and now at Harvard University, for prehistoric human bone samples from the Georgia coast. Knowing of the work that Thomas and I were doing on St. Catherines Island, Nik was keenly interested in documenting patterns of dietary change in this region. He had done the pioneering work with J. C. Vogel on carbon isotope analysis of human bone samples showing distinctive isotopic changes in later prehistory in New York state and revealing, with remarkable clarity, the timing of the adoption and increased dependence on corn by ancient populations.

Nik van der Merwe's analysis of the Georgia coastal bone samples showed that like his findings from New York state, the carbon isotope ratios became increasingly higher in later prehistory (see chapter 2). The increasing values were interesting and suggested a shift to corn agriculture, but they could not be considered conclusive. Chief among the reasons for not accepting his results outright is the problem underlying use of stable carbon isotopes in populations that eat corn and marine foods simultaneously. The ratio of the stable isotopes of carbon (^{12}C and ^{13}C) is a terrific discriminator between plants with the different photosynthetic pathways and the animals and humans that eat these plants (see chapter 2). As discussed previously, C_4 plants (and their consumers) have stable isotope ratios that differ from stable isotope ratios of C_3 plants in significant ways. The bones from humans eating these plants also show ratio differences, albeit not as extreme as those in the plants themselves. Herein lies the problem: Stable carbon isotope ratios are also different between marine and terrestrial foods (and the animals and humans eating them). Marine fish and mammals have higher stable carbon isotope ratios than do animals feeding on terrestrial C_3 foods. The values, therefore, overlap with those derived for C_4 plants (such as corn) and consumers of C_4 plants. The values are not as high as C_4 isotopic signatures, but certainly approach them. Put another way, there is enough overlap in the stable isotope ratios of the bones of people eating marine foods and the bones of people eating C_4 plants, that the higher values in the later period that van der Merwe's lab was coming up with *could* be interpreted as more marine foods—not corn—in the diets of later prehistoric populations living in the Georgia Bight.

Margaret Schoeninger offered a simple solution to the problem. In collaboration with Michael DeNiro, then at UCLA, she had done pioneering work on stable isotopes of nitrogen in the food chains of various regions globally. Marine and terrestrial (land-based) organisms metabolize nitrogen differently, resulting in clear differences in ratios of the stable isotopes of nitrogen, ^{15}N to ^{14}N, for species from these different settings. Based on their findings, Margaret suggested that we analyze our human bone samples for *both* carbon and nitrogen and simply work up two-dimensional plots of stable isotopes of carbon and nitrogen for the Georgia coastal skeletons. If we could show that the nitrogen isotope ratio values either remained the same or were reduced in the Georgia coastal series—reflecting the same or increasing dependence on terrestrial foods—and, simultaneously, the carbon isotope ratio increased, then we could make a good case for increasing dependence on corn. My gut feeling told me that just such a dietary change had happened in the prehistoric Georgia coast, but I needed the hard evidence provided by bone chemistry and stable isotope analysis.

With this new idea in front of us, I pulled some additional bone samples for chemical analysis. By this time, Margaret had the necessary equipment set up in her lab—the analysis requires an instrument called a mass spectrometer—first at Harvard and later at Wisconsin, and we went to work doing more isotope analysis.

We have now analyzed bone samples from many prehistoric archaeological sites on the Georgia coast, covering the chronological sequence and in different ecological settings and dietary regimes using bivariate plots of stable carbon and nitrogen isotope ratios. Skeletons from several early prehistoric (400 B.C.–A.D. 1000) St. Catherines Island coastal sites, and one site located slightly inland at the mouth of the Savannah River representing a terrestrial setting, were compared with late prehistoric (A.D. 1000–1450) sites from St. Catherines Island and St. Simons Island (coastal) and from the Irene Mound site (terrestrial). The results are compelling: First, the isotopic differences between the early prehistoric foragers living on the coast and the contemporary population living slightly inland reflect the coastal/terrestrial dichotomy—coastal foragers have higher carbon and nitrogen isotope ratio values than the contemporary terrestrial foragers living on the mainland. Second, the late prehistoric farmers show a clear shift toward even higher carbon isotope values, but the nitrogen isotope values remain about the same throughout the sequence. This isotopic profile reflects a clear shift to corn agriculture in late prehistory, but maintaining the same level of consumption of marine foods as before. The check provided by simultaneous use of both carbon and nitrogen stable isotopes demonstrated that these people indeed became increasingly dependent on corn. Nik's original conclusions about prehistoric dietary change were vindicated.

The dietary changes that we have documented via stable isotope analysis for the Georgia coast have profound implications for the health and behavior of native populations living in the region prior to European contact. Corn is deficient in calcium; it is deficient or lacking in the three (of nine) essential amino acids, lysine, tryptophan, and isoleucine; niacin (vitamin B_3) is chemically bound, which prevents its bioavailability; it contains the chemical phytate, which prohibits iron absorption; and it has a large amount of sugar. These negative attributes should adversely affect the health and well-being of people whose dietary base includes a great deal of corn. Additionally, the kind of physical labor and activity that goes into foraging and collecting should be very different from the kind of physical labor and activity that goes into corn farming. The workload changes in the earlier foragers versus the later farmers should be revealed by changes in the prevalence of osteoarthritis and bone structure. Let's see what the record says.

TRACKING PHYSIOLOGICAL STRESS FROM TEETH

As I illustrated in our study of the Great Basin people in the last chapter, enamel defects called hypoplasias are a highly sensitive indicator of physiological stress, especially stress that occurs during the first years of life when the teeth are forming. Although the cause of hypoplasias is difficult to identify, hypoplasias provide a good overall indicator of general levels of health. Dale Hutchinson and I have examined the frequency of incisors and canines with hypoplasias in an effort to document change in physiological stress over time. Contrary to what we had expected to see, the frequency of hypoplasias actually *decreased* in comparing the prehistoric Georgia coastal foragers to farmers. For the upper and lower canines, for example, this decrease is statistically significant (maxilla = 88 percent to 70 percent; mandible = 91 percent to 77 percent). This finding suggests the possibility that stress may have declined in this setting with the shift from foraging to farming.

In order to examine growth disruption of teeth in a more detailed fashion, we decided to analyze the size of individual hypoplasias microscopically. We fit the eyepiece of a dissecting light microscope with a measurement scale in order to document the widths of hypoplasias—measured from the top to the bottom of the groove—in the prehistoric foragers and farmers. Tooth enamel is deposited incrementally, beginning at the tip of the tooth crown and concluding at the junction of the crown and root. The enamel in the teeth of most people and other primates develops at a fairly uniform rate, depending on the location on the tooth crown. Grace Suckling and her research collaborators in New Zealand have identified an association between hypoplasia size and the severity of stress in laboratory animals—the worse the stress, the larger the hypoplasias. Therefore, we surmised that a wide hypoplasia should represent an episode of stress that is worse than that indicated by a narrow hypoplasia.

Our results were more consistent with what we would expect to see in a population undergoing increased stress in the foraging-to-farming transition. For the Georgia coastal people, the prehistoric farmers have distinctively wider hypoplasias than the prehistoric foragers do. The differences are not profound, but they are statistically significant (for example, the width of hypoplasias in the mandibular canine increased, on average, from .50 mm to .79 mm).

In order to corroborate our findings based on enamel hypoplasia size, we looked at tooth size as a measure of stress. Tooth size is influenced by a complex interplay between environment and heredity, but heredity is the major determinant of how big teeth are in a person—the children of large-toothed parents tend to have large teeth. Despite the significant influence of genes in the determination of tooth size, environment appears to play a small, but important, role. Research conducted by Stanley Garn and his associates at the University of Michigan in the 1970s showed that in living people, children born to mothers who were in poor health or had poor nutrition had relatively small teeth. Over the course of human evolution—especially over the last two million years or so—our teeth have decreased in size, reflecting their decreased importance as culture took on an increasing role in the preparation of food. Simply, as humans developed stone tools—and, later, metal implements—to process food before it enters the mouth, our teeth have been reduced to their present size. This has been a slow, gradual process, indicating that the diminutive size of our teeth is largely due to evolutionary change. However, in a number of regions of the world, where tooth size reduction has occurred rapidly (within a few generations), the influence of environmental factors is strongly suggested in determining tooth size.

Comparisons of tooth size—based on length and breadth measurements of the crowns of deciduous (baby) and permanent (adult) teeth—show a reduction in comparing the earlier Georgia coastal foragers with the later farmers. This very rapid change—

it took place within a matter of decades—in the later prehistoric people suggests that the environmental component may be much more important than the genetic component in explaining these observed changes. The crowns of deciduous teeth are formed while the fetus is growing and are mostly formed by the time of birth. We suggest, therefore, consistent with Garn's findings, that the reduction in the size of these teeth reflects changes in maternal health status (and not genes) as a result of the shift from foraging to farming. Like the hypoplasia research, these findings underscore the fact that the growth of dental tissues is sensitive to physiological stress, including during the period of life prior to birth.

IRON SUFFICIENCY

In the 1970s, physical anthropologist Mahmoud El-Najjar proposed an interesting dietary hypothesis for explaining high frequencies of porotic hyperostosis and cribra orbitalia, based especially on his study of prehistoric native peoples from the American Southwest. These are the porosities in skulls that I discussed in the previous chapter, reflecting abnormally high production of red blood cells in the skull bones. El-Najjar documented a high positive correlation between the degree of dependency on corn of prehistoric people and frequencies of porotic hyperostosis and cribra orbitalia: People who eat lots of corn have high frequencies of porotic hyperostosis and cribra orbitalia. When first published in the scientific journals, El-Najjar's dietary hypothesis made perfect sense because the presence of iron-inhibiting phytate in corn should promote iron deficiency anemia.

Recent work by bioarchaeologists and others has shown, however, that food—such as corn—is just one of a suite of factors that influence iron status in humans. For example, in their study of prehistoric populations from the Santa Barbara Channel Islands region off the coast of southern California, Patricia Lambert and Phillip Walker have provided strong evidence to suggest that parasitism can lead to iron deficiency. And other circumstances having nothing to do with iron status—such as scurvy and bone inflammation—may well cause bone lesions that are similar to the ones caused by iron deficiency anemia.

Our study of the skulls of the prehistoric Georgia coastal foragers and farmers reveals a very low frequency of pathological lesions associated with iron deficiency in both groups: Only 6 percent of the skulls of the prehistoric foragers have cribra orbitalia and none of their skulls have porotic hyperostosis. In the prehistoric farmers, the frequencies are also quite low (3 percent for both cribra orbitalia and porotic hyperostosis). The lack of increase from the earlier to the later group—in fact, there is a slight decline—lends support to the idea that iron deficiency is not necessarily linked to diet and, in particular, to the consumption of corn.

Compelling research on living people who eat mostly corn versus those who simultaneously eat corn and seafood (especially fish) provides an important clue about why some corn-consuming populations—such as our late prehistoric Georgians—have such low frequencies of porotic hyperostosis. Nutrition scientists Miguel Layrisse, Carlos Martínez-Torres, and Marcel Roche found that people who consume corn alone have abysmal iron absorption. However, people who eat corn along with fish increase their iron absorption by about *300 percent*. This evidence has important implications for food consumption and iron absorption in ancient humans. All else being equal—for example, if parasitism is the same—then we predict that if the Georgia coastal groups ate significant amounts of seafood in both the earlier and later periods of prehistory, then skeletal evidence of iron deficiency should remain low in both the foragers and farmers. As discussed above, the isotope ratios of carbon and nitrogen provide strong evidence to indicate that both the early prehistoric foragers and the late prehistoric farmers living on the Georgia coast used marine foods heavily, and we believe that the use of these foods contributed to maintaining normal, healthy iron status.

DISEASE: DENTAL CARIES

Dental caries, or tooth decay, is linked to two factors: (1) the kind of food eaten, and (2) how the food is prepared. Carbohydrates, especially simple sugars, bear most of the responsibility for dietary factors that cause tooth decay. Fats have no association with dental caries, and protein seems to inhibit caries in some circumstances. Carious lesions develop when the normal flora in the mouth (e.g., the bacterium *Streptococcus mutans*) metabolizes the sugar, producing acids that dissolve the enamel and underlying dentine. The manner in which food is prepared can also be highly influential in cariogenesis. Soft, pasty foods are more conducive to the aggregation of colonies of bacteria (plaque) that generate the acid responsible for the cavities in the teeth called carious lesions. Thus, populations that boil their foods, especially carbohydrates, into soft mushes are more susceptible to caries.

Prehistoric Georgia coastal farmers have substantially more carious lesions than their foraging predecessors. In adding up all the teeth (incisors + canines + premolars + molars), only 1.2 percent of foragers' teeth are carious, in contrast to 9.6 percent of farmers' teeth. Bioarchaeologist Mark Griffin of San Francisco State University and I surveyed the frequencies of a range of Eastern Woodlands archaeological populations and found that those with caries frequencies below 7 percent tended to be foragers (no corn consumption) and those above 7 percent tended to be farmers (corn consumers). The high frequency from the late prehistoric Georgia coast fits squarely within the realm of caries frequencies for corn consumers.

The higher caries frequency in the Georgia coastal farmers is somewhat less than that which has been found in late prehistoric Mississippian period populations from interior, noncoastal Georgia. Physical anthropologist Matt Williamson of Georgia Southern University has found that 24 percent of the molars he studied from late prehistoric upland Georgians have carious lesions, whereas their contemporaries from the coast have 18 percent carious molars. Both frequencies are high, to be sure, but the interior groups appear to be more caries-prone than the coastal groups. Similarly, other samples from late prehistoric Eastern Woodlands sites tend to show somewhat greater frequencies of dental caries, suggesting that the late prehistoric coastal Georgians consumed somewhat lower amounts of corn. This conclusion is supported by comparison of stable carbon isotope ratios from the Georgia coast and interior Mississippian samples: The interior Mississippian samples tend to have higher carbon isotope ratios than those from the Georgia coastal farmers. Matt and I concluded that these differences likely reflect the greater use of seafood, and somewhat better diet, for the coastal late prehistoric Indians.

Comparison of males and females in the late prehistoric Georgia coastal sample shows that males have less tooth decay than females (8 percent vs. 13 percent of teeth are affected in males and females, respectively). This pattern suggests that Georgia coastal men ate less corn than women, a finding that is consistent with the gender differences in activities associated with food production in native peoples living in the American Southeast. In native southeastern United States groups, ethnographers and early chroniclers commented on the strict sexual division of labor: Women were responsible for most plant gathering, planting and care of crops, and food preparation; males did the hunting. Because of the greater intimacy with domesticated food that women had in these societies, they would have been exposed more than men to factors that cause tooth decay. This idea is also consistent with ethnographic accounts that males involved in hunting receive more meat than women and others not involved in hunting. Moreover, unlike men, women likely snacked on the foods they were preparing. Experimental and clinical studies show that the frequency of food consumption can be just as important in the promotion of tooth decay as the actual kind of food being consumed. It may have also been the case that women in this setting may not have been allowed to eat as much protein as men. Food prohibitions exist in a variety of places worldwide in traditional societies today, whereby women are limited in the amount of meat or fish they can eat. Food restrictions and dietary inequalities could also contribute to poorer dental health in women than in men.

DISEASE: BONE INFECTIONS

The limb bones of skeletons from archaeological sites are often swollen and have periosteal reactions, the pathological lesions caused by infection, such as from the "staph" bacteria known as *Staphylococcus aureus*. The specific characteristics of the diseased bones help the bioarchaeologist identify cause of the infection. For example, in skeletons from the American Southeast and Midwest, Mary Lucas Powell and Dale Hutchinson have described tibia bones that are swollen and bowed ("saber-shin"), a pattern that is found today in people who have one of the several forms of a treponematosis—venereal syphilis, nonvenereal (endemic) treponematosis, or yaws. The specific characteristics of bone pathology in the American Southeast indicate that the disease is likely the nonvenereal form of syphilis. Paleopathological studies suggest that venereal syphilis made its first appearance in both Europe and the Americas in the late 1400s. The bacterial organism causing the disease may have evolved rapidly out of the bacterial organism responsible for the nonvenereal form of the disease.

A number of skeletons from the late prehistoric Georgia coastal Irene Mound site have evidence of this specific infection. However, most of the skeletons from the Irene Mound site and other localities have the much more common periosteal reactions, which we cannot diagnose, except to say that they are probably due to infection of some unknown variety.

In the Georgia coastal setting, all long bone types show an increase in the frequency of periosteal reactions, but the most profound increase is in the tibia, increasing from 9.5 percent to 20 percent. Bioarchaeologists don't really know why the tibia is so much more prone to infection than other long bones. The greater frequency of infection in the tibia may be due to the fact that unlike the other long bones, the tibia is not surrounded by large amounts of soft tissue (such as muscles), and thus may be cooler and more susceptible to infection-causing pathogens.

Although the increase in frequency of periosteal reactions could reflect the appearance of a new disease in this setting, this increase more likely represents a general decline in community health as the Georgia coastal populations became larger, more sedentary, and more aggregated in permanent or semipermanent communities. These larger aggregates of human hosts increased the kind of constant interpersonal contact that it takes to spread infectious pathogens from one person to the next. Moreover, the accumulation of human waste, including trash and fecal matter, especially in comparison with the more mobile foragers, would have contributed to more infections. If, for example, someone sustained an injury, such as an abrasion or cut, the chances of the wound becoming infected—and of the infection spreading to the bones—would increase because of poor hygiene. Thus, I believe that the higher rates of infection on the late prehistoric Georgia coast were due not so much to the change in the kinds of foods being eaten, but rather to the change in settlement pattern and lifestyle. This pattern of change in infection is seen, in fact, in people who are currently going from living a nomadic lifestyle to a sedentary lifestyle. Biological anthropologists Paul Leslie of the University of North Carolina and Mike Little of the State University of New York have found that infectious disease has increased as the Turkana tribespeople of Kenya shift their settlement pattern from one involving high mobility to living in permanent and crowded communities.

The increase in frequency of bone infection and duration or severity of physiological stress also reflects the well-known synergistic relationship between infection and malnutrition: Simply, malnourished people are less resistant to infection, and chronic infection worsens nutritional status. That is, individuals with an infection have an increased need for protein and other nutrients for the production of antibodies that help fight the infection. If an individual is malnourished, the immune system is suppressed and the person has a reduced ability to provide protein and nutrients; as a consequence, the infection worsens. In the Georgia coast, where there was likely a reduction in nutritional quality with the shift to farming, the ability to fight infection was decreased.

MORTALITY

One important indicator of quality of life is how long a person and other members of the society live. When someone in the United States is born today, he or she can expect to live about seventy-five years. How long could a Georgia coastal Indian expect to live after he or she was born? In my analysis of the skeletons of prehistoric foragers and farmers, age at death based on indicators such as amount of tooth wear and various age changes in the skull and bones covered the range, from newborns to seventy-year-olds. The average age at death declined slightly, from twenty-three years in the foragers to twenty-two years in the farmers, and the number of older adults (greater than forty-five years) declined slightly, from 13 percent of the population to 7 percent of the population. This suggests that people might expect to live for a somewhat shorter time once agriculture comes into play. Unfortunately, when studying archaeological skeletons, the link between age and death and mortality is unclear. The average age at death of a collection of skeletons from an archaeological site is strongly influenced by the number of children being born when the population was alive. If the birthrate of a population increases over a time period—the period from foraging to farming, in this instance—then this means that there would be an increasing number of babies and other juveniles in the living population, and quite possibly in the skeletal sample representing that living population. Hypothetically, the presence of more children in the later group of skeletons—brought about by an increased number of births in the later period—would bring down the average age at death. Thus, the decline in average age at death may not represent an increase in mortality, but rather an increase in fertility. We will revisit this issue in the next chapter, when I discuss the pattern of demographic change seen in other regions of the globe.

In summary, the analysis of bioarchaeological indicators of health in comparing prehistoric foragers and farmers living on the Georgia coast prior to European contact strongly suggests that the quality of life declined in this setting, confirming my early suspicions about health made back when I was just beginning graduate school. Fertility and birth rates may have increased—which would have caused the population size to increase—but the cost of increased population, sedentism, and shift in diet had an overall negative impact on the quality of life in this setting of North America.

Workload and Activity

MEASURING WORKLOAD AND ACTIVITY: OSTEOARTHRITIS

In the previous chapter, I argued that osteoarthritis is a compelling indicator of physical activity in past humans. The visible changes associated with the disorder—namely, growths of bone on the margins of joints and degeneration of joint surfaces—allow bioarchaeologists to assess behavioral patterns and changes in earlier societies.

In the Georgia coast skeletons, we compared the frequency of osteoarthritis for foragers and farmers in the major joints of their skeletons: the spine, shoulder, hip, wrist, and hand. Controlling for age, since osteoarthritis is age-driven—the older one gets, the greater the chance of having the disorder—this comparison reveals an appreciable decrease in frequency of osteoarthritis for most joints examined:

Cervical: 26.0 percent to 16.4 percent
Thoracic: 15.6 percent to 11.4 percent
Lumbar: 41.9 percent to 24.5 percent
Shoulder: 9.7 percent to 5.3 percent
Hip: 12.0 percent to 6.8 percent
Wrist: 5.9 percent to 1.1 percent
Hand: 5.0 percent to 3.0 percent

In consideration of the fact that the mechanical environment plays such an important role in the development of osteoarthritis, this trend suggests a decrease in mechanical loading of the joints of the skeleton in prehistoric Georgia coastal populations.

Thus, while the general picture of health appears to have deteriorated in the transition from foraging to farming, the situation relating to workload—or other factors that could be involved in the mechanical environment—shows an improvement, if reduced workload can be considered an improvement. This may be cultural bias from my perspective as a sedentary American professor, but I would conclude that having to work less hard is better than having to work hard, at least in the physical sense.

MEASURING WORKLOAD: BIOMECHANICS

Part of my dissertation study of Georgia coastal skeletons assessed changes over time in the size of bones. This analysis revealed an unambiguous pattern of skeletal size reduction in the late prehistoric farmers relative to the earlier prehistoric foragers. At the time, and in light of the decrease in osteoarthritis, I tentatively interpreted this change to reflect a decrease in skeletal robusticity that was due to a decrease in workload and activity.

The general decrease in bone size in the Georgia coastal populations indicates a functional cause related to activity, namely that decreased skeletal robusticity resulted from the shift from a foraging to a farming lifestyle and a decrease in workload and activity generally. Thus, the change in skeletal size and structure was due to the behavioral consequences of a shift in diet, and not directly to the foods eaten. In consideration of the scientific breakthrough in bone biomechanics discussed in the previous chapter, and particularly the application of beam theory and cross-sectional geometric analysis to archaeological skeletons, external bone size is almost certainly only a part of the picture of the effects of the mechanical environment on the developing individual. That is, external measurements do not provide a full representation of the way bone is distributed in cross sections of long bones. The distribution provides an important perspective on how the bone is loaded in life. Just because a bone may be large externally does not necessarily mean that it is especially well adapted to heavy loading—the biomechanical picture is not represented by what we see on the surface.

On the other hand, a human population may be composed of mostly small people—and hence, small bones—not because of minimal mechanical loading, but rather because of poor nutrition. A change in robusticity may be due not to behavior, but rather to the direct effects of dietary and nutritional shifts. Anthropologists and others have observed that human populations with poor nutrition tend to be shorter and have smaller bones than populations with good nutrition. And, certainly, the reduction in bone size and height in this setting—the average height of the Georgia coastal dweller declined by about an inch for males (from 5 feet 6 inches to 5 feet 5 inches) and by about two inches for females (from 5 feet 2 inches to 5 feet 0 inches)—may be explained, at least in part, by the shift to a less nutritious diet.

Biomechanical analysis of long bones presents us with a very powerful tool for reconstructing and interpreting the activity patterns and lifestyles of past populations because it is useful for disentangling the nutritional from the mechanical environments and identifying their respective influences on bone development. Our study of cross-sectional geometry of Georgia coastal femora and humeri from prehistoric foragers and farmers provides an important perspective on this issue. Unlike the Nevada skeletons, where we used computed axial tomography (CT or CAT) scans to produce the bone cross sections for analysis, in the Georgia study we were able to cut the bones, examine the actual sections, and calculate the cross-sectional geometric properties, the areas, and second moments of area. The exposed bone sections, two sections for each femur and one section for each humerus, were photographed, and the images of the sections were projected onto a screen in Ruff's lab at Johns Hopkins University. The contours of the subperiosteal (outer) and endosteal (inner) surfaces were then hand-traced with an electronic digitizer pen hooked up to a desktop computer. The statistical package loaded into the computer then automatically calculated the series of cross-sectional geometric properties for determining bending and torsional stress (see chapter 2).

Analysis of femora and humeri from the Georgia coastal sites reveals several important biomechanical trends over time that are generally consistent with our suspicions about activity, especially with regard to our finding on osteoarthritis and decreased workload. That is, second moments of area (properties that measure bone strength) declined for both the femur and humerus, but the changes were especially pronounced for the humerus. This pattern indicates a decline in bone strength, and especially so in the upper arm. Second, there is an appreciable decline in the mobility index, the ratio of I_x/I_y, indicating that adults on the Georgia coast became increasingly sedentary with the shift from foraging to farming. Finally, the long bones decrease in length over time, indicating a stature reduction for the prehistoric farmers relative to the prehistoric foragers. Thus, people are shorter, have reduced bone strength, and are less mobile over time.

Our work on skeletal structure indicates that the distribution of bone in a cross section represents a complex interplay of both nutritional and mechanical factors, and this setting is no exception. The reduction in bone strength, coupled with the decrease in mobility, indicates important behavioral modifications that accompanied the shift from foraging to farming on the Georgia coast. On the other hand, the stature reduction suggests that nutritional quality decreased in a significant fashion with the adoption of corn agriculture. This combination of behavioral and nutritional changes fits our expectations that the adoption of an agricultural lifestyle involved more sedentary behavior and is associated with reduced nutrition.

The biomechanical analysis has other important implications for our bioarchaeological investigation of prehistoric Georgia coastal Indians. I made the case earlier in this chapter that increasing sedentism is a necessary requisite for the substantial increases in infectious disease that we observe here and elsewhere in the Eastern Woodlands. Our biomechanical analysis supports this argument by showing that, indeed, populations were more sedentary in the later prehistoric period. We had strongly suspected that late prehistoric populations were more sedentary than their predecessors, especially in consideration of the archaeological evidence in the region showing larger and more densely occupied habitation sites in later times. But, prior to our work, the argument for increasing population size and declining mobility was based solely on this indirect archaeological evidence. One more piece of the puzzle is now in place about the lives and lifestyles of prehistoric Georgians.

In summary, our work in the Georgia Bight suggests a widespread pattern of decline in the quality of life in the few centuries prior to the arrival of Europeans and the establishment of mission centers in the sixteenth century. This is reflected in a general deterioration of health and nutritional quality in this region. There is a silver lining in every cloud, however. Our study of the skeletons from the region suggests that workload lessened in the transition. So, although health declined in the late prehistoric period, the local populations did not work as hard as before. What about the world picture of changing subsistence and patterns of altering health and lifestyle? Are the trends we have identified from the Georgia coast unique to this region, or are they part of a larger worldwide development? Let us now take a look at the shift from foraging to farming from the perspective of global trends in health and activity in order to answer these questions.

Note

1. In total, the prehistoric skeletal sample from the Georgia coast includes 847 individuals from forty-three burial sites. Some of the skeletons are from the first millennium B.C. However, most of the skeletons postdate A.D. 700, and they provide a continuous human biological record to the time of European contact in the early to middle sixteenth century.

References

Bar-Yosef, O. (1998) The Natufian culture in the Levant, threshold to the origins of agriculture. *Evolutionary Anthropology* 6:159–177.

Braidwood, R. J. (1967) *Prehistoric Men* (7th edition). Glenview, Illinois: Scott, Foresman.

Chen, B., and Jiang, Q. (1997) Antiquity of the earliest cultivated rice in central China and its implications. *Economic Botany* 51:307–310.

Childe, V. G. (1953) *New Light on the Most Ancient Near East*. New York: Praeger.

Cordain, L. (1999) Cereal grains: humanity's double-edged sword. *World Review of Nutrition and Diet* 84:19–73.

Cohen, M. N., and Armelagos, G. J., eds. (1984) *Paleopathology at the Origins of Agriculture*. Orlando, Florida: Academic Press.

Cook, D. C., and Hunt, K. D. (1998) Sex differences in trace elements: status differences or self-selection? In A. L. Grauer and P. Stuart-Macadam, eds. *Sex and Gender in Paleopathological Perspective*. Cambridge: Cambridge University Press, pp. 64–78.

El-Najjar, M. Y. (1976) Maize, malaria and the anemias in the pre-Columbian New World. *Yearbook of Physical Anthropology* 20:329–337.

Garn, S. M., Osborne, R. H., Alvesalo, L., and Horowitz, S. L. (1980) Maternal and gestational influences on deciduous and permanent tooth size. *Journal of Dental Research* 59:142–143.

Garn, S. M., Osborne, R. H., and McCabe, K. D. (1979) The effect of prenatal factors on crown dimensions. *American Journal of Physical Anthropology* 51:665–678.

Hutchinson, D. L., Larsen, C. S., Schoeninger, M. J., and Norr, L. (1998) Regional variation in the pattern of maize adoption and use in Florida and Georgia. *American Antiquity* 63:397–416.

Lambert, P. M., and Walker, P. L. (1991) Physical anthropological evidence for the evolution of social complexity in coastal southern California. *Antiquity* 65:963–973.

Larsen, C. S. (1982) *The Anthropology of St. Catherines Island: 3. Prehistoric Human Biological Adaptation*. Anthropological Papers of the American Museum of Natural History, vol. 57, part 3.

———. (1983) Deciduous tooth size and subsistence change in prehistoric Georgia coast populations. *Current Anthropology* 24:225–226.

———. (1995) Biological changes in human populations with agriculture. *Annual Review of Anthropology* 24:185–213.

———. (1997) *Bioarchaeology: Interpreting Behavior from the Human Skeleton*. Cambridge: Cambridge University Press.

Larsen, C. S., Crosby, A. W., Griffin, M. C., Hutchinson, D. L., Ruff, C. B., Russell, K. F., Schoeninger, M. J., Sering, L. E., Simpson, S. W., Takács, J. L., and Teaford, M. F. (n.d.) A biohistory of health and behavior in the Georgia Bight: the agricultural transition and the impact of European contact. In R. H. Steckel, J. C. Rose, and P. W. Sciulli, eds. *The Backbone of History: Health and Nutrition in the Western Hemisphere*. New York: Cambridge University Press, forthcoming.

Larsen, C. S., and Harn, D. E. (1994) Health in transition: disease and nutrition in the Georgia Bight. In K. D. Sobolik, ed. *Paleonutrition: The Diet and Health of Prehistoric Americans*. Southern Illinois University at Carbondale, Center for Archaeological Investigations, Occasional Paper, no. 22, pp. 222–234.

Larsen, C. S., and Hutchinson, D. L. (1992) Dental evidence for physiological disruption: biocultural interpretations from the eastern Spanish borderlands, U.S.A. In A. H. Goodman and L. L. Capasso, eds. *Recent Contributions to the Study of Enamel Developmental Defects. Journal of Paleopathology, Monographic Publications*, no. 2, pp. 151–169.

Larsen, C. S., and Ruff, C. B. (1994) The stresses of conquest in Spanish Florida: structural adaptation and change before and after contact. In C. S. Larsen and G. R. Milner, eds. *In the Wake of Contact: Biological Responses to Conquest*. New York: Wiley-Liss, pp. 21–34.

Larsen, C. S., Ruff, C. B., and Griffin, M. C. (1996) Implications of changing biomechanical and nutritional environments for activity and lifeway in the eastern Spanish borderlands. In B. J. Baker and L. L. Kealhofer, eds. *Bioarchaeology of Native American Adaptation in the Spanish Borderlands*. Gainesville: University Press of Florida, pp. 95–125.

Larsen, C. S., Schoeninger, M. J., van der Merwe, N. J., Moore, K. M., and Lee-Thorp, J. A. (1992) Carbon and nitrogen stable isotopic signatures of human dietary change in the Georgia Bight. *American Journal of Physical Anthropology* 89:197–214.

Larsen, C. S., and Sering, L. E. (1999) Inferring iron deficiency anemia from human skeletal remains: the case of the Georgia Bight. In P. M. Lambert, ed. *Bioarchaeological Studies in Life in the Age of Agriculture*. Tuscaloosa: University of Alabama Press.

Larsen, C. S., Shavit, R., and Griffin, M. C. (1991) Dental caries evidence for dietary change: an archaeological context. In M. A. Kelley and C. S. Larsen, eds. *Advances in Dental Anthropology*. New York: Wiley-Liss, pp. 179–202.

Larson, L. H. (1980) *Aboriginal Subsistence Technology on the Southeastern Coastal Plain during the Late Prehistoric Period*. Gainesville: University Presses of Florida.

Layrisse, M., Martínez-Torres, C., and Roche, M. (1968) Effect of interaction of various foods on iron absorption. *American Journal of Clinical Nutrition* 21:1175–1183.

Little, M. A., and Leslie, P. W., eds. (1999) *Turkana Herders of the Dry Savanna: Ecology and Biobehavioural Response of Nomads to an Uncertain Environment*. Oxford: Oxford University Press.

Morgan, L. H. (1877) *Ancient Society*. New York: Henry Holt.

Powell, M. L. (1988) *Status and Health in Prehistory: A Case Study of the Moundville Chiefdom*. Washington, D. C.: Smithsonian Institution Press.

Ruff, C. B. (1992) Biomechanical analyses of archaeological human skeletal samples. In S. R. Saunders and M. A. Katzenberg, eds. *The Skeletal Biology of Past Peoples: Advances in Research Methods*. New York: Wiley-Liss, pp. 37–58.

Ruff, C. B., and Larsen, C. S. (1990) Postcranial biomechanical adaptations to subsistence changes on the Georgia coast. In C. S. Larsen, ed. *The Archaeology of Mission Santa Catalina de Guale: 2. Biocultural Interpretations of a Population in Transition*. Anthropological Papers of the American Museum of Natural History, no. 68, pp. 94–120.

———. (n.d.) The mechanical environment of La Florida. In C. S. Larsen, ed. *Bioarchaeology of La Florida*. Gainesville: University Press of Florida, forthcoming.

Ruff, C. B., Larsen, C. S., and Hayes, W. C. (1984) Structural changes in the femur with the transition to agriculture on the Georgia coast. *American Journal of Physical Anthropology* 64:125–136.

Ryan, A. S. (1997) Iron-deficiency anemia in infant development: implications for growth, cognitive development, resistance to infection, and iron supplementation. *Yearbook of Physical Anthropology* 40:25–62.

Schoeninger, M. J., van der Merwe, N. J., Moore, K. M., Lee-Thorp, J. A., and Larsen, C. S. (1990) Decrease in diet quality between the prehistoric and contact periods. In C. S. Larsen, ed. *The Archaeology of Mission Santa Catalina de Guale: 2. Biocultural Interpretations of a Population in Transition.* Anthropological Papers of the American Museum of Natural History, no. 68, pp. 78–93.

Shipman, P. (1986) Scavenging or hunting in early hominids: theoretical framework and tests. *American Anthropologist.* 88:27–43.

Smith, B. D. (1995) *The Emergence of Agriculture.* New York: Scientific American Library.

———. (1998) Between Foraging and Farming. *Science* 279:1651–1652.

Suckling, G. W., Elliot, D. C., and Thurley, D. C. (1986) The macroscopic appearance and associated histological changes in the enamel organ of hypoplastic lesions of sheep incisor teeth resulting from induced parasitism. *Archives of Oral Biology* 31:427–439.

Thomas, D. H. (1987) *The Archaeology of Mission Santa Catalina de Guale: 1. Search and Discovery.* Anthropological Papers of the American Museum of Natural History, vol. 63, part 2.

Thomas, D. H., Jones, G. D., Durham, R. S., and Larsen, C. S. (1978) *The Anthropology of St. Catherines Island: 1. Natural and Cultural History.* Anthropological Papers of the American Museum of Natural History, vol. 55, part 2.

Vogel, J. C., and van der Merwe, N. J. (1977) Isotopic evidence for early maize cultivation in New York State. *American Antiquity.* 42:238–242.

Williamson, M. A. (1998) *Regional Variation in Health and Lifeways among Late Prehistoric Georgia Agriculturalists.* Ph.D. dissertation, Purdue University, West Lafayette, Indiana.

4

Going Global: Bioarchaeology of the Foraging-to-Farming Transition

THE WORK that my associates and I did on the Georgia coast provides a compelling example of the health costs associated with the foraging-to-farming transition. But how do our findings compare with those in other regions of the world? Could the Georgia setting just represent an isolated instance of declining health, and that the rise of agriculture actually was, in all ways, an improvement in the human condition elsewhere? This chapter addresses these questions in the broad perspective of what bioarchaeologists have learned about this important adaptive change in the history of our species in the last ten thousand years. It suggests that Georgia was not an isolated instance of changing health accompanying the foraging-to-farming shift. Rather, wherever farming was adopted, health was affected—for the worse in many instances—and workloads changed in dramatic ways for most members of our species.

When I began my work in Georgia early in graduate school in the mid-1970s, nearly all bioarchaeological studies that had previously considered the foraging-to-farming transition had focused on specific and sometimes overly narrow aspects of biological change. Few bioarchaeologists had attempted to look at the broad picture of stress and biocultural adaptation, combining a number of health and stress indicators, such as infection, caries, osteoarthritis, and skeletal size and robusticity, all within one research program.[1]

A major basis for comparison began in the spring of 1982, when archaeologist Mark Cohen and bioarchaeologist George Armelagos organized a conference held in an old farmhouse on the shore of Lake Champlain near Plattsburgh, New York. The conference brought together for the first time a group of bioarchaeologists working in different areas of the world on the foraging-to-farming transition. Cohen and Armelagos asked all of the scientists participating in the conference to pull information on health and activity for each of the regions in which they were working.

The coverage was impressive, including regions in North America, South America, Africa, Europe, and Asia. All continents where the shift from foraging to farming took place were represented. At the time, my dissertation had just been published by the American Museum of Natural History, and I was anxious to discuss my results with colleagues working in these different areas. The conference and the publication of its proceedings turned out to be a major boon to our understanding of the outcome of the transition in many corners of the globe. My results from the tiny region of coastal Georgia were similar to what others were finding about health and lifestyles in the foraging-to-farming transition elsewhere. Since the conference, much additional work has been initiated by bioarchaeologists and others, creating a growing picture of the human biology of the shift to agriculture.[2]

In this chapter, I will discuss what all these bioarchaeologists have learned about the impact of the shift from foraging to farming on human health and activity.

The Global Picture in Patterns of Health

Growth and Development

THE SKELETON

Most human groups involved in the foraging-to-farming shift saw a decline in nutritional quality. Prehistoric people shifted from a diverse diet including various plants and animals to a diet involving the consumption of a much narrower range of foods. For many settings, this decrease in dietary diversity is indicated by the dependence on one major plant, such as corn in North America, rice in Asia, wheat in temperate Asia and Europe, and millet, sorghum, or corn in Africa. This narrowing of dietary breadth also involved a decrease in access to animal sources of protein, arguably the most complete kind of protein. All domesticated plants have nutritional deficiencies: Corn-dependent populations have reduced iron absorption levels (in the absence of significant access to marine foods), among other problems; milled grains like millet and wheat contain very little iron; and rice is deficient in protein. Although human populations living in the regions dependent on these different foods undertake various strategies for improving the nutritional content of these foods, such as consumption of beans where corn and/or rice dependency are present, or special processing (e.g., alkali processing in corn), the shortfalls in nutritional quality are almost never completely compensated for.

Comparisons of long bone lengths of children of different ages provide an indication of the rates of growth in North America, where most studies have been conducted. Children's long bones from prehistoric sites in Illinois studied by Della Cook and Alan Goodman, for example, tend to be shorter and less robust in later agricultural populations than in earlier hunter-gatherers, which is strongly suggestive of generalized growth retardation. The shorter children in the later farmers also tend to have other evidence of growth disturbance, such as more porotic hyperostosis, enamel defects, and bone infections.

These decreases in growth in juveniles would suggest that as adults, they would be short. For many regions where farming was adopted, adult heights indeed decreased in many settings: for example, western Europe, the eastern Mediterranean, Nubia, South Asia, Mesoamerica, the Ohio River valley, and central Illinois. Some authorities have suggested that under conditions of food shortages or poor nutrition, shortened height may have been beneficial to a person's well-being. In their study of adult heights of precontact Maya from the Yucatán peninsula of Mexico, physical anthropologists Lourdes Márquez and Andrés del Ángel found a general decline in height over time. They argued that the reduction was due to declining quality of living circumstances and diet and suggested that the decrease in height may be a kind of an adaptation to marginal living conditions. Simply, shorter and smaller bodies require less food—the later people were small, but healthy.

But, under these marginal environmental circumstances, do shorter, smaller bodies confer an advantage? My answer to this question is an emphatic *no*. The fact that short height in peasant societies living in Mesoamerica (or elsewhere) is strongly associated with high levels of infectious disease and malnutrition argues against the conclusion regarding the benefits of small body size. Moreover, these short adults had undergone growth deficiencies in childhood, and there are no known human populations living anywhere in the world today that show a combination of slow childhood growth and good health.

Some regions of the world show either no change or an actual increase in height with the shift from foraging to farming in prehistory: for example, the central Ohio River valley, west-central Illinois, the lower Mississippi River valley, Ecuador, and Portugal. This variability, showing different responses in height to reduced food quality, reflects the fact that terminal body height is the end product of various factors that affect growth and development during childhood and adolescence. Humans have an enormous capacity for catch-up growth during critical periods prior to reaching adulthood. Economic historian Richard Steckel of Ohio State University showed that remarkable levels of catch-up growth are possible even under dire environmental circumstances. He analyzed height data on more than fifty thousand slaves from Africa, finding that despite their very small size throughout childhood, during adolescence there were huge rebounds in growth, reaching height standards for developed nations today. At the time of their growth increase between the ages of fifteen and seventeen, adolescents apparently received extra food, which seemingly had a profoundly positive influence on growth rates for the period just prior to adulthood. This finding underscores the fact that growth may be stunted in childhood, but if key resources are provided at critical periods of a person's development, then height can recover and nearly full growth attained.

Bone mass, such as that measured by thickness or the distance from the endosteal to subperiosteal surface, is a highly sensitive indicator of health and well-being. Bioarchaeological studies of bone mass reveal clear trends, either with respect to the foraging-to-farming transition or with other adaptive shifts. In these settings, thin cortical bone has been interpreted by some to represent the result of a lifetime of poor nutrition (for example, west-central Illinois, Nubia, the American Great Plains), whereas thick cortical bone has been viewed as representing good nutrition (for instance, Portugal, Great Plains). On the face of it, these conclusions linking bone mass to good nutritional health seem warranted. Indeed, in living populations, poorly nourished people have thinner cortical bone and low bone mass. However, Chris Ruff and others have amply demonstrated that the distribution of bone tissue, when viewed in cross section, is strongly influenced by the level and type of physical activity—the mechanical environment—in addition to nutrition.

If we look at the change in location of the outer subperiosteal and inner endosteal surfaces of a long bone shaft over the course of an individual's lifetime, these surfaces are displaced outwardly away from an imaginary center line running along the midline of the bone shaft over the course of childhood and adulthood. Put another way, the cortical bone expands as a person ages. Before age forty, the amount of bone gain on the subperiosteal surface is greater than the loss on the endosteal surface, thus providing a net gain in bone mass. After age forty or so, the losses are greater than the gains, resulting in a net loss in bone tissue. These losses can be especially problematic because they make the bones of the skeleton susceptible to fracture.

Despite the bone losses in people after age forty, the cortical bone continues to expand outwardly, so that in a very real sense, the bone continues to grow. Thus, the diameter of a person's femur midshaft will be greater at age eighty than at age forty. Skeletal biologists believe that the continuous expansion of the subperiosteal surface is a compensatory response to bone loss—by expanding the bone subperiosteal diameter, mechanical strength to the bone is maintained, despite the loss of bone. Recall from chapter 2 that bone placed further from the central axis provides a stronger cross section and a bone that is better able to resist mechanical forces of bending and torsion. In these age-related changes, the thinner cortical bone has nothing to do with nutrition and everything to do with redistribution in response to the mechanical environment. It is true that low bone mass can result from low quality of nutrition, but lifestyle and activity are also key considerations when interpreting size, thickness, and mass of bone tissue. Contrary to the assertions of many, then, thick cortical bone does not necessarily mean good nutrition.

DENTITION

Just as we see a general decrease in skeletal size in many settings following the shift to farming, there is also a reduction in tooth size. Unlike skeletal size, human tooth size reduction is a nearly universal phenomenon, which began about two million years ago in our hominid ancestors and continues to the present day. Some of the most dramatic reduction has taken place just in the last ten thousand years. In some settings, this reduction has been extraordinarily fast and has tended to occur in populations that made the transition from foraging to farming. Physical anthropologist Loring Brace at the University of Michigan has found that human populations that made the shift to farming earliest tend to have the smallest teeth. For example, Chinese have extremely small teeth in comparison with Europeans, reflecting the longer period that the Chinese have had agriculture.

Tooth size reduction over the last ten thousand years was not simply due to nonevolutionary factors. In his study of ancient Nubian teeth, James Calcagno of Loyola University of Chicago identified a relatively greater reduction in the size of the teeth in the back of the mouth (premolars and molars) compared with the size of the teeth in the front of the mouth (incisors and canines). The later intensive agriculturalists in Nubia have many diseased and impacted teeth. Calcagno argues that smaller back teeth should be less susceptible to decay (smaller teeth have less surface area for colonization by cariogenic bacteria), and hence, there would be a selective advantage for having smaller teeth. This may be the case for Nubia, but in the bigger picture, the rapid reductions taking place within such a short time framework in a number of settings globally (for example, on the Georgia coast) suggest the role of nonevolutionary, environmentally related factors in influencing tooth size, and not changes in genes (evolution).

Markers of Deprivation and Disruption

IRON STATUS

Populations from various settings worldwide involved in the shift from foraging to farming show substantial increases in porotic hyperostosis and cribra orbitalia, much of which likely reflects increased iron deficiency anemia (for example, the eastern Mediterranean, central Europe, Nubia, Syria, South Asia, the central Ohio River valley, west-central Illinois, central Illinois, the lower Mississippi River valley, and Costa Rica). One of the best-documented settings showing high frequency of cribra orbitalia is from the Wandersleben site in Germany. Here, physical anthropologist Petra Carli-Thiele of the University of Göttingen found that half of the skulls of children from early agriculturalists living in central Europe at about 6000 B.C. have cribra orbitalia. Her microscopic analysis of cribra orbitalia and porotic hyperostosis in skulls reveals that most of the children probably suffered from anemia, and many of them also displayed skeletal symptoms of scurvy (vitamin C deficiency) and infection. Archaeological and paleopathological diagnoses suggest that iron deficiency likely resulted from a combination of factors, including protein deficiency, low health status, and poor living conditions in general. Clearly, the focus on the cereal grains (wheat, barley, and rye), combined with a more sedentary lifestyle and poorer health overall, led to a decline in well-being.

Not all prehistoric agriculturalists have high frequencies of cribra orbitalia or porotic hyperostosis. Like the prehistoric agriculturalists from the Georgia coast, intensive agriculturalists from the Mississippian center located at Moundville, Alabama, and the Pre-classic Maya site of Cuello, have quite low frequencies of porotic hyperostosis and cribra orbitalia. Thus, these groups tend to have more porotic hyperostosis or cribra orbitalia in later farmers than in earlier foragers, confirming the point raised in the previous chapter that dependence on corn agriculture is not a prerequisite for iron deficiency, although it may be an important predisposing condition.

ENAMEL DEFECTS

Hypoplasias increase in many regions in the shift from foraging to farming: for example, the Ohio River valley, west-central Illinois, central Illinois, the lower Mississippi River valley, Ecuador, South Asia, and southwest Asia. Thus, this indicator shows a general increase in physiological stress in the later agricultural populations. The position of the enamel defect on the tooth crown provides detailed information on the age of the person when the defect formed. At the Dickson Mounds in central Illinois, Alan Goodman plotted the age of occurrence of hypoplasias for each individual and found that they tended to occur at earlier ages—by several years—in the later intensive agriculturalists than in the earlier foragers. This is a significant finding, because it suggests that the agricultural adaptation was more stressful than the forager adaptation in this setting. Moreover, the Dickson people with more and earlier-occurring hypoplasias died at younger ages than individuals with fewer and later-occurring hypoplasias. This, too, is significant, because it is consistent with a growing body of clinical research showing that children with earlier episodes of stress have an increased risk for chronic illness and early death. At Dickson Mounds—as with most other sites studied by bioarchaeologists—the enamel defects appear to peak in frequency during the period of about two years to four years of age. This tightly constricted age pattern coincides with the period of weaning in humans generally. Thus, the pattern of age distribution may reflect stresses associated with the transition from human milk provided by the mother to a more-or-less adult diet. In many human societies, weaning foods—gruels made from cereal grains—are less nutritious and likely contribute to poorer health.

In recent years, bioarchaeologists and paleopathologists have been looking at the finer details of enamel developmental disrup-

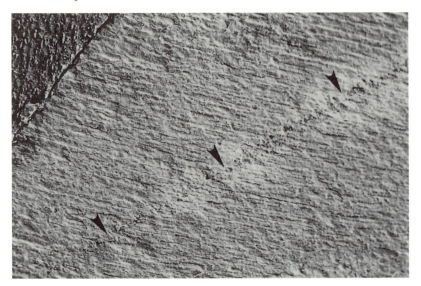

Scanning electron micrograph (230×) of a permanent maxillary central incisor showing accentuated Retzius line (arrows; see also page 18). Micrograph by Scott W. Simpson; from Larsen 1997, and reproduced with permission of Cambridge University Press.

tion by examining the microscopic characteristics of enamel formation. Like the growth of trees, the growth of enamel is periodic—layers of wood in trees are laid down in a way that is analogous to layers of enamel laid down in teeth. The growth layers in trees are easily seen with the naked eye. The growth layers in teeth can be seen only under high-powered magnification with the use of a microscope. The enamel sandwiched between two growth lines in teeth—called Retzius lines—represents the period of time when the enamel was being deposited, or about one week of growth. When growth is disrupted by some physiological disturbance, the lines appear as dark or broad bands, representing stress episodes lasting anywhere from several hours to several days. One very common example of these accentuated Retzius lines is the so-called neonatal line, which represents the trauma of birth of the infant.

Consistent with the hypoplasia evidence, accentuated Retzius lines are more frequent in prehistoric farmers than in foragers. In their study of the Dickson Mounds teeth, Jerome Rose and his colleagues found a nearly fourfold increase in lines in the later intensive corn agriculturalists compared to these in the earlier incipient agriculturalists. Similarly, physical anthropologist Scott Simpson at Case Western Reserve University found that more intensive agriculturalists in Florida have more enamel microdefects than the earlier less-intensive agriculturalists or foragers (see chapter 6).

Disease

DENTAL CARIES AND ORAL HEALTH

One of the most comprehensive health changes to take place in ancient populations undergoing the shift to farming was a decline in dental health, resulting largely from an increased emphasis on dietary carbohydrates. From a sample of populations worldwide, Christy Turner of Arizona State University has determined average frequencies of teeth that are decayed:

Foragers, 1.7 percent
Mixed foraging and agriculture, 4.8 percent
Agricultural, 8.6 percent

Populations with a high prevalence of dental caries also tend to have a high prevalence of adult tooth loss. This association reflects the fact that untreated caries can eventually lead to tooth loss. The association between caries and tooth loss also indicates that caries-promoting factors, such as various bacteria, also result in gingivitis and periodontitis, leading causes of tooth loss.

BONE INFECTIONS

One of the hallmarks of the agricultural transition is population size increase and sedentism. Because crowding is a circumstance that promotes the spread of infection and infectious disease, we would expect to see increases in bone infection in this transition. Indeed, for almost every setting, there are increases in bone infection: for example, the eastern Mediterranean, west-central Illinois, the central Ohio River valley, central Illinois, western Europe, the lower Mississippi River valley, and Ecuador.

Most of the bone infections seen in these different settings are fairly basic affairs, consisting of simple periosteal reactions. However, some of the infections—especially in the American Midwest and Southeast—involve a characteristic pattern of swelling on the tibias, and sometimes a distinctive group of pitted lesions on frontal bones. This pattern suggests a nonvenereal form of syphilis, which is highly prevalent in these regions, but is mostly missing from Europe. Bioarchaeologists Brenda Baker and George Armelagos speculate that the venereal form of syphilis may have evolved rapidly in Europe following Columbus's first voyage to the New World.

An interesting exception to the pattern of increase in bone infections is found in the Oaxaca Valley of Mexico. Bioarchaeologist Denise Hodges of Northern Illnois University regards the lack of increase as a reflection of the fact that the adoption of agriculture in this region was a very slow process—having taken place over a period of six thousand years—contrary to other regions in North America, where populations shifted from foraging to farming in a few hundred years or less. She speculates that populations that underwent the transition from foraging to farming in a slow manner had sufficient time to adjust to disease-causing factors.

Demography

ESTIMATING MORTALITY (OR FERTILITY?)

Looking at skeletons from around the world, one very common trend is a reduction in average age at death in the comparison of early foragers and later farmers. Most bioarchaeologists have interpreted this to reflect an increase in mortality and declining life expectancy. That may well be the best explanation. However, increasing fertility and birthrate may also be a cause. As I discussed for the Georgia coast, if there is an increase in number of births in a population, then the cemeteries representing the populations undergoing demographic change should contain a higher proportion of juveniles than those from earlier periods. I suspect that farmers experience both increased mortality and increased fertility relative to their foraging ancestors, making it virtually impossible to interpret changes in average age at death. However, one clear trend that has occurred in humans following the invention and adoption of agriculture is population increase. Population increase is brought about by an increase in birthrate. Thus, the decline in average age at death that we see globally, including in the Georgia Bight discussed in the last chapter, likely underlies population growth in later prehistory worldwide.

ACTIVITY CHANGES WITH AGRICULTURE: BELOW THE NECK

Osteoarthritis

Degenerative disease involving surfaces and margins of the joint of the skeleton has been documented from a wide range of settings by bioarchaeologists. Bioarchaeologists have found decreases in osteoarthritis in some settings and increases in others that accompanied the shift from foraging to farming. Some settings show no change at all. At the site of Abu Hureyra, Syria, physical anthropologist Theya Molleson of the Museum of Natural History in London has found that both the late prehistoric foragers and the slightly later Neolithic farmers have a great deal of osteoarthritis, which can be linked with specific aspects of lifestyle, such as stone-grinding of grains. The lack of a definitive temporal pattern in osteoarthritis prevalence suggests to me that osteoarthritis is largely determined on the basis of local factors and patterns of physical activity unique to specific regions (see below). That is, the type of labor involved in agricultural production was likely very different from one region to the next.

Bone Form and Function

BONE SIZE

The size and structure of bone have been studied extensively by bioarchaeologists, especially regarding the external dimensions of long bones. Generally, comparisons of the skeletons of earlier foragers and later farmers from some archaeological contexts indicate a pattern of decreased bone robusticity and size, especially in long bones, which presumably reflects a decline in physical activity and workload (for example, the Ohio River valley, Virginia, Levant, and Ukraine). This is by no means a universal phenomenon, since some regions show either no change or an increase in external robusticity of bones (for example, Tennessee and Alabama). Thus, in comparing different regions of the world, there is a lack of a pattern of external skeletal robusticity and osteoarthritis, which confirms my overall impression that workload is driven by local factors involving work and physical activity.

BONE SHAPE

There are some shape changes in the bones of prehistoric farmers that appear to represent a universal pattern of behavioral adaptation, especially in the femur bone. Various physical anthropologists and anatomists over the years have noted that the midshafts of femurs (the region of the mid-thigh) in farming populations tend to be rounder than in foraging populations. The femur midshafts in prehistoric foragers tend to be somewhat flatter from side to side. This pattern of variation between prehistoric foragers and farmers represents a worldwide trend of increasing circularity of the femur midshaft since the end of the Pleistocene epoch. The greater side-to-side flattening in the femur midshaft of prehistoric foragers has been interpreted by some authorities to represent poor nutrition. However, cross-sectional geometric analysis of the I_x/I_y mobility ratio, where I_x represents a measure of bone strength from front to back and I_y represents bone strength from side to side in the femur midshaft (see chapter 2), indicates that the morphological change reflects a shift from a mobile to a sedentary lifestyle and has nothing to do with nutrition. Simply, people who do a lot of walking or running have more mechanical loading of the midshaft of their femurs due to increased bending relative to those who do little walking or running. So, the bone remodels over a person's lifetime, placing more bone on the front and back of the femur midshaft and giving a flattened cross section.

Many authorities suspect that adults from archaeological contexts having large and robust long bones were physically active during their lifetimes. The new developments in biomechanics and the analysis of cross-sectional geometric properties have provided strong support for this assertion. For example, the large and robust postcrania studied by us in the Stillwater Marsh region of the American Great Basin are indeed "strong," at least in the biomechanical sense (see chapter 2). The important advantage of using cross-sectional geometric analysis for making inferences about the mechanical environment of a past human population is the added insight about physical activity and behavior.

Owing to the relative newness of the technology required for biomechanical analysis, there are only a handful of bioarchaeological studies, aside from the Georgia coastal research, that address the foraging-to-farming transition and its behavioral consequences. Bioarchaeologist Patricia Bridges of Queens College in New York analyzed the cross-sectional geometric properties of a large series of skeletons representing early prehistoric foragers and late prehistoric farmers from Alabama. In contrast to our findings from the Georgia coast, Bridges discovered a pronounced *increase* in bone strength in the transition to farming in this setting. In his study of foragers and later farmers from western New York, physical anthropologist David Barondess of Wayne State University found no change in bone strength. Thus, for these three regions of the Eastern Woodlands—where all populations made a shift from foraging to corn agriculture—the findings are different. Although there are only a handful of biomechanical studies, their different patterns confirm my assertion that localized adaptation best explains the variation in skeletal morphology in the foraging-to-farming shift.

One important difference in lifestyle and living circumstances between the inhabitants of western New York and those of the two southeastern samples is the fact that the prehistoric New Yorkers lived in a temperate climate, in contrast to populations living in the Alabama and Georgia subtropical settings. This is not to say that climate was chiefly responsible for the differences in skeletal adaptation in the three regions; rather, climate played a dominant role in determining what kinds of plant and animal resources were available to local populations. Differences in climate and environment generally would have meant that the technologies used to extract essential resources—such as food—would have been different among these three settings. Likewise, the mechanical loads associated with the work environment may have been different as well. The biomechanical evidence gathered by bioarchaeologists indicates this to be the case.

ACTIVITY CHANGES WITH AGRICULTURE: ABOVE THE NECK

Chewing, Skull Shape, Tooth Wear, and Malocclusion

The masticatory apparatus—the jaws and teeth and the chewing muscles—provides the means for initial preparation of the food entering the mouth, followed by the final reduction of food before it is swallowed. The rates and patterns of tooth wear are highly variable across human populations, and depend mostly on the texture of foods being eaten. The texture of foods is determined largely by the characteristics of the foods themselves (such as by the presence of naturally occurring abrasives in plants) or the way the food is prepared (such as the use of grinding stones for making flour from cereal grains). Tooth wear can also be very subtle, as revealed by scanning electron microscopy. Comparison of microwear on the teeth of foragers and farmers reveals a high degree of variation. In many settings, the number of microscopically visible features (mostly grooves and pits) associated with highly abrasive diets decline in frequency with the shift to farming or with more intensive farming (for example, in west-central Illinois, western Japan, and the lower Mississippi River valley). In contrast, these features increase in frequency in other settings, indicating the shift to a more abrasive diet (for example, in South Asia and Syria). In the latter, the pattern of increased microwear appears to reflect the use of grinding stones and the shift from eating many small-grained wild cereals to eating few large-grained domesticated cereals.

There is abundant evidence indicating a decrease in tooth wear in many regions of the world with the shift from foraging to farming or with agricultural intensification (for example, Japan, South Asia, Nubia, Portugal, Denmark, Peru, Mesoamerica, the Ohio River valley, Tennessee, Alabama, Texas, the lower Mississippi River valley, and Ontario). This trend indicates that food became softer and less textured in the foraging-to-farming transition. For many of the regions, the decline in tooth wear is undoubtedly related to food preparation techniques used by agriculturalists versus those employed by foragers. In some cases, the introduction of ceramics or improved ceramic technology facilitated extended cooking, where food—plant carbohydrates—could be cooked for hours on end, producing a soft mush with fewer abrasives. This change in food and the technology used to process it resulted in teeth with less-worn occlusal surfaces.

The decrease in functional demand on teeth in the chewing process also had important implications for the rest of the masticatory apparatus—the chewing muscles and the bones to which these muscles attach on faces and jaws. Earlier in this century, the influential British anatomist and physical anthropologist Sir Arthur Keith observed a reduction in size of the jaws of recent British compared to ancient British. He suggested that the decrease in jaw size was due to the replacement of tough foods (meat) eaten by earlier people with soft cereal grains eaten by later people. This is an early application of Wolff's Law to the masticatory apparatus— eating soft foods make faces and jaws smaller.

Keith's findings have been confirmed time and time again by physical anthropologists who study human and nonhuman primate species from paleontological, archaeological, and living settings. Importantly, his observations of ancient and modern British people are part of the worldwide trend of decreasing craniofacial size and robusticity. Accompanying this decrease is a clear change in the shape of the human skull that is related to the shift from foraging to farming or to intensified farming. The human skull

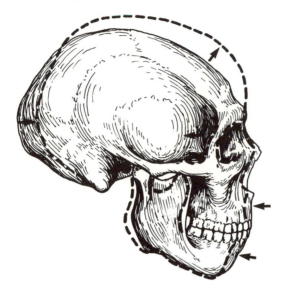

Skull changes in ancient Nubia, comparing a robust Mesolithic period (ca. 10,000 B.C.) forager with a later gracile
Meroitic-Christian period (A.D. 0–1500) farmer (dashed
line). Note the more globular and shorter skull of the
farmer. These changes are due to a decrease in demand,
from chewing softer, more processed foods in the later period. Similar changes occurred in many settings worldwide,
including the Georgia Bight. Adapted from Carlson and
Van Gerven 1977; reproduced with permission of the authors and John Wiley & Sons, Inc.

has changed in shape from long and narrow to short and wide; in
other words, in many settings, the part of the human skull that
houses the brain—called the cranial vault—has become rounder
in the last ten thousand years or so.

There have been various interpretations explaining these trends
in skull shape over the last ten thousand years. Some concluded
that it just may represent a change associated with the increasing
efficiency of bipedal walking. A much better interpretation explaining the change in skull form came from the study of skulls of
ancient Sudanese Nubians of northern Africa by David Carlson of
Baylor University and Dennis Van Gerven of the University of
Colorado. They interpreted the shortening and decreasing ro-

busticity of the skull as representing a response to decreased mechanical demands placed on the chewing muscles as populations shifted from consumption of hard-textured wild sources of food to consumption of soft-textured, agricultural foods. Carlson and Van Gerven's hypothesis is strongly supported by other lines of evidence showing what happens to skulls in humans, laboratory animals, and wild animals whose diets involve different textures of foods. For example, primates, including humans, who confine their diets to eating soft-textured foods have shorter and more gracile skulls than others eating hard-textured foods. Carlson and Van Gerven's study also has important implications for interpreting facial anatomy and size in modern humans, which are markedly smaller than those in populations living ten thousand years ago. Indeed, it suggests that the facial appearance of modern humans is at least in part determined by our culinary history, the foods we eat, and how these foods are processed.

I see other implications for the reductions in skull robusticity brought about by the shift from foraging to farming in our ancestors. Chief among them is the phenomenal increase in the incidence of malocclusion, tooth crowding, and impaction (especially in the "wisdom teeth," or the third molars) in people worldwide. This increase has been especially dramatic in the last couple of centuries. Indeed, orthodontics in the United States and other developed nations is a booming business—more and more of us have crowded, poorly aligned teeth that need to be fixed. Experimental research involving feeding soft- and hard-textured foods to laboratory animals indicates the tremendous importance of food texture and its influence on the masticatory complex. This research provides unequivocal evidence that habitual consumption of overly soft or otherwise highly processed foods promotes occlusal abnormalities—crooked teeth, misaligned jaws, and chewing problems. The bioarchaeological results are especially revealing—with few exceptions, when people shifted from eating hard-textured foods (mostly hunter-gatherers) to eating soft-textured foods (mostly agriculturalists), there was an increase in occlusal abnormalities. In more recent times, as our food has become increasingly processed, malocclusions have increased apace.

Looking at living human populations helps us to put these changes within a broader environmental context. Nonindustrial populations or groups eating unprocessed, hard-textured foods have an "edge-to-edge" bite, in which the upper incisors come into direct contact with the lower incisors when the jaws are fully closed. Chances are that this is not your bite pattern, or at least one that is comfortable for any extended period of time. In our own society, or other societies that eat highly processed foods, the edge-to-edge bite is extremely rare and occlusal abnormalities are exceedingly common. In the United States, a slight overbite, where the upper incisors overlap the lower incisors, has become the desired cosmetic pattern—most orthodontists will make every effort to achieve this occlusal arrangement for their patients.

From my reading of the experimental, clinical, and bioarchaeological evidence, the reasons for the increase in occlusal problems are multiple and complex. However, the decreased demand placed on the masticatory apparatus by humans over the last ten thousand years of their history has likely played the most important role in contributing to these changes. The increases seen in malocclusion in ancient and living humans are likely related to two sets of factors—development and genetics. Tooth size is under greater genetic control than that of the bone tissue comprising the upper and lower jaws that provide support for the teeth. Analysis of thousands of archaeological skulls worldwide indicates that there has been a greater amount of decrease in jaw size than tooth size over time. This relatively greater reduction in the size of the bones of the skeletal structures supporting the teeth than that of the teeth themselves has created a kind of a "disharmony" between these two components of the masticatory complex, skeletal and dental. Also contributing to the disharmony between the teeth and jaws in recent versus ancient populations is the fact that very few people nowadays, especially in developed nations, wear down their teeth to any appreciable degree. In traditional societies, and for most of human history, substantial wear of the occlusal and interstitial (between-teeth) surfaces results in an actual reduction in the size of teeth over the course of an individual's lifetime.

Tooth wear is, however, secondary to the role of mechanical demand in promoting maximum bone growth and larger jaws for support of the teeth.

LOOKING FOR PATTERNS

A number of dietary changes occurred during the last ten thousand years in human beings, such as the development of alcoholic beverages and salt and sugar production. Each of these changes was new in our evolution, and had important consequences for the health of our species. The development of alcoholic beverages, salt, and processed sugar and their consequences for human health pale, however, in comparison to the major dietary changes involving plant cultivation and food processing. There are some rather clear patterns in health and activity that emerge in this global overview of the bioarchaeology of the foraging-to-farming transition, which we can summarize here.

First, some widespread changes took place, including a decrease in oral and general health and an increase in physiological stress. Many populations show increased tooth decay and skeletal infection. The former are directly related to the food consumed and how it is prepared; the latter reflect the indirect consequences of the agricultural transition, especially increased sedentism, population crowding, and poor hygienic conditions. Many populations studied by bioarchaeologists also show an increased incidence of growth arrest in teeth, which is also caused by negative living circumstances.

Second, there are changes that appear to be caused by localized factors, especially in regard to physical activity and workload. Variation in the prevalence of osteoarthritis and structural geometry of long bones appears to be much more tied to local circumstances involving food production and the differences in lifestyle between foragers and farmers. Thus, the shift to agriculture beginning at the Pleistocene-Holocene boundary some ten thousand years ago and the associated biological changes show differences among regions of the world, suggesting that dietary shifts and accompanying biological changes in bones and teeth were at least in part configured by local circumstances.

Third, there are some important implications that come out of the Georgia coastal research and other regional studies regarding the costs and benefits for humans of this adaptive shift. Namely, the transition from foraging to farming was not the positive change that has been traditionally presented in the popular and scientific literature. On the other hand, I do not mean to imply that life beginning in the Holocene went from all good to all bad in the foraging-to-farming shift. To draw this conclusion would represent the same kind overly simplistic conclusions drawn earlier about the foraging-to-farming transition. Indeed, the work by my collaborators and me on skeletons of foragers from the American Great Basin indicates evidence of poor nutrition and bone mass reduction, a pattern that is present in other foragers. Anthropological demographer James Wood has stated: "On balance, most hunter-gatherers were probably just as miserable as most agriculturalists."[3] The bioarchaeological research shows that hunter-gatherers and agriculturalists were probably "miserable," but for very different reasons. I am convinced that there was an increased health burden, as well as consequences for activity, for many of the human populations that underwent the transition from foraging to farming. Thus, in answer to the questions posed at the end of the last chapter, it seems reasonable to conclude that the developments my research team and I documented in the Georgia coastal region of North America are part of a worldwide trend of decreasing quality of life.

Nor do I mean to imply that the changes in health in the foraging-to-farming transition were solely related to the quality of diet. Diet certainly is key to the broader consideration of what happened to the health of our species in the last ten thousand years, but other factors, such as politics, culture, society, and local environmental factors were also important.

Would people have known that the health of their friends and neighbors was growing increasingly worse—at least as we bioarchaeologists measure the change? No. Bioarchaeologists are almost always looking at aggregates of deaths, deaths that cover many years and span many generations. I would be hard-pressed to be able to imagine that any one individual or society would notice the kinds of subtle changes in health and behavior taking place. On the other hand, the beauty of bioarchaeology and its sister disciplines (e.g., paleontology) is that we have the important perspective of long and unbroken stretches of time. This perspective of time allows us to study and interpret biological changes in the long duration.

Finally, with regard to the New World evidence, these findings address a myth that continues to persist about Native Americans before the arrival of Europeans: that prehistoric Native Americans lived in a disease-free environment. To be sure, some of the dreadful Old World diseases (e.g., smallpox, measles, and malaria) were absent from the Americas prior to European contact. However, the presence of both nonspecific and specific infections, iron deficiency anemia, and other evidence of morbidity throughout the Americas provides substantial evidence contradicting the perception that native peoples were disease-free prior to European contact.

With the arrival of Spaniards on the Atlantic coast to what are now the modern states of Florida and Georgia, native peoples faced many novel challenges to their health and well-being that were to affect nearly every fabric of their lives. Spain's modus operandi for control of this region of the New World—named La Florida by explorer Juan Ponce de León in 1513—was colonization of new territories and exploitation of native populations for economic gain. In the next chapter, I will set the stage for understanding the human biology of this contact period, especially regarding the cultural, environmental, and historical factors that helped to shape the changes seen in native populations in the Americas, in the region of La Florida.

NOTES

1. The research conducted by bioarchaeologists George Armelagos and his collaborators in Sudanese Nubia and in the Dickson Mounds population from Illinois, and by Jane Buikstra and her collaborators in the lower Illinois River

valley of west-central Illinois, represent two important exceptions. Their comprehensive analyses of biological change presented patterns of declining health and robusticity that were broadly similar to my findings from coastal Georgia.

2. Much of the work completed by bioarchaeologists and others working on the foraging-to-farming transition has been summarized in a review article, Larsen 1995. Specific references to regions and bioarchaeologists can be found in that article. Another source is Cohen 1989.

3. Wood 1998, p. 103.

REFERENCES

Barker, D. J. P. (1996) The origins of coronary heart disease in early life. In C. J. K. Henry and S. J. Ulijaszek, eds. *Long-term Consequences of Early Environment: Growth, Development and the Lifespan Developmental Perspective*. Cambridge: Cambridge University Press, pp. 155–162.

Barondess, D. A. (1998) *Anthropometric and Biomechanical Assessment of Skeletal Structural Adaptations in Bioarchaeological Populations from Michigan and Western New York*. Ph.D. dissertation, Michigan State University, East Lansing.

Brace, C. L., Rosenberg, K. R., and Hunt, K. D. (1987) Gradual change in human tooth size in the late Pleistocene and post-Pleistocene. *Evolution* 41:705–720.

Bridges, P. S. (1989) Changes in activities with the shift to agriculture in the southeastern United States. *Current Anthropology* 30:385–394.

Calcagno, J. M. (1989) *Mechanisms of Human Dental Reduction: A Case Study from Post-Pleistocene Nubia*. University of Kansas Publications in Anthropology, no. 18.

Carli-Thiele, P. (1996) *Spuren von Mangelerkrankungen an steinzeitlichen Kinderskeleton (Vestiges of Deficiency Diseases in Stone Age Child Skeletons)*. Göttingen, Germany: Verlag Erich Goltze.

Carlson, D. S., and Van Gerven, D. P. (1977) Masticatory function and post-Pleistocene evolution in Nubia. *American Journal of Physical Anthropology* 46:495–506.

———. (1979) Diffusion, biological determinism, and biocultural adaptation in the Nubian Corridor. *American Anthropologist* 81:561–580.

Cohen, M. N. (1989) *Health and the Rise of Civilization*. New Haven, Connecticut: Yale University Press.

Cohen, M. N., and Armelagos, G. J., eds. (1984) *Paleopathology at the Origins of Agriculture*. Orlando, Florida: Academic Press.

Cook, D. C. (1984) Subsistence and health in the lower Illinois Valley: osteological evidence. In M. N. Cohen and G. J. Armelagos, eds. *Paleopathology at the Origins of Agriculture.* Orlando, Florida: Academic Press, pp. 235–269.

Danforth, M. E. (1994) Stature change in prehistoric Maya of the southern Lowlands. *Latin American Antiquity* 5:206–211.

———. (1997) Late Classic Maya health patterns: evidence from enamel microdefects. In S. L. Whittington and D. M. Reed, eds. *Bones of the Maya: Studies of Ancient Skeletons.* Washington, D. C.: Smithsonian Institution Press, pp. 127–137.

Goodman, A. H. (1994) Cartesian reductionism and vulgar adaptationism: issues in the interpretation of nutritional status in prehistory. In K. D. Sobolik, ed. *Paleonutrition: The Diet and Health of Prehistoric Americans.* Southern Illinois University at Carbondale, Center for Archaeological Investigations, Occasional Paper, no. 22, pp. 163–177.

———. (1996) Early life stress and adult health: insights from dental enamel development. In C. J. K. Henry and S. J. Ulijaszek, eds. *Long-term Consequences of Early Environment: Growth, Development and the Lifespan Developmental Perspective.* Cambridge: Cambridge University Press, pp. 163–182.

Goodman, A. H., Lallo, J., Armelagos, G. J., and Rose, J. C. (1984) Health changes at Dickson Mounds, Illinois (A.D. 950–1300). In M. N. Cohen and G. J. Armelagos, eds. *Paleopathology at the Origins of Agriculture.* Orlando, Florida: Academic Press, pp. 271–305.

Hinton, R. J., Smith, M. O., and Smith, F. H. (1980) Tooth size changes in prehistoric Tennessee Indians. *Human Biology* 52:229–245.

Hodges, D. C. (1989) *Agricultural Intensification and Prehistoric Health in the Valley of Oaxaca, Mexico.* University of Michigan, Memoirs of the Museum of Anthropology, no. 22.

Hutchinson, D. L., Larsen, C. S., Schoeninger, M. J., and Norr, L. (1998) Regional variation in the pattern of maize adoption and use in Florida and Georgia. *American Antiquity* 63:397–416.

Keith, A. (1916) Is the British facial form changing? *Nature* 98:198.

Larsen, C. S. (1995) Biological changes in human populations with agriculture. *Annual Review of Anthropology* 24:185–213.

———. (1997) *Bioarchaeology: Interpreting Behavior from the Human Skeleton.* Cambridge: Cambridge University Press.

Lubell, D., Jackes, M., and Meiklejohn, C. (1989) Archaeology and human biology of the Mesolithic-Neolithic transition in southern Portugal: a preliminary report. In C. Bonsall, ed. *The Mesolithic Europe: Papers Presented at the Third International Symposium.* Edinburgh, Scotland: John Donald Publishers Ltd., pp. 632–640.

Lukacs, J. R. (1985) Tooth size variation in prehistoric India. *American Anthropologist* 87:1–15.

Márquez, L., and del Ángel, A. (1997) Height among prehispanic Maya of the Yucatán peninsula: a reconsideration. In S. L. Whittington and D. M.

Reed, eds. *Bones of the Maya: Studies of Ancient Skeletons*. Washington, D. C.: Smithsonian Institution Press, pp. 51–61.

Martin, D. L., Armelagos, G. J., Goodman, A. H., and Van Gerven, D. P. (1984) The effects of socioeconomic change in prehistoric Africa: Sudanese Nubia as a case study. In M. N. Cohen and G. J. Armelagos, eds. *Paleopathology at the Origins of Agriculture*. Orlando, Florida: Academic Press, pp. 193–214.

Molleson, T. (1994) The eloquent bones of Abu Hureya. *Scientific American* 271(2):70–75.

Owsley, D. W. (1991) Temporal variation in femoral cortical thickness of North American Plains Indians. In D. J. Ortner and A. C. Aufderheide, eds. *Human Paleopathology: Current Syntheses and Future Options*. Washington, D. C.: Smithsonian Institution Press, pp. 105–110.

Powell, M. L. (1988) *Status and Health in Prehistory: A Case Study of the Moundville Chiefdom*. Washington, D. C.: Smithsonian Institution Press.

Rose, J. C., Armelagos, G. J., and Lallo, J. W. (1978) Histological enamel indicator of childhood stress in prehistoric skeletal samples. *American Journal of Physical Anthropology* 49:511–516.

Ruff, C. B. (1987) Sexual dimorphism in human lower limb bone structure: relationship to subsistence strategy and sexual division of labor. *Journal of Human Evolution* 16:391–416.

Saul, F. P., and Saul, J. M. (1997) The Preclassic skeletons from Cuello. In S. L. Whittington and D. M. Reed, eds. *Bones of the Maya: Studies of Ancient Skeletons*. Washington, D. C.: Smithsonian Institution Press, pp. 28–50.

Sciulli, P. W. (1997) Dental evolution in prehistoric Native Americans of the Ohio Valley area. I. Wear and pathology. *International Journal of Osteoarchaeology* 7:507–524.

Simpson, S. W. (n.d.) Patterns of growth perturbation in La Florida: evidence from enamel microstructure. In C. S. Larsen, ed. *Bioarchaeology of La Florida*. Gainesville: University Press of Florida, forthcoming.

Steckel, R. H. (1987) Growth depression and recovery: the remarkable case of American slaves. *Annals of Human Biology* 14:111–132.

Turner, C. G., II (1979) Dental anthropological indications of agriculture among the Jomon people of central Japan: X. Peopling of the Pacific. *American Journal of Physical Anthropology*. 51:619–636.

Weidenreich, F. (1945) The brachycephalization of recent mankind. *Southwestern Journal of Anthropology* 1:1–54.

Wood, J. W. (1998) A theory of preindustrial population dynamics. *Current Anthropology* 39:99–135.

5

Europeans Arrive:
Circumstances and Settings
for Native Population
Collapse in the Americas

THE STORY of the arrival of Europeans in the New World can be told in alternative ways—from the perspective of the Europeans, who were interested in securing lands and territories, or from the view of the Native Americans, who experienced loss and deprivation. Regardless of the viewpoint, the spread of people from Europe to North America and elsewhere in the world had profound implications for the health and well-being of native peoples wherever Europeans set foot. In the 1980s, the discovery of Spanish mission sites by archaeologists in the American Southeast allowed the investigation of the consequences of contact for native peoples. The study of skeletons from these sites provides a unique viewpoint from the perspective of the skeletal biology of the native populations from La Florida, the region of the American Southeast colonized by Spain over a period of more than two centuries. This chapter looks at the historical and archaeological contexts for studying the health and biology of native peoples in the region. Although the historical record—written sources—is important for understanding the impact of colonization, bones provide a picture of the changing lives and lifestyles of the native peoples.

While doing fieldwork on St. Catherines Island in the 1970s, I would often imagine what life might have been like for me had I

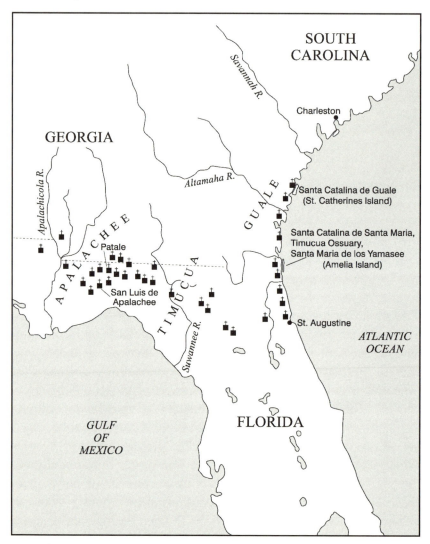

Map of La Florida showing locations of major tribes (Guale, Timucua, Apalachee) and mission sites.

been a Guale Indian living there during the last century before the arrival of Europeans. As a male in my mid-twenties, I would have had a number of responsibilities that would have required some long-distance travel in order to hunt or trade. Because a significant part of the diets of my fellow villagers was based on corn (beans and squash were also favored foods among many tribes in the Eastern Woodlands), I might have occasionally helped adult women in planting and care of crops at my home village, although this type of work was primarily the women's responsibility. My teeth wouldn't have been in the best of shape—many were likely either decayed or missing—and I may have suffered from a chronic infection at some point in my life. Unlike my contemporaries living to the west in interior Georgia, I probably did not have iron deficiency anemia. While I was a youngster, however, I would have had my share of nutritional problems, leading to physiological stress and growth disruption.

Had I been present on the island in April 1566, when the Spaniard Pedro Menéndez de Avilés visited St. Catherines Island in order to establish a mission and small military outpost, my life would have changed immediately. One could only imagine my shock when I first saw Menéndez and his fellow Europeans arriving in their big wooden vessels, wearing freakish clothing, speaking an unintelligible language, and waving pieces of cloth on long sticks. This would surely have been one of those life-defining events—right up there with birth of a son or daughter or the death of a loved one. Things would never be the same for my family, my fellow Guale tribesmen, or me.

Bringing my thoughts back to the late twentieth century and putting on my bioarchaeology "hat," I could also envision the insight that could be gained about the human biology of the contact period from the study of the remains of native populations who once inhabited the island. At the time, I was preoccupied with my study of the foraging-to-farming transition, and the idea of ever looking at substantial numbers of mission period skeletons seemed remote. For one thing, the site of the mission, named Santa Catalina de Guale by the Spaniards, had not yet been discovered, let alone the *campo santo*—the cemetery—holding the remains of its long-dead occupants. Archaeologists working on the island at various times in the 1950s and 1960s—Lewis Larson, John Griffin, and Joseph Caldwell—had been able to identify the general location of the mission, but that was all. In the late 1970s, David Thomas of the American Museum of Natural History had completed a large systematic archaeological survey of the island, locating many sites, including several with mission-period artifacts. Still, the precise location of the mission remained shrouded in mystery.

Our knowledge of the location of the mission and extent of the Spanish presence on St. Catherines Island changed dramatically in the early 1980s with the application of newly developed nondestructive remote sensing approaches to locating archaeological sites, employing proton magnetometry and soil resistivity. The suspected location of the mission was "mapped" using this technology, and the resulting reams of computer printouts were studied. Thomas struck archaeological pay dirt. With remarkable clarity, the outlines of several structures were revealed in bold detail on the maps generated by this amazing technology. Thomas began excavation in the largest of the apparent structures, which he called Structure 1. It turned out to occupy a great deal of my attention for some years to come.

Around the day that I presented the results of my dissertation research at the conference near Plattsburgh, New York, in the spring of 1982, Dave phoned me at my office in Dartmouth, Massachusetts (I was then teaching at the University of Massachusetts branch campus), to inform me that fragments of skeletal remains and rosary beads were appearing in his initial digging in the interior of Structure 1; could I come to the island in May to begin a bioarchaeological excavation? Thomas went on to explain that his initial test excavations in Structure 1 provided convincing evidence that this was the mission *iglesia*, or church. If his hunch proved correct, then this was also the site of the *campo santo*, or cemetery, where the Guale converts would have been interred in the same manner as any other Roman Catholic in the New World or back in Spain. It took me a nanosecond to respond to his request: Yes—I was again on my way south.

Beginning in May 1982 and continuing through 1986, in collaboration with Thomas, who excavated the architectural remains of Structure 1, I directed the excavation of what had indeed turned out to be the mission cemetery. I undertook a bioarchaeological study in order to look at the biocultural impact of contact and missionization on these native populations. I couldn't think of a more appropriate location for the investigation, especially in light of the comprehensive data set we had already developed and analyzed for the precontact ancestors of these people. Following the first field season at Santa Catalina, I telephoned all the members of the scientific team who had been involved in the study of the prehistoric Guale. They agreed to continue working with me on this new and exciting research, which we called the La Florida Bioarchaeology Project. It was to be an unprecedented investigation involving fieldwork and laboratory research, applying bioarchaeological methods and theory to this important colonial setting of the Spanish Americas. Other contact-era native cemeteries had been reported and analyzed in the New World, but ours was to be the first modern analysis involving a comprehensive approach to the study of the human biology and lifestyles of native populations following European contact.

CONTACT AND HEALTH: SO MUCH MORE TO GO ON THAN JUST WRITTEN RECORDS

The scholarship on the human biology of contact has largely focused on the impact of European-introduced infectious diseases to native peoples. This work has played a pivotal role in placing the understanding of native population change within the realm of human biology. With regard to New Spain, Spanish colonizers have often been viewed as sadistic murderers and exploiters of Indians, leading to the deaths of millions. Historians working with documentary records argue that disease was far more important than what is depicted in the "Black Legend," in which Spanish cruelty was principally responsible for the deaths of countless Native Americans. As historian Noble David Cook summarizes in his book, *Born to Die*:

> Amerindians died wherever Europeans trod. They succumbed (from disease) following contact with the Portuguese, then the English, the French, and the Dutch. Substantial numbers of deaths continued, no matter which European territory was involved, regardless of the location of the region. It seemed to make no difference what type of

colonial regime was created; those who lived in the mission territories under the supposedly benign and caring administration of friars seemed to die as rapidly as those subjected to forced labor in dangerous silver and gold production.[1]

In his book, Cook identifies the sources from which we can evaluate postcontact demography and population biology—letters from early settlers, native codices, and other written documentation. Although these sources are important, the human skeletal record can provide another important perspective on the contact period. Moreover, as we developed our research agenda for the La Florida Bioarchaeology Project, we became increasingly convinced that the biohistory of postcontact native societies was far more complicated—and interesting—than the singular focus on Old World disease and its aftermath.

I strongly agree with my colleagues in history and anthropology that the topic of demographic collapse is an important one, and certainly European infectious diseases explain much of the population collapse, but its emphasis in the popular and scholarly literature has overshadowed questions and discussion of other highly significant aspects of contact-period human biology. Namely, what is the larger biocultural context for population change? What is known about the *surviving* populations that were in contact with Europeans, sometimes over a period of generations? In what ways did these survivors adapt to wholly new circumstances affecting their lifestyles? We believed that bioarchaeology could provide answers to these questions in ways that historians have not considered in substantive ways. The perspective on postcontact demography and human biology presented by Cook and other historians is not wrong. Rather, I argue here that we can greatly expand our understanding of this critical period of human history by looking at a wider range of sources, including documentary, archaeological, and bioarchaeological.

As we began the huge project facing us, and especially in reading the enormous background literature, it became apparent to me that biological anthropology was very much underrepresented in the discussion of the impact of European contact on native peoples in the Americas. This underrepresentation seemed surprising given that much of this impact was biological, involving such issues as population collapse, disease, diet, and labor, and that the study of skeletons could tell us a lot about these topics. However, this isn't so surprising when one considers the fact that until twenty-five years ago or so, physical anthropologists dealt mostly with topics not relating to life history; the field was far more concerned with determining racial types and population classification. Moreover, few large, well-documented contact period skeletal samples had been professionally excavated, and if they had been, there were no prehistoric comparative samples from which to evaluate biological change. If excavated skeletal samples were available from a contact period site, the results of their study were often relegated to an appendix buried in the back of some obscure archaeological site report. Finally, many of the methods bioarchaeologists use in their studies of ancient populations—such as bone chemistry, scanning electron microscopy, and cross-sectional geometry—were not developed until recently.

Laid out in front of us was an important opportunity to contribute to a more informed understanding of this period of human history, when two very different worlds—European and Indian—confronted each other. In addition to having comprehensive skeletal samples representing the contact period at Santa Catalina, my collaborators and I had the great fortune of being able to draw on an extraordinarily rich archaeological and historical record for interpreting our findings. This record proved to be important in many ways over the course of our research.

THE LA FLORIDA BIOARCHAEOLOGY PROJECT

The Setting

EXPLORATION AND COLONIZATION

When the Spanish Crown first employed the term *La Florida* in the early 1500s, it identified a vast region of the North American continent, from the Atlantic coast to the Mississippi River and from the southern tip of Florida to Newfoundland. By mid-century, the enterprise had contracted considerably; control had shrunk to include mostly the modern state of Florida, the Georgia coast, and part of coastal South Carolina. This was still a great deal of turf, encompassing thousands of square miles that were inhabited by numerous and highly variable Indian tribes.

Although Spain had enjoyed enormous successes in the Americas, the "conquest" of La Florida proved difficult. The first forays by Europeans into the region involved a series of expeditions, with an eye toward colonization and immediate economic gain. These expeditions—led by some of Spain's finest (and not so finest), such as Vásquez de Ayllón in 1526, Pánfilo de Narváez in 1528, and Hernando de Soto in 1539–1543—were short-term affairs, and no permanent colonies resulted. Ayllón and six hundred followers, including men, women, and African slaves, attempted to establish one such colony, perhaps located somewhere in Guale territory on the Georgia coast. As with the others, time, starvation, sickness, and other factors led to the collapse of this effort.

Spain's long-term colonization began in 1565 with the ousting of the French at the Battle of Fort Caroline on the St. Johns River in northern Florida and the founding of the first permanent European colony at St. Augustine (which remains a vibrant community to this day). Pedro Menéndez orchestrated both events. Menéndez and his entourage, mostly military folk whose interests were primarily personal gain, recognized the economic potential of the region and its native peoples. The strategy of subjugating native populations by missionization and brute force began in earnest. Over the next 140 years, a series of more than one hundred sites having *doctrinas* (mission centers with a resident priest), *visitas* (villages with churches visited by priests), or European settlements (e.g., St. Augustine and San Luis) was established in La Florida. The primary mission centers were systematically placed among agricultural populations with access to St. Augustine, the capital of the colony on the north Florida Atlantic coast. Spain's colonial strategy focused on sedentary agriculturalists in north Florida and coastal Georgia, in large part because it was easier to control sedentary traditional farmers than nonsedentary foragers living in southern Florida, such as the Calusa.

Long-lasting missions were established among three principal tribes, the Guale along the Georgia coast, the Timucua on the north Florida Atlantic coast and extending inland to the Florida panhandle, and the Apalachee in the Florida panhandle. The missionization of these groups would irrevocably alter the cultural and biological landscapes of this corner of the New World.

BELIEF SYSTEMS AND BURIAL PRACTICES

Unlike the colonial efforts undertaken by Britain and France in New England and New France, respectively, Spain was very interested in rooting out and destroying the native belief systems and religious practices and replacing these systems and practices with Roman Catholicism. As is indicated by the abundant archaeological record of burial practices in the La Florida missions, this replacement was highly successful—most burials are Christian-style interments, versus traditional burial in earthen mounds. The widespread practice of Christian burial rapidly adopted by the native populations indicates that this burial program was high on the list of the priorities of missionaries when they set out to introduce Roman Catholicism to Native American populations in the La Florida colony.

Historical sources indicate that Indian converts were strongly encouraged to follow church guidelines for treatment of the remains of the deceased. That is, when individuals died, they were given last rites, burial ceremonies were held, and their remains were placed in shallow pits, on their backs with hands folded on their chests and their legs extended. The cemeteries are often located within large churches, as in the case of Santa Catalina de Guale on St. Catherines Island and San Martín de Timucua and San Luis de Apalachee in northern Florida. Archaeologists have identified and excavated more than a dozen mission cemeteries in Spanish Florida. These missions show a remarkable uniformity in the burial mode, and all include individuals of all ages and both sexes.

Most remains of deceased individuals buried in the Spanish missions are without grave accompaniments. The missions of Santa

Catalina de Guale and San Luis de Apalachee are two important exceptions to this pattern. Mission cemeteries at both localities contain graves with an elaborate and rich material culture, such as glass beads, crosses, European ceramic plates, mirrors, and elaborate majolica eating and drinking utensils. At Santa Catalina, my bioarchaeological crews found one high-status child buried with a shell disk, called a "gorget," showing an incised Mississippian-style motif of a rattlesnake head. This artifact had been made well before the arrival of the Europeans, and clearly represented an heirloom, where a succession of people—probably related in some fashion—passed it from one generation to the next. The presence of this and other grave inclusions must have represented a major concession to the Indians on the part of the mission priests, since European Catholics, then as now, bury their dead with either nothing or a simple rosary.

The material culture from the Santa Catalina *campo santo* is especially remarkable, which probably speaks to the strategic location of the mission on the Atlantic coast. In addition to saving souls, Spain had a vested interest in maintaining its territorial control, and the missions served as an important buffer, protecting Spain's economic and political hold on the region. To the north, Great Britain was making large gains in its territorial expansion, and to the west, France continued to be a significant threat. This material wealth likely reflects the fact that Santa Catalina was associated with the principal town of the Guale. The wealth of material culture associated with the remains of the deceased at Santa Catalina may also signify a greater effort on the part of the Spanish Crown to keep native populations loyal to Spain.

Similarly, the San Luis cemetery, excavated by crews under the direction of Bonnie McEwan of the Florida Bureau of Archaeological Research and me, was located in the church of the principal Apalachee town at the western end of the missions. The material culture found with some of the remains may at least in part reflect Spain's interest in this area of the colony and any encroachment from European powers controlling territory to the west of La Florida, especially France. Interestingly, people from both the Santa Catalina and San Luis missions have a relatively low incidence of tooth decay. At least with respect to their teeth, their health was better than Indians living at other missions.

The Santa Catalina and San Luis missions also contain the only cemeteries where a very select few people were buried in coffins, large wooden boxes specially designed to contain the remains of specific deceased persons. One person (of 432) located close to the altar at Santa Catalina was interred in a coffin; at San Luis, seven people (of 210) were in coffins, also at the altar end of the church. The strategic location and special treatment given these interments reflect their higher position in native society—rank had its privileges in death as it must have had in life. Underscoring the differences in status at these missions, individuals interred with material culture tend to be located closest to the ritual nucleus of the church, the sanctuary and altar.

With the exception of three adult males at San Luis, all persons in the Spanish Florida missions were buried with their heads in an easterly direction. The orientation of the majority in these mission settings was meant to position the deceased so that on the day of reckoning, the congregation would rise up and face the priest and the altar behind him. The three exceptions in the San Luis cemetery are oriented with their heads to the west. Two of these individuals were also buried in coffins. The unusual burial treatment of these individuals may indicate that they were high-ranking Apalachee, having special ties to the church. One of the three—an adult male—died of an apparent gunshot wound; a .44-caliber lead shot was found lodged in his lower vertebrae. His high status did little to protect him from a violent end.

SOME VARIATION IN THE
BURIAL PRACTICES IN LA FLORIDA:
THE AMELIA ISLAND OSSUARY

One important and unusual exception to the apparently rigid burial program imposed on the native populations in Spanish Florida is from Amelia Island, Florida, another barrier island located immediately south of the present Georgia-Florida state boundary. There, a large, rectangular pit containing a jumbled mass of loose (or disarticulated) bones representing the remains of about sixty Timucua Indians predating a later Guale cemetery was archaeologically investigated by my bioarchaeological crews in a collaborative project with archaeologists Jerald Milanich and Rebecca Saunders of the Florida Museum of Natural History.

Close inspection of the bones during the course of fieldwork and in the follow-up laboratory study has helped us to rule out two alternative scenarios for the circumstances surrounding the burial of these people. First, it is highly unlikely that the bones are the remains of people who died during one of the epidemics that swept the region on a periodic basis. Epidemic deaths usually take place over a period of weeks or months, and the pattern of disarticulation in these skeletons did not fit the time frame representing epidemic deaths. Had these deaths been due to an epidemic, we would have seen the pit filled with articulated skeletons. This was not the case—most of the bones were not articulated as discrete skeletons, but rather were completely disarticulated. In other words, the bones of nearly everyone were not joined, but rather were loose. These disarticulated remains represent the people who had been dead for the longest period of time, whereby the soft tissues were completely decayed.

Careful excavation and study in the field revealed that parts of some skeletons were still partially articulated when excavated, such as parts of hands, feet, and vertebral columns. These partial articulations suggest that some of the connective tissue holding the joints together—such as cartilage between some of the hand bones—was still present when the remains were physically moved by a person or persons for burial to the ossuary pit from some unknown location. These partial articulations represent the remains of people who died somewhat later than those people whose skeletons were completely disarticulated. Finally, the skeletal remains of two completely articulated adult males were found in the bottom of the ossuary pit in the remains of a large wooden box. These individuals obviously represent deaths that had occurred a very short time before their burial.

Drawing on what forensic anthropologists have learned about body decomposition rates and skeletonization in this area of the

American South, we can estimate roughly the amount of time it took for the deaths represented in the Amelia Island ossuary to accumulate. The length of the postmortem interval in soft-tissue decomposition is highly dependent on the season of the year. Forensic entomologists (people who study bugs from crime sites) Paul Catts and Neil Haskell have shown that tissue-eating insects (mostly fly larvae, commonly known as "maggots") are much more active "consumers" during the hot summer months than during the winter months. Given the right conditions, such as the season of the year, temperature, humidity, and shade, maggots can skeletonize a human corpse in a matter of weeks, or even days. Keeping these factors in mind, along with the presence of the partially articulated joints we observed in the field, I estimate that these skeletal remains represent an accumulation of deaths taking place over a period of perhaps as short as a year to as long as two or three years. Thus, these deaths cannot be accounted for by some epidemic sweeping through the region.

Second, it is unlikely that the skeletons represent people who had once been buried elsewhere, dug up by their fellow Timucua tribesmen from some other location, transported to the ossuary pit, and reburied there. If that had been the case, then I would expected to have seen damaged bones among the remains that I studied. As any seasoned archaeologist knows, if bones are not fully exposed and then carefully removed from the ground during excavation, they are easily broken or otherwise damaged. The bones of the face are especially fragile. Even the best field archaeologists have been known to damage these and other bones during excavation. I observed none of the kind of damage that would have been present had the skeletal remains been dug out of the ground by a nonarchaeologist. I believe, therefore, that the secondary interment scenario—excavation and reburial in the ossuary pit—can be eliminated.

With these two alternatives ruled out—epidemics or secondary burial—the most likely sequence of events can be reconstructed as follows: First, within a few days following the deaths of the two adult males, a wooden box was constructed, their remains were placed in the box, and the box was lowered to the bottom of a rectangular pit dug specifically for the occasion. Second, the remains of the partially and completely disarticulated individuals were collected (probably from an aboveground mortuary house) and placed around and on top of the wooden box containing the two males. Lastly, the ossuary pit was refilled.

At the same time that the ossuary pit was being excavated by our bioarchaeological team, we were also excavating a Guale cemetery located next to it. One of the burials in the Guale cemetery intruded into the upper fill of the ossuary pit. The presence of this intrusive Christian-style burial in the ossuary pit indicates that the Amelia Island ossuary was created relatively early in the contact period. Just how early is hard to say, but the presence of large wrought-iron nails used in the construction of the burial box containing the two adult males indicates that the ossuary is certainly from the contact period. This indicates that the ossuary likely dates to the middle or late 1500s, before full-blown missionization began—certainly no priest who took his job seriously would have allowed this kind of non-Christian burial. The ultimate reasons for ossuary burial elude us. Whatever they were, they were quickly superseded by the powerful edicts on burial and mortuary style handed down by the Roman Catholic church and passed on to this region of the New World and its inhabitants.

LIVING AND DYING IN THE GUALE CHIEFDOM:
1566–1702

By the time the European powers of Spain, Britain, and France had sorted out who controlled what territory in the middle to late sixteenth century, the northernmost Spanish presence on the Atlantic seaboard was located at the Santa Catalina mission and its associated village on St. Catherines Island. When Pedro Menéndez arrived with his countrymen in 1566, he met Indians who had a broad-based subsistence economy based on farming, hunting, gathering, and fishing. The stable carbon and nitrogen isotopic analysis of late prehistoric skeletons (see below), along with a careful interpretation of historical sources by ethnohistorian Grant Jones of Davidson College, indicates that corn was key in the subsistence economy and diet of the people that Pedro Menéndez met in the mid-1500s. Moreover, corn was grown in sufficient quantities for long-term storage, and chiefs redistributed it to the general population. The historical sources also indicate that the demands for food tribute by Spanish military and others, in addition to the encouragement by mission priests to grow crops in a more intensified manner, contributed to an increase in corn production.

From the beginning of colonialism, native labor was a central element in Spain's economic interest and perceived success in La Florida. Historical sources provide a vivid and compelling picture of work and activity by Indians on St. Catherines Island and elsewhere. Here, and at other places throughout New Spain, the *repartimiento* labor draft was implemented by the Spaniards. In this system, able-bodied Indians (mostly adult men) were required to provide obligatory labor for a range of activities, including road construction, carrying heavy materials over long distances, agricultural labor, military service, and building projects—the huge fortress at St. Augustine known as the Castillo de San Marcos was built mostly by the hard work of the Indians. This labor draft involved the relocation of men from their home villages for lengthy periods of time. The compensation for these efforts was marginal, and the physical toll on the laborers was enormous. Europeans had little interest in common labor, and by all accounts, the native labor was central to food production. Indians provided the food for the military garrisons stationed at the missions, for the priests living at the missions, and for tribute to the Spanish Crown. Governor Gonzalo Méndez de Canzo remarked in his 1602 report to the king:

> But with all this and the grain from the maize [corn], the labor that they endure in the many cultivations that are given are great, and, if it were not for the help of the Indians that I make them give, and they come from the province of Guale . . . it would not be possible to be able to sow any grain.[2]

The Guale living on St. Catherines Island and the contemporary populations living elsewhere in the mission system suffered tremendous losses due to European-introduced epidemic diseases.

As discussed in the previous chapter, native populations were not newcomers to infectious disease. Ample evidence exists for the presence of nonspecific infections as well as some specific infectious diseases, and diagnosis by bioarchaeologist Mary Lucas Powell from the late prehistoric Irene Mound site on the north Georgia coast indicates the presence of two diseases of radically different mortal and morbid effects, tuberculosis and nonvenereal treponematosis. However, the experience with these diseases in the few centuries prior to the arrival of the Spaniards did little to prepare the native populations living on St. Catherines Island or elsewhere for the coming invasion of Old World pathogens.

During the 1600s, there was a remarkable decline in population size during and following epidemics. At least two measles epidemics hammered the region of La Florida between 1613 and 1617. The governor wrote in late 1655 that a series of smallpox epidemics had contributed to substantial mortality. These, and other epidemics, wreaked havoc on the labor force that was involved in various projects throughout the provinces, and on food production for local villages.

The huge population losses due to Old World pathogens in this and other regions has been the focus of discussion by medical historians and others. A consensus has developed suggesting that Indian populations had greater genetic susceptibility because of their lack of immunological experience. I think this consensus is wrong, however, in that it is unlikely that the native populations lacked some inherent genetic resistance in comparison with Europeans. Rather, Europeans had the advantage of having had previous experience with the pathogens that caused such diseases as smallpox and measles, resulting in acquired immunities for them. Moreover, the native population lacked the medical knowhow for caring for these particular kinds of viral and bacterial infections, namely rest, warmth, and fluid consumption. In New England, colonists were well aware of the efficacy of these behaviors for treating the sick; native populations were not.

Throughout the seventeenth century, there was a reduction in the number of missions and native villages. By the mid-1670s, only six Guale settlements were present, and this number was reduced even further, to just four settlements north of Cumberland Island, by 1680. This reduction in settlements reflects the significant population reduction in the seventeenth century. It also reflects the practice of aggregation of populations from scattered villages into larger communities. Priests believed that population concentration would facilitate religious conversion; civil authorities viewed the practice as facilitating political control. After all, it would be easier to subjugate peoples who lived in a few concentrated villages, rather than being dispersed over a wide region. From the perspective of health, this aggregation of Indians into a few densely populated mission centers would have exacerbated poor sanitation conditions and encouraged the spread of infectious disease.

The excavations at Santa Catalina by Thomas revealed another factor that would have contributed to deteriorating health conditions. On the east side of the Santa Catalina mission complex, Thomas's field crews excavated the remains of a shallow plank-lined well. The well was a source for drinking water, which would have negative consequences for the health of the mission occupants. People living in the subtropics of the Georgia coast today know that drinking water drawn from a shallow well is risky business, mainly because these wells are easily contaminated by parasites and other disease-causing microorganisms. On the southern margin of the mission is one of the island's larger freshwater streams, which also likely served as a water source. Evidence indicates that the stream was dammed during the mission period, if not before. Scattered about the perimeter of the stream is an abundance of contact-era trash, including food remains and other debris, dating to the time of the occupation of the mission. These kinds of circumstances—slow moving water and dumping of trash—would have also promoted parasitic infection. Importantly, parasitic infection and associated blood loss from the bowels can very easily move the malnourished child into a condition of profound anemia, as seen in populations living today in poor rural and urban environments in Brazil and other underdeveloped settings.

At various times and places in La Florida, the Guale and other tribes expressed their strong dissatisfaction with the Spaniards by

instigating revolts. Among the Guale, the most ambitious revolt
was led by Juanillo, an heir to one of the Guale chiefdoms. A series
of well-coordinated attacks on four missions in 1597 resulted in
the deaths of four Spanish priests at the hands of Indians. In retali-
ation, the Spanish commenced a brutal and effective campaign
against the Guale; villages, crops, and food stores were burned,
and men, women, and children were killed. The discord between
Spaniards and Guale quieted over the following years, and by 1607
or so, a new group of missionaries had reestablished mission life
at Santa Catalina.

Throughout the late 1500s and 1600s, various factors—epidemics, forced labor, military and other forms of harassment, and
widespread social disruption—resulted in population reduction on
an unprecedented level. Beginning in 1661, yet a new series of
events added to the deteriorating circumstances for the Guale.
Equipped with firearms and other weaponry, "a nation of warrior
Indians," probably the Rechahecrians from Virginia, attacked various Guale settlements, "sacking the churches and convents and
killing the Christian Indians."[3] Although the invaders eventually
retreated, the damage was widespread, forcing relocations of
Guale Indians.

In 1670, a geopolitical development on the southeastern Atlantic coast was to ultimately spell doom for the Spaniards and Span-
ish-allied Indians, including the Guale and other tribal groups.
In that year, British colonists founded the city of Charles Town
(Charleston, South Carolina) with an eye toward expansion southward into Spanish-controlled territory. Attacks on Spanish interests to the south began, and in 1680, following a decade of harassment, a force of three hundred British troops and British-allied
Yamasee Indians led by Colonel James Moore attacked St. Catherines Island and its mission. The small Spanish garrison protecting
the mission and Guale temporarily equipped with firearms with-
held the attack in a day-long battle. However, the handwriting was
on the wall regarding the bleak future on the island, and subse-
quent to the attack, the Indians, priests, and soldiers fled southward to Sapelo Island. By 1684, along with other refugee groups,

the Guale re-established a new Santa Catalina mission and village on Amelia Island, giving it the old name of Santa Catalina de Guale. (In order to avoid confusion, archaeologists and historians call the Amelia Island mission Santa Catalina de Santa Maria.)

The movement southward of Guale from St. Catherines Island reflects the state of turmoil for native populations during the late seventeenth century. The turmoil would re-emerge some eighteen years later, when on an early November morning in 1702, on their way to attacking St. Augustine, British troops and allied-Indians, again led by Colonel James Moore, invaded and overran Amelia Island, forcing the Indians and Spaniards to flee yet again. Escaping southward, they eventually settled near St. Augustine, bringing the Guale chiefdom to an end.

The Guale Skeletal Remains

Our excavations on St. Catherines and Amelia Islands involved thorough documentation of location and context for individual burials. At Santa Catalina on St. Catherines Island, detailed study of construction and architectural features by Dave Thomas suggested that most of the more than four hundred burials are from the post-1597 rebellion, and are contemporary with the second wattle-and-daub structure built around 1607 on the site of the earlier mission burnt during the rebellion period.[4] The terminal date of burial is 1680, the year of abandonment of the mission, thus bracketing the skeletal series to mostly between 1607 and 1680.

The cemetery is restricted to an area of about 36 feet by 65 feet, corresponding to the width and length of the church building. The façade of the church faced southeast, and was of wattlework (sticks and planks) in construction. All other walls were wattle-and-daub (sticks and mud). Most of the daub encountered by Thomas in his excavations was burnt, indicating that the building had burned to the ground, probably at the time of abandonment. A large, rectangular churchyard, covered with water-rolled shell collected from nearby natural marine-shell deposits, fronted the church. The shell had a huge effect on preservation of human remains, particularly at the southeast end of the cemetery. Under normal conditions, the very acidic soils of St. Catherines Island destroy bones and teeth. But in this setting of the churchyard and adjacent cemetery, the shell chemistry—shell is composed largely of calcium carbonate—very effectively neutralized the acidic soil, creating excellent conditions for preservation of skeletons at this end of the cemetery.

Burials were oriented parallel to the long axis of the church (northwest-southeast). Remains of the deceased were all in Christian-style postures described above, with the heads to the east-southeast away from the altar. One grave located at the extreme northern end of the cemetery was a non-Christian style burial: The remains were disarticulated and had probably been wrapped into a bundle prior to interment in a shallow pit. This individual probably postdates the burial of the other 431 individuals in the mission cemetery. Half of the skeletons were disturbed to varying degrees by superimposition of later burials. This high degree of disturbance reflects the long occupation of the mission and use of a limited burial area.

The "discovery" of the lost Santa Catalina mission on St. Catherines Island was not accidental. The process of site identification had involved years of study, careful consideration of historical records, and well-planned archaeology informed by state-of-the-art remote sensing technology. In contrast, the site of the later Santa Catalina mission on Amelia Island was found quite by accident. In the mid-1980s, the Dorion family bought a few acres of land on Amelia Island, hoping to build a home. In the process of initial preparation for house construction, a human skeleton was encountered by workmen. The landowner got in touch with contract archaeologist Kenneth Hardin before continuing with construction. Preliminary testing and analysis of artifacts indicated to him that the proposed location of the house sat atop the *campo santo* of the reestablished Santa Catalina. Historical records housed in the archives of the University of Florida clearly indicated that this was indeed the site of the newly established Santa Catalina; these records even included a detailed map showing the church location and other key parts of the mission.

Knowing of my work on St. Catherines Island—my bioarchaeological crews were excavating there at the time—Ken called me to ask if my crew and I might consult with him regarding further work on the new mission site. The landowner was intent on construction, but wanted to do the right thing by way of archaeological mitigation of this important site. My group and I traveled to Amelia Island; we were immediately dumbstruck by the incredible similarity between the mission cemetery complexes of Amelia Island and St. Catherines Island. Moreover, the physical similarity of skeletons from the two sites was striking—the two missions were clearly related.

With the permission and the generous financial backing of the landowner, we went to work—Ken Hardin, personnel from the Florida Museum of Natural History, Northern Florida University, Williams College, and my group excavated the Guale cemetery at the new Santa Catalina mission. Shortly into the project, we encountered the Timucua ossuary containing the aforementioned disarticulated skeletons in the northeastern corner of the cemetery. Moreover, eroding out of the nearby creek bank, the skeletons from yet another mission cemetery, probably the first mission—known as Santa Maria de Yamasee—on the island prior to the arrival of Guale Indians from St. Catherines Island, were appearing. The Indians living at Santa Maria de Yamasee were Yamasee Indians from interior South Carolina and Georgia, who had moved southward to Amelia Island. Amelia Island was an attractive haven for displaced Indians. This was a complicated place!

Bioarchaeological excavations of the Santa Catalina mission on Amelia Island resulted in the recovery of 121 individuals of all ages and both sexes, along with the remains from the earlier Timucua ossuary (see below). The discovery of a brass stamp with the image of the patron saint, Santa Catalina, confirmed our assessment that this was the mission founded by Indians and Spaniards from St. Catherines Island. The long axis of the cemetery was oriented southeast-northwest, with heads of the deceased directed toward the southeast. Unlike the St. Catherines cemetery, relatively little disturbance—only 8 percent—from intrusive burial was present in this cemetery. This low level of disturbance reflects the short-term use of the cemetery, less than twenty years, by a smaller group of people than the one that was present at the original Santa Catalina mission on St. Catherines Island.

Unlike many other contact-era settings in the Americas, the Guale did not represent an aggregation of a hodgepodge of groups drawn from different cultures. As ethnohistorian John Worth has pointed out, the social, political, and cultural continuity of the Guale is well indicated by the persistence over time of chiefly lineages, despite substantial population loss and change. The core towns identified in the seventeenth-century Guale, including those living on St. Catherines Island, represent an aggregate of the more dispersed villages of earlier times, reflecting the high degree of cultural adaptability under stress. In addition, continuity in pottery styles through the mission period, identified by archaeologist Rebecca Saunders, argues for the maintenance of a strong sense of ethnic identity of the Guale Indians until their abandonment of Santa Catalina on Amelia Island in 1702.

The discussion in this chapter provides the essential context for our study of contact-period Indians of Spanish Florida. In the next chapter, we will look at what the study of skeletons from Spanish Florida tells us about the impact of colonization on native populations, how our findings compare with other regions of the New World, and the ongoing consequences of contact for living native peoples in the Americas today.

Notes

1. Cook 1998, p. 5.
2. John Hann, unpublished translation; cited in Larsen 1990, p. 16.
3. Worth 1995, p. 15.
4. David Hurst Thomas, personal communication.

References

Bushnell, A. T. (1994) *Situado and Sabana: Spain's Support System for the Presidio and Mission Provinces of Florida.* Anthropological Papers of the American Museum of Natural History, no. 74.

Catts, E. P., and Haskell, N. H. (1990) *Entomology and Death: A Procedural Guide*. Clemson, South Carolina: Joyce's Print Shop, Inc.

Cook, N. D. (1998) *Born to Die: Disease and New World Conquest, 1492–1650*. Cambridge: Cambridge University Press.

Dunlop, Captain (1929) Journal of Capt. Dunlop's voyage to the Southward, 1687. *South Carolina Historical and Genealogical Magazine* 30(3):127–133.

Hann, J. H. (1990) Summary guide to Spanish Florida missions and *visitas*, with churches in the sixteenth and seventeenth centuries. *The Americas* 56:417–513.

Jones, G. D. (1978) The ethnohistory of the Guale coast through 1684. In D. H. Thomas, G. D. Jones, R. S. Durham, and C. S. Larsen, eds. *The Anthropology of St. Catherines Island: Natural and Cultural History*. Anthropological Papers of the American Museum of Natural History, vol. 55, part 2, pp. 178–210.

Larsen, C. S., ed. 1990 *The Archaeology of Mission Santa Catalina de Guale: 2. Biocultural Interpretations of a Population in Transition*. Anthropological Papers of the American Museum of Natural History, no. 68.

———. (1993) On the frontier of contact: mission bioarchaeology in La Florida. In B. G. McEwan, ed. *The Spanish Missions of La Florida*. Gainesville: University Press of Florida, pp. 322–356.

———. (1997) *Bioarchaeology: Interpreting Behavior from the Human Skeleton*. Cambridge: Cambridge University Press.

Larsen, C. S., Huynh, H. P., and McEwan, B. G. (1996) Death by gunshot: biocultural implications of trauma at Mission San Luis. *International Journal of Osteoarchaeology* 6:42–50.

Larsen, C. S., Schoeninger, M. J., Hutchinson, D. L., Russell, K. F., and Ruff, C. B. (1990) Beyond demographic collapse: biological adaptation and change in native populations of La Florida. In D. H. Thomas, ed. *Columbian Consequences, Volume 2: Archaeological and Historical Perspectives on the Spanish Borderlands East*. Washington, D. C.: Smithsonian Institution Press, pp. 409–428.

McEwan, B. G. (1999) The archaeology of the historic period Apalachee. In B. G. McEwan, ed. *Indians of the Greater Southeast during the Historic Period: Archaeology and Ethnohistory*. Gainesville: University Press of Florida.

Milanich, J. T. (1995) *Florida Indians and the Invasion from Europe*. Gainesville: University Press of Florida.

Milanich, J. T., and Milbrath, S. (1989) *First Encounters: Spanish Explorations in the Caribbean and the United States, 1492–1570*. Gainesville: University Press of Florida.

Pennie, R. A., Pearson, R. D., McAuliffe, I. T., and Guerrant, R. L. (1996) The illness burden in poor rural and urban communities: enteric parasitic infections. In R. L. Guerrant, M. A. de Souza, and M. K. Nations, eds. *At the Edge of Development: Health Crises in a Transitional Society.* Durham, North Carolina: Carolina Academic Press, pp. 149–159.

Powell, M. L. (1990) On the eve of conquest: life and death at Irene Mound, Georgia. In C. S. Larsen, ed. *The Archaeology of Mission Santa Catalina de Guale: 2. Biocultural Interpretations of a Population in Transition.* Anthropological Papers of the American Museum of Natural History, no. 68, pp. 26–35.

Saunders, R. A. (1992) *Continuity and Change in Guale Indian Pottery,* A.D. 1350–1702. Ph.D. dissertation, University of Florida, Gainesville.

Thomas, D. H. (1987) *The Archaeology of Mission Santa Catalina de Guale: 1. Search and Discovery.* Anthropological Papers of the American Museum of Natural History, vol. 63, part 2.

———. (1990) The Spanish missions of La Florida: an overview. In D. H. Thomas, ed. *Columbian Consequences, Volume 2: Archaeological and Historical Perspectives on the Spanish Borderlands East.* Washington, D. C.: Smithsonian Institution Press, pp. 357–397.

Weber, D. J. (1992) *The Spanish Frontier in North America.* New Haven, Connecticut: Yale University Press.

6

Bioarchaeology of Population Decline and Extinction in Spanish Florida

THE EXCAVATION and study of Spanish missions by archaeologists, historians, and bioarchaeologists offers an important chance to understand more fully the cultural and biological implications of colonization and missionization in this important region of North America for the lives and lifestyles of native peoples. The establishment of missions among native groups in Spanish Florida resulted in a decline in quality of life—a trend that had preceded the arrival of the Europeans. These changes were brought about by alterations in diet, agricultural intensification, nutritional decline, population concentration around mission centers, labor exploitation, and the introduction and spread of diseases originating in Europe and brought to North America with the colonists. Although health declined for native populations, some evidence based on the study of skeletons suggests an accommodation of sorts during the two-hundred-year period of Spanish presence in the American Southeast. This chapter looks at the bioarchaeological findings from La Florida, and especially for the Guale, the tribe that lived along the Georgia and northern Florida Atlantic coast. Bioarchaeology presents a picture of complex change—in health, diet, and activity—for native populations in the region, in ways not anticipated through the study of historical or written sources.

Before our bioarchaeological study of the Guale, there had been only one other substantive investigation of native skeletons from Spanish Florida. Based on her study of skeletons from the Apalachee mission of San Pedro y San Pablo de Patale (or more simply, Patale), physical anthropologist Rebecca Storey of the University of Houston suggested that the health of native populations may have actually improved compared to that of the late prehistoric Indians from the Lake Jackson site, the nearby major Mississippian center and mound complex in northern Florida. The improved health, she suggested, may have been related to greater access to protein derived from domesticated animals (such as chickens) imported from the Old World or raised in the New World.

The documentary record for Spanish Florida indicates that missions are often mentioned as sources of Old World domesticated animals, such as chickens, pigs, and cattle. However, analysis of animal bones from various missions by zooarchaeologist Elizabeth Reitz at the University of Georgia suggests that these documentary sources probably exaggerated the importance of Old World domesticated animals in the diets of mission Indians. That is, although archaeology of the missions reveals evidence of the use of domestic chickens, pigs, and cattle in native diets, the contribution of these animals appears to have been minuscule in relation to animals that were native to the region, such as deer. There is at least one important exception, however. The people at San Luis seemed to have eaten a fair amount of beef—cattle bone has been identified by Reitz in the food refuse from the site. Moreover, her analysis of animal remains indicates that there is a great deal of variation in the specific animals used for food across Spanish Florida, suggesting that subsistence strategies were highly localized and that native knowledge was more important than European knowledge of foods eaten. The high degree of variability in diet is also indicated by studies of plant remains by Margaret Scarry of the University of North Carolina and Donna Ruhl of the University of Florida, as well as in our analysis of stable carbon and nitrogen isotopes from the human bones (see below). By these various accounts, there is little reason to believe that dietary quality improved in the mission Indians compared with their prehistoric predecessors.

We projected that our work in Guale could provide an additional and, perhaps, broader perspective than what was available in Storey's study of skeletons from the Patale mission. By looking at a range of health indicators, coupled with an assessment of activity and physical behavior, we would be in a position to understand what must have been a complex picture of adaptation and stress. Thus, the overall goal of the La Florida Bioarchaeology Project was to characterize the health and activity of native populations based on a study of skeletons, framed within the larger setting of the colonial period in the New World.[1] Dietary reconstruction, the foundation for understanding health and activity in this complex setting, was our first order of business.

DIET IN LA FLORIDA: BIG CHANGES AND NUTRITIONAL STRESS

Bone Chemistry, Tooth Microwear, and Food

STABLE ISOTOPES, CORN, AND SEAFOOD

Various historical records suggest that the mission populations increased their production and consumption of corn. We hypothesized that the isotopic values should indicate a major reorientation of diet, reflecting the increase in production of this important food source. Analysis of stable carbon and nitrogen isotope ratios in the prehistoric populations from the region showed a clear increase in C_4 consumption—corn—and no change in marine food consumption (see chapter 3). Margaret Schoeninger analyzed additional bone samples in her lab from the Santa Catalina missions and late prehistoric sites in the region. As is usually the case in a scientific investigation, there were both expected and unexpected results that emerged from this analysis. Additional materials from the late-period Irene site were analyzed and compared to materials from the early (Savannah) period from the same locality. As expected, there was an increase in stable carbon isotope ratios (more corn) in the Savannah period (A.D. 1150–1300), but unexpectedly, there was a decrease in isotope ratios (less corn) in the following Irene period (post-A.D. 1300). We had incorrectly assumed that both periods would show relatively strong indications of corn consumption. Moreover, the late prehistoric Irene stable carbon isotope values were considerably lower than contemporary late prehistoric populations living on the coastal islands. Thus, these other localities indicated significant corn consumption at a time when the major Mississippian center at Irene was experiencing a decline in this key food.

Archaeologist David Anderson of the National Park Service had earlier reconstructed a comprehensive environmental profile for the Savannah River valley (the Irene site is located in the mouth of the valley on the north Georgia coast). His work strongly suggested that the region had experienced a major period of drought, environmental deterioration, and social disruption during the late prehistoric period at Irene and elsewhere in the valley. Our hunch is that the drought was severe enough that corn crops failed miserably for a time, forcing the local prehistoric populations to shift back to the use of nondomesticated C_3 foods. Our isotopic findings certainly indicate that a C_4-to-C_3 dietary shift occurred, and we think it was due to the corn being eliminated, or nearly so, from the diet.

Moving into the mission period, comparison of late prehistoric Georgia coastal populations, earlier historic Guale from St. Catherines Island and later historic Guale from Amelia Island, reveals clear trends in stable isotope values of carbon and nitrogen: Average stable carbon isotope ratios increased and stable nitrogen isotope ratios decreased slightly. These trends can mean only one thing: The late prehistoric and mission period Guale became increasingly dependent on corn, but simultaneously consumed somewhat smaller amounts of marine foods.

BARIUM, STRONTIUM, AND SEAFOOD

Other evidence involving bone chemistry also points to a major shift in diet for these people. Knowing of our growing studies involving stable isotopic analysis, archaeologists Joseph Ezzo of Statistical Research, Inc., in Tucson, Arizona, and James Burton of

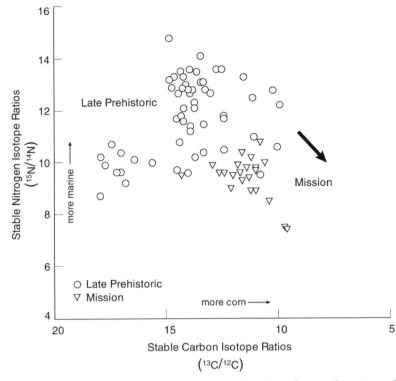

Stable carbon and nitrogen isotope ratio values from late prehistoric and mission period farmers from the Georgia Bight. The arrow indicates the tendency for decreasing nitrogen isotope ratios and increasing carbon isotope ratios in the mission period Guale. These changes depict a shift from eating less marine foods and more corn over time.

the University of Wisconsin, Madison, suggested that we do a pilot study of the alkaline elements barium (Ba) and strontium (Sr) in our skeletal samples. The ratio of these elements is closely linked with diet in the following manner: In terrestrial plants and animals, barium and strontium are present in approximately equal levels; the ratio of Ba/Sr is equal to 1. In seawater and marine organisms, however, the Ba/Sr ratio is extremely small, less than 0.001. The lower ratio results from the combination of high sulfate content of ocean water and low solubility of barite (barium sulfate), which essentially removes most barium from ocean water.

Since barium and strontium leave a biogenic signature in human skeletal tissue, the measurement of the Ba/Sr ratio could help identify the relative use of terrestrial and marine foods in the native populations we were studying.

Analysis of bone samples from Johns Mound, a prehistoric pre-agricultural population from St. Catherines Island, and from mission-era Guale from St. Catherines and Amelia Islands at the lab in Madison revealed relatively low Ba/Sr ratios in the pre-mission and mission Guale. These findings suggested that marine foods continued to be included in Guale diets in the mission period, and in a very big way.

MICROWEAR AND TOOTH USE

Other lines of evidence confirmed a major shift in diet during the mission period. Physical anthropologist Mark Teaford at Johns Hopkins University has devoted a considerable part of his professional career to studying microwear on chewing surfaces of teeth of a range of fossil and extant primate and human species. This research has proven enormously informative about how people use their teeth and the impact of different kinds of foods. Although he had previously done little work on recent humans, Teaford agreed to join our bioarchaeological project and compare the patterns and frequency of microwear features of Guale teeth in order to help us firm up our understanding of diet in this setting. At his scanning electron microscopy lab, Teaford documented patterns and frequencies of scratches, pits, and grooves in the upper first molars from the preagricultural Johns Mound population from St. Catherines Island and from the two Santa Catalina missions, from St. Catherines and Amelia Islands. We expected to see a decrease in microwear features with the increased focus on corn and cooking foods into soft mushes. Moreover, if these people were eating less seafood, it might be expected to see less grit in the diet, as shellfish are notorious for containing many fine sand particles that can wear occlusal surfaces of teeth. Teaford's preliminary assessment showed a gradual, but distinctive, decrease in the frequency and size of microwear features: There are fewer scratches and pits, and grooves are narrower in the mission teeth. This finding shows in dramatic detail the change in tooth use in the mission period. People were eating softer foods with less grit, which I believe points to corn boiled in ceramic pots.

These bone chemistry and microwear studies fit perfectly with our expectations based on the historical sources regarding the importance of agriculture in historic-period Indians in the Georgia Bight. One of the most compelling sources that gives a picture of the extent of agricultural production in the mission complex on St. Catherines Island was provided by visitors during the first few decades following the mission's abandonment by the Spaniards and Guale Indians. Stopping there briefly in 1687, Captain Dunlop saw cleared areas of seven or eight miles for agriculture. Following his shipwreck on the north Florida coast, Englishman Jonathan Dickinson remarked about his stay on the island: "We got to the place called St. Catelena [sic], where hath been a great settlement of Indians, for the land hath been cleared for planting, for some miles distant."[2] Although he did not report on the consumption of corn per se, the extent of production is indicated by the amount of clearing of land specifically devoted to agriculture. Even today, the imprint of these large agricultural fields on the landscape is still evident. Royce Hayes, the superintendent of St. Catherines Island, has long observed subtle differences in vegetation in a large region surrounding the mission compared to the rest of the island, indicating the location of former agricultural fields.

Contrary to an earlier reconstruction of the Guale diet, our findings indicate that the establishment of mission centers had a profound effect on native subsistence systems. Grant Jones's assessment of the historical records and his conclusions regarding the importance of corn were confirmed by our bioarchaeological analysis. Importantly, the increased emphasis on corn, along with other stressors, had an impact on overall health and activity for the Guale. This bioarchaeological research, then, provides a context for addressing issues such as quality of diet, health status, and behavioral changes in these populations. The shift to an increasingly narrower diet dominated by corn may have contributed to the decline and extinction of these populations.

HEALTH IN THE MISSIONS

Growth and Development

TOOTH SIZE IN JUVENILES AND ADULTS

Tooth sizes in the mission Indians from St. Catherines and Amelia Islands show slight increases compared to those of the precontact foragers and farmers. Given the well-known relationship between tooth size and body size in humans and other primates, these increases likely reflect an increase in body size over the time span, which is indicated by greater long bone lengths in the mission Guale (see below). Thus, the change does not reflect nutritional quality. But there is another aspect of tooth size that provides insight into health and stress. Clinical research shows that the environment in which we grow, develop, and mature—beginning at conception—has profound consequences throughout the entire life span. Persons who receive inadequate nutrition during early childhood can be smaller, more prone to disease, and have a shorter life expectancy than persons with adequate nutrition. The hypothesis that members of a population who are more physiologically stressed are more likely to die at an earlier age than less-stressed members of a population can be tested by comparing the size of juvenile teeth and adult teeth. That is, individuals with small teeth—those who did not grow to their full genetic potential—had a reduced life span. This is not to say that because people have smaller teeth, they die earlier. Rather, it simply indicates the failure of teeth to reach their genetically determined size potential.

Comparison of size (measured as maximum breadth) of maxillary permanent teeth of juveniles (<16 years) and adults (>16 years) reveals that adults of the prehistoric and mission Guale have teeth that are between 2 percent and 6 percent larger than those of juveniles, depending on the tooth (we measured permanent incisors, canines, premolars, and molars). This finding suggests that indeed, as predicted by our hypothesis, members of a population who are physiologically compromised from poor diets or disease (resulting in small teeth) tend to die at younger ages than other members of the population. Interestingly, the Guale from Amelia Island show an especially large disparity in tooth size between juveniles and adults. For example, the tooth sizes for adult maxillary left incisors and canines all exceed a 4 percent juvenile-adult difference. Most other teeth in the St. Catherines Guale and prehistoric foragers and farmers show a 2 percent (or less) size difference between juvenile and adult teeth.

ENAMEL DEFECTS

I have shown in previous chapters that study of enamel defects can be highly informative about levels of environmental disruption. Compared to the prehistoric Indians, mission Indians have a large number of hypoplasias. This change in frequency suggests an increase in physiological stress, especially in relation to long-lasting stress. In order to look at the finer details of physiological stress, we decided to look at accentuated Retzius lines, enamel defects representing short-term stress (see chapter 4). Scott Simpson at Case Western Reserve University has been developing a microscopic technique for studying Retzius lines, which appear as very small irregularities in enamel structure and represent brief and acute metabolic disruptions that occur over a period of less than a few days.[3] Earlier research done by Simpson and others on other human populations indicates that the defects are most common in enamel forming between twelve and thirty months of age.

Simpson has studied Retzius lines from individuals drawn from various prehistoric and contact-era sites in Florida, including the Santa Catalina mission on Amelia Island and the adjacent Timucua ossuary. His findings show that only half the ossuary individuals have enamel with lines, but *all* the individuals of the Amelia Island mission Guale have lines. Although the finding is preliminary, this difference between the two sites suggests a substantial difference in health, with the later population being far less healthy than the earlier population. This is consistent with the idea that stress would have increased as health declined.

What caused the stress that we are seeing in these people? Simpson believes that infants and young children in the Spanish missions suffered from bouts of diarrhea caused by viral and bacterial diseases. Infantile diarrhea is often rapid, lasting no more than several days. The chief drawback of diarrhea is the rapid systemic dehydration that occurs in the infant, leading to severe fluid loss that affects nearly every tissue of the body, including teeth. Physiologically, these losses result in fluid movement from intracellular to extracellular spaces, resulting in disruption of the cells of the body, including the ameloblast cells that produce enamel. With the introduction of new foods and water to the infant in the weaning process in these missions, along with other negative circumstances associated with life in the missions (such as poor sanitation), infants must have been exposed to factors contributing to diarrhea, which we believe explains the high prevalence of accentuated Retzius lines in the Amelia Island mission Indians.

Iron Status

Our dietary reconstruction, showing an increase in emphasis on corn in the mission Indians coupled with a decrease in emphasis on marine foods, suggested to us that the mission Indians may have suffered from iron deficiency anemia. As discussed in the previous chapter, iron deficiency is prevalent in many corn-dependent populations, but the consumption of marine foods serves to enhance iron absorption. We believe that the availability of marine foods in late prehistoric times provided a means of increasing iron bioavailability. However, parasite-contaminated water taken from wells may have dramatically affected iron status in the mission-period Guale.

Comparisons of the prehistoric and mission-era Guale reveal a striking dichotomy in the prevalence of porotic hyperostosis and cribra orbitalia, pathological conditions linked to iron deficiency anemia. The precontact crania show well under 10 percent with either porotic hyperostosis or cribra orbitalia, indicating very little iron deficiency. In sharp contrast, the St. Catherines Island and Amelia Island Guale show 27 percent affected for both groups; well over 50 percent of juveniles less than ten years of age at death have porotic hyperostosis or cribra orbitalia. The greater frequency of pathology in juveniles—a pattern seen in virtually every skeletal series studied by bioarchaeologists—reflects the fact that the bone is undergoing rapid growth and development at this stage and young juveniles are especially susceptible to iron depletion. Our findings indicated that iron deficiency anemia became a problem only after the arrival of Europeans and the establishment of missions among native populations.

Here, I re-emphasize the point that some porotic hyperostosis or cribra orbitalia may not be related to iron deficiency anemia. In order to identify other specific diseases that could have caused porotic hyperostosis and cribra orbitalia in this setting, physical anthropologist Michael Schultz at the University of Göttingen completed a detailed microscopic study of thin sections of cranial bone from four mission-period skulls in his laboratory. One of the children with porotic hyperostosis is from the Yamasee mission on Amelia Island—Santa Maria de Yamasee—which slightly predates the nearby Santa Catalina mission. The skull shows extensive porotic hyperostosis. Microscopic study revealed the characteristic pattern of parallel alignment of bone spicules usually associated with iron deficiency anemia, called the hair-on-end effect when viewed in X rays. Other skulls in the analysis indicated evidence of superficial inflammation of bone, and not iron deficiency.

These bioarchaeological findings strongly suggest a dramatic increase in iron deficiency anemia in the mission-period Guale. Decreased marine food consumption, parasitic infection, and the overall deteriorating living conditions in the missions conjoined to produce poor iron status. The presence of widespread anemia had other important implications for the health of the native children living during the mission period. Iron deficiency is also associated with delays in cognitive and behavioral development in infants and young children. Delays in motor and mental development persist well into the fifth year of life in iron-deficient infants. Clearly, the high prevalence of anemia in the mission Indians con-

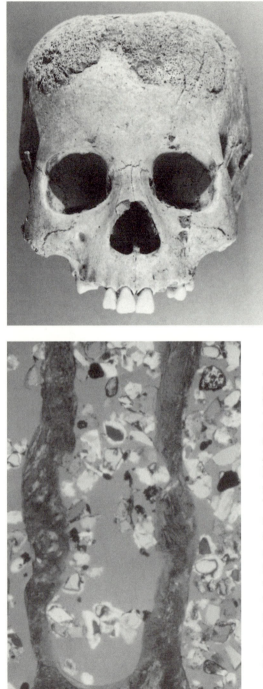

Top: Porotic hyperostosis in juvenile skull from Amelia Island. The entire upper area of the skull is covered with expanded bone. Bottom: Microscopic section of porotic bone from top of skull from the same individual (70×). The parallel orientation of the bone (dark material) is typical of people with iron deficiency anemia. The irregularly shaped objects within the hollow spaces are tiny sand particles originating from the burial matrix. Preparation of microscopic section and photograph courtesy of Michael Schultz.

tributed to part of the health burden, and the children growing up in this environment were disadvantaged in many ways.

Physical anthropologist Patty Stuart-Macadam at the University of Toronto has suggested that the reduced iron status may confer some benefits for someone who has an infection. Clinicians have long observed that low iron in the blood of an individual reduces the availability of this essential nutrient not only for the human, but also for the pathogenic microbes being carried by the individual. Thus, moderate levels of iron deficiency may also cut off or substantially reduce the supply of iron to these microbes. By doing so, iron deficiency may provide an advantage to the person with an infection.

However, even slight iron deficiencies have other health costs, such as affecting the production of a number of key enzymes for various biological functions. Therefore, although iron deficiency anemia may be beneficial in some respects, it has other health costs for the individual that are likely more consequential for their well-being.

Disease

DENTAL CARIES

The bone chemistry and microwear analyses suggested that both the diet, and probably the manner in which food was prepared, changed significantly in the mission-period Indians. Comparison of dental caries prevalence in the precontact farmers with that in the early mission and late mission Guale revealed a slight decline in frequency of carious lesions in the St. Catherines Island mission Indians, from 9.6 percent to 7.6 percent. We believe that the slight decline is not especially significant, and certainly the percentage of teeth affected in the St. Catherines Guale is well within the range for populations that are dependent on corn agriculture, at least with respect to those in the Eastern Woodlands (and see chapter 4).

The late mission Guale from Amelia Island have a very different level of tooth decay than the earlier population from St. Catherines Island. Nearly one-third (31 percent) of the teeth of the Amelia Island Guale display carious lesions. Moreover, the lesions are severe, and for the first time, we see individuals with the tooth crowns and entire teeth that are missing altogether. The increase in prevalence of poor oral health may be due to the fact that there were more older adults in the Amelia Island mission than in the late prehistoric and St. Catherines missions. However, age-controlled analysis verified that indeed, many more teeth—and more individuals—had dental disease in the Amelia Island population than in the earlier groups. This high frequency is also in sharp contrast to the frequency that Tiffiny Tung and I have determined for the Apalachee from San Luis, about 5 percent.

The increase in caries reflects the increased consumption of high-carbohydrate foods during the late seventeenth century for the Indians living on Amelia Island. Additionally, the manner in which the food was prepared may have also changed. In this regard, Teaford's microwear analysis shows that the Amelia Island population has the least number of microwear features, such as scratches, grooves, or pits, of the populations from the Georgia Bight. The isotope evidence shows similar levels of consumption of corn, which suggests to me that the change seen in microwear resulted from a major alteration in the way the food was processed. Either the foods were softer, or the native populations were more successful at removing grit particles that might cause the wear. Regardless, a softer food consistency would greatly enhance the cariogenicity of diet and the microorganisms that cause tooth decay. Whatever the cause of increased decay may have been, the evidence provides a clear picture of declining oral health in the late mission Guale.

BONE INFECTIONS

In addition to the caries evidence, some of the most compelling evidence for a decline in health and overall quality of life in the mission period is derived from our study of nonspecific bone infections, periosteal reactions on the major bones. The foraging-to-farming transition in the Georgia Bight involved an increase in infection. We expected to see a continuation of this trend in the missions of St. Catherines and Amelia Islands, especially in light of the practice of relocation and concentration of native populations in and around mission centers and the increase in disease. That is, the prevalence of infection should increase in the period of missionization.

Comparison of frequency of periosteal reactions between the late prehistoric farmers and the early mission Guale from St. Catherines revealed a reduction from 20 percent to 14.4 percent. Some 60 percent of the tibias of the Amelia Island mission Indians display periosteal reactions, however, most of which are probably caused by infection. This represents a huge increase in bone infections in the late mission Guale. I think that there can be only one conclusion that can be drawn from this study of trends in the contact-period Guale—health declined in the contact period. We might speculate, however, that the relatively low frequency of periosteal reactions in the St. Catherines Island Guale may reflect relatively better health status compared with other mission populations. As pointed out earlier, Santa Catalina on St. Catherines Island was the northernmost outpost in Spanish Florida for more than a century. Perhaps the mission people enjoyed relatively better provisioning or other factors that would enhance their health in comparison with other native populations living elsewhere in the colony. The historical records are silent on this point, and this suggestion regarding better health on St. Catherines Island must, at least for now, remain purely speculative.

The extraordinarily high frequency of tibia periosteal reactions in the Amelia Island Guale reflects the exceedingly poor circumstances of living in the Spanish missions during the late seventeenth century. One must keep in mind that by the late 1600s, this population had been exposed to a century and a half of social and biological disruption involving social and physical dislocation, population concentration, and deteriorating environmental circumstances. Moreover, the synergy between poor nutrition of this corn-dependent population and the increase in disease suggests to me that some of the increased prevalence of bone infection may reflect the combined interaction of poor diet and increased exposure to infectious disease. The increase in bone infection tells us that conditions in the late mission period had worsened considerably.

Demography

LIFESPAN AND BIRTHRATES

The stresses of life deriving from poor health and well-being have a tremendous impact on birth and death rates, representing what demographers call fertility and mortality, respectively. As discussed earlier, age at death in archaeological assemblages of skeletons is strongly influenced by fertility—skeletal series with many younger individuals reflect high birth rates, and conversely, skeletal series with many older individuals reflect low birth rates. In collaboration with Katherine Russell and Scott Simpson, we determined the age at death of the skeletons from the missions on St. Catherines and Amelia Islands and found that there are large numbers of older adults in the later mission, especially when compared to the earlier mission. This indicates that many old people were inhabiting the later mission. Moreover, the age structure in the St. Catherines mission Indians was similar to that of the prehistoric foragers and farmers that I had studied earlier. For the four populations from the Georgia Bight, the following percentages of individuals older than thirty-five years were present (number in the parentheses is average age at death for the population):

Prehistoric foragers: 26 percent (23 years)
Prehistoric farmers: 23 percent (23 years)
Santa Catalina, St. Catherines Island: 16 percent (21 years)
Santa Catalina, Amelia Island: 56 percent (30 years)

The presence of many older adults in the Amelia Island mission—well over half the assemblage is made up of individuals older than thirty-five years—suggests that they had very low birth rates. The low birth rates—caused by all sorts of negative factors affecting the health of reproductive-age women—likely contributed to the decline in population numbers during the mission period. Other factors were no doubt involved, but this analysis suggests the importance of birth rate in maintenance of population size. Almost certainly, reproduction was likely a significant factor in the depopulation of La Florida.

WORKLOAD AND ACTIVITY IN THE GEORGIA MISSIONS

Osteoarthritis

As discussed in other chapters of this book, the study of osteoarthritis in archaeological collections provides an important perspective on the mechanical environment in past populations: High levels of osteoarthritis reflect a more demanding physical lifestyle and workload than low levels of osteoarthritis. Because the skeletal joints from the St. Catherines mission Guale were generally very poorly preserved, our understanding of osteoarthritis is based on our observations of the skeletons from the Guale living on Amelia Island in the late 1600s. I showed in chapter 3 that there were appreciable declines in the frequency of osteoarthritis in comparing prehistoric farmers with earlier foragers from the Georgia coast. Comparison of the late mission Guale with the precontact farmers reveals a profound increase in osteoarthritis for all of the major skeletal joints:

Cervical: 16.4 percent to 68.3 percent
Thoracic:11.4 percent to 68.3 percent
Lumbar: 24.5 percent to 67.2 percent
Shoulder: 5.3 percent to 15.2 percent
Hip: 6.8 percent to 10.5 percent
Wrist: 1.1 percent to 13.2 percent
Hand: 3.0 percent to 5.9 percent

In light of the presence of a large number of older adults in the Amelia Island mission, this increase might be interpreted as reflecting the older age structure of these Indians. However, con-

Engraving from 1591 showing Timucua Indians laboring in agricultural fields. Note that both women and men are working. Prehistorically, this may have been an activity involving mostly women. Exploitation of native populations as a labor source by the Spanish resulted in heavy labor for many adults.

trolling for age by comparing the number of people within the same five-year age groups shows that, in fact, more Amelia Island mission Indians had osteoarthritis than those in the other time periods. Given the primacy of the mechanical environment in promoting osteoarthritis, we believe that these increases in the Amelia Island Guale indicate a major increase in workload and level of physical activity affecting all joints of their skeletons. The biomechanical analysis below helps sort out some of the factors involved in interpreting activity in the mission period.

Bone Structure

Cross-sectional geometric analysis offers a means for identifying the level and type of workload, along with inferences about mobility, in the mission Indians. We selected well-preserved femora and humeri from the St. Catherines and Amelia Island missions in order to examine bone strength and to infer key factors in activity in mission populations. As we did with the prehistoric long bones, we cut the shafts of these long bones, using two sections in the femur (the area of the femur shaft that is located immediately below the hip end of the bone, and the midshaft corresponding to the mid-thigh region) and in the humerus (the area of bone near the elbow). The sections were photographed, electronically digitized, and cross-sectional geometric properties calculated in Chris Ruff's lab at Johns Hopkins University.

The structural analysis reveals several important findings. First, average long bone lengths increased in the early mission period, and declined slightly in the late mission period. Generally, then, heights calculated from lengths of long bones were greater in the mission Indians than in the prehistoric Indians. Second, the bone mass—as measured by cortical area—changed very little over the time span from late prehistoric to early and late mission Guale. Third, an analysis of J, the mechanical measurement of the bone's ability to resist torsion (twisting)—and also a good overall indicator of bone strength—shows an increase in the femur for both adult males and females. Thus, the cross-sectional properties indicate a marked increase in bone strength.

Fourth, comparison of Ruff's mobility index of I_x/I_y (measuring anterior-posterior versus medial-lateral bending strength) in the femur midshaft shows some important changes through time. The mobility index for adult females shows a continuous decrease from the prehistoric farmers to the early mission period and again in the late mission period. We interpret this to mean that women became increasingly sedentary over the time span. Males, however, show an increase in the mobility index in the early mission Guale, which is followed by a decrease in the late mission Guale. On closer examination of individual data for the mobility index in St. Catherines Island mission males, the increase in the mobility index appears to be due to the bias of five Guale males who had very high mobility index ratios (index values exceeding 1.30). Thus, males from St. Catherines Island include two groups—one with a high average mobility index and the other with a low average mobility index.

These changes in bone strength and mobility reflect some important aspects of behavior and activity not revealed in our analysis of osteoarthritis. On the face of it, the increase in height (determined from femur lengths) suggests an improvement in nutrition. Our dietary reconstruction based on bone chemistry and dental caries indicates that the *quality* of diet, however, certainly did not improve. Thus, we speculate that the quantity of food available to mission Indians may have increased, causing weight gain (and higher stature). Overall, however, there was a decline in mobility, but with at least some males in the St. Catherines mission still involved in long-distance travel. Historical records tell us that some, but not all, males from the missions were recruited for labor projects involving long-distance travel. We speculate that the five males with high mobility indexes were men who had been involved in these kinds of travel over long distances during their lifetimes.

The increases in bone strength are likely due to the increased demands and physical labor placed on the Indians during the mission period. As noted above, some of these increases may also be due to weight gains in these more sedentary populations.[4] It is difficult to test the hypothesis involving weight gain and its influence on cross-sectional geometry, especially since we are not able to measure body weights in these skeletal populations (that is one drawback of studying the dead when drawing conclusions about health and lifestyle). However, our argument is consistent with the observed increases in body weight and decline in nutritional quality in North American native populations who underwent (or are currently undergoing) comparable transitions involving increased sedentism. Aleš Hrdlička, a physical anthropologist at the Smithsonian Institution, made numerous observations of Native American populations living in the American Southwest at the turn of the century. He especially noted increases in body weight as these groups became more sedentary and shifted away from eating traditional foods acquired from hunting and gathering to eating processed carbohydrates. Since World War II, obesity in native populations shifting from reservation living to urban settings has increased dramatically. The pattern of weight gain is directly tied to increased sedentism and access to carbohydrates and fats. The increased consumption of carbohydrates and more sedentary lifestyle in the Spanish Florida mission system may well have resulted in increased weight gain. Thus, Bishop Calderón's remark made in 1675 in reference to the Indians of Spanish Florida, that "[t]hey are fleshy, and rarely is there a small one,"[5] may reflect these changing settlement and dietary conditions identified through bioarchaeological analysis.

In summary, what we have found out about the Guale based on their bone structure is important because it addresses the questions posed above regarding health and lifestyle changes. In a very real sense, these findings underscore the importance of looking at native peoples that were adapting to changing conditions during a very critical period of their history. As shown in this and in the previous chapters, bioarchaeological research allows us to examine responses to alterations in the biomechanical and nutritional environments of pre- and postcontact native peoples. These studies of skeletal biomechanics demonstrate that the arrival of Europeans and the establishment of mission centers resulted in significant behavioral modifications. An increase in body weight in the more sedentary mission Indians may explain some of the increase in cross-sectional geometric properties. Importantly, these bone strength increases reflect the increase in workload due to labor exploitation by the Spanish. Whatever the cause, the bone structural changes were dramatic, and were almost certainly due to the profound influence of changes in lifestyle, both before and after contact by Europeans.

A consensus has built over the last several decades that disease brought by Europeans from the Old World was the cause of population collapse, social disruption, and extinction of many native populations in the Americas. From what my research team and I have learned, I would argue that equally important to the understanding of proximate cause of the remarkable population decline in native groups from the sixteenth through the nineteenth centuries (Native American population size has actually rebounded in the twentieth century) is the wide array of other factors that provided the context for and ultimate causation of this collapse. These factors include excessive workload and labor exploitation, reduced nutritional quality, violent European-Indian interactions, warfare, soil depletion, population crowding and reduced sanitation, sedentism, social disruption, physiological stress, and reduced fertility. The bottom line is that if we really want to gain a broad-based perspective on the human biology of the contact period, we must move away from monocausal explanations—introduction of Old World disease and population collapse—of biological change and investigate the full range of sources that better inform our understanding of this important period of world history. The bioarchaeology of human remains recovered from contact-era sites offers an important means toward achieving this goal.

COMPARISONS WITH OTHER REGIONS OF THE NEW WORLD

The volume of research on the contact period, including bioarchaeology, has grown by leaps and bounds in the last decade or so, in large part because of the interest generated by the commemoration in 1992 of the five-hundredth anniversary of Columbus's landfall in the Americas. In contrast to the fourth Columbian centenary, an event that excluded native peoples, the decade of the 1990s was filled with new insight into the impact of the arrival of Europeans on native New World populations. The bioarchaeology of the contact period generated out of this new interest in colonialism indicates a great deal of variation in health and lifestyle across the Americas following contact by Europeans. In part, the mosaic of biological change can be attributed to the different approaches to colonization by the various European nations involved. Although there were many players, chief among them were the powerful nations of Great Britain, France, and Spain. Other nations also had a role to play in colonialism. For example, for a time, Holland and Sweden controlled large areas of the American Northeast (e.g., New York and New Jersey). However, as with Spanish Florida, Great Britain eventually squeezed these smaller nations out of the competition for control of eastern North America.

Contacts between native populations and Europeans in the American Northeast tended to be entrepreneurial in focus, involving trade relationships and little governmental control. In New Spain, covering southern North America, Central America, and most of South America (excluding Brazil), contacts with native populations tended to be more closely monitored by governmental and religious authorities. The land and the native peoples came under the protection of Spain, unlike in New England, where colonists sought to displace the indigenous populations. These influences had profound effects on the cultural and biological landscapes of native populations in their respective regions.

Variability in the biological response to contact can also be explained by the preexisting characteristics of the various native groups encountered by Europeans. The habitats, population size and distribution, social complexity, dietary composition, and other parameters vary tremendously across the Americas. Even within relatively limited areas where native groups shared cultural identities, the foods consumed and habitats exploited were variable. These differences indicate that the colonial period and resulting biological changes were not a uniform process with predictable outcomes, but rather a patchwork affair that depended on the nature of the particular European exploitative strategies as well as the cultural, biological, and ecological circumstances of the setting and the people being exploited.

A comparison of various regions in the Americas that were colonized by European powers during the sixteenth and seventeenth centuries shows some interesting similarities and differences. Typically, initial explorations resulted in contacts—sometimes friendly, but often violent—between Europeans and Indians. This exploratory period was then followed by long-term interaction in the form of permanent European settlements and sustained contact. Bioarchaeological evidence indicates that most settings involving prolonged interactions between Europeans and Indians led to the decline in quality of life and changes in activities for the latter. The other side of the picture—the changes in health and behavior for Europeans—is not as clearly known (the next chapter will explore some of the possibilities). For most native peoples, diet was dramatically altered, as in the case of La Florida. Analysis of stable isotopes for prehistoric and mission-era Guale (see above), Timucua, Yamasee, and Apalachee reveal a strong degree of variability prior to contact. Late prehistoric people ate corn in coastal Georgia, but not in Florida (except for people living at the Mississippian period center at the Lake Jackson site in the Florida panhandle). At the height of the mission era in the seventeenth century, our isotope analysis shows, however, that most native peoples were eating corn throughout the provinces of Georgia and Florida. Archaeological evidence indicates that plant and animal species eaten varied across La Florida, but there was a common focus on corn in the region generally.

The increasing similarity of diet in the contact period, at least with respect to the consumption of corn, occurred in other areas of the Americas, with some important exceptions. For example, the levels of corn consumption of the Maya of Mesoamerica did not change with contact. Corn use actually declined among Southwestern Pueblo and Great Plains tribes during the contact period.

Most contact-era populations studied by bioarchaeologists show some evidence of increased physiological stress. In La Florida and the Maya mission population of Lamanai (Belize), the frequency of accentuated Retzius lines increased dramatically, but Tipu Maya (also in Belize) had low numbers of these defects. The relatively low frequency of these defects in the Tipu Maya suggests that children did not experience the same high levels of physiological stress as at Lamanai or other mission settings. These relatively low levels of stress may reflect the fact that the Tipu mission was in a remote location. The missions of La Florida and at Lamanai were in much closer contact with Spanish activity, owing to their important economic roles in the support of Spain's colonial effort in these respective regions.

Comparisons of health indicators of prehistoric and mission populations in Texas by physical anthropologist Elizabeth Miller at California State University in Los Angeles show some interesting parallels with our findings from La Florida. At the San Juan

Capistrano and San Francisco Xavier de Horcasitas missions, increases in prevalence of porotic hyperostosis, infection, hypoplasia, and caries are substantial in comparison with the prehistoric Indians. In Texas, as in Spanish Florida, dietary change and sedentism, along with disease, played an enormously important role in contributing to the health declines seen in the mission-era native populations.

Few bioarchaeologists have considered the skeletal correlates of activity in addressing issues relating to adaptive shifts in native peoples and the arrival of Europeans in the New World. Skeletons from only two other settings have been systematically studied. Like La Florida, contact-era native populations from Michigan analyzed by David Barondess show dramatic increases in bone strength and skeletal robusticity relative to the prehistoric Indians. The contact settings of Florida and Michigan are very different, which is important to consider. In Florida, the native populations were living under a highly exploitive system directly administered by Spanish government and church authorities. Increased workload and behavioral adaptations resulted from direct changes involving labor exploitation and decreased population mobility. In Michigan, on the other hand, native populations did not live under direct political and social control of a European power. The increase in skeletal size and robusticity in this setting reflects increased involvement by native people in the growing fur trade with the French. Native populations, Barondess suggests, may have intensified their physical activities, especially those involved in the production of items important for the fur trade. A likely activity would have been increased hunting and preparation of furs, as well as production of food for sale to the French and other Europeans living in the region. The decision to participate in the fur trade was motivated by economic interest on the part of the native population, and not by demands placed on them by Europeans.

The skeletal remains of the Ponca and Omaha Indians studied by Karl Reinhard and his collaborators at the University of Nebraska show a marked change in the pattern of osteoarthritis relative to prehistoric Indians, suggesting shifts in the kinds of workload or activities that cause the disorder. In particular, the historic tribes express a pattern of osteoarthritis involving the hip and lower back, which largely reflects the acquisition of the horse as a means of transportation.

Ongoing Consequences

By the middle of the nineteenth century, few native groups living in the Americas had escaped the (mostly negative) effects of contact with Europeans or Euroamericans as the colonizers moved westward from the Atlantic coast. The consequences of these contacts for native peoples throughout the Americas continue to the present day. In the first decade of the present century, Hrdlička observed the "appalling" levels of tuberculosis in native populations of the greater American Southwest, including northern Mexico. This apparent increase in tuberculosis can be explained only by the decreased quality of living conditions that were conducive to the spread of the opportunistic microbes that causes tuberculosis. Hrdlička also remarked on the presence of obese people, relating the condition to sedentism and the new lifestyle associated with reservation living.

Although the American public is currently experiencing an epidemic of obesity—according to body mass index measurements more than half the American population is overweight—Native Americans since World War II have been particularly hard-hit. In the Southwestern Pimas, the increase in body mass has been dramatic, especially in comparison of pre- and post-1945 birth cohorts. The trend in these tribes and other native populations is tied to increased sedentism and consumption of high-fat, high-carbohydrate diets, a development that has its roots in the increased access to Western or nontraditional foods.

The increase in obesity in Native Americans is especially problematic because excessive body weight is a major health risk for non-insulin-dependent (type 2) diabetes mellitus. Diabetes mellitus involves abnormally high blood sugar (glucose) due to deficiency of or reduced response to insulin, the chemical in the body that regulates carbohydrate metabolism. Although the disease was originally thought to have been a minor, harmless trait in Native Americans, it is now clear that it can lead to kidney failure, eye disease and blindness, and cardiovascular disease. Diabetes mellitus usually occurs in obese, sedentary adults who are over forty years of age. The increases in diabetes in Native American groups are especially profound in comparison with the greater American population. In the early 1900s, Hrdlička could find only one individual with diabetes among all the Pima that he met in his survey of the greater Southwest. By the 1970s, 50 percent of adults in the tribe over the age of thirty-five were diabetic. Today, the disease is common in other tribes, such as the Cherokee in North Carolina.

The reasons for such a remarkable increase in the prevalence of diabetes in Native Americans are complex. For one, native groups appear to have a genetic susceptibility to the disease. However, physical anthropologist Emőke Szathmáry of the University of Manitoba suggests that the current epidemic seen in Native Americans is due mostly to lifestyle changes since World War II, involving increased sedentism, overconsumption of fats and protein, and excessive weight gain.

For many Native American societies, lives continue to be disrupted in ways that are hauntingly similar to events that took place during the sixteenth and seventeenth centuries. In the last several decades, many thousands of Mayan Indians living in Guatemala have died as a result of terrorism sponsored by local and national governments. Tragically, some one million Maya have either fled or been displaced in some other manner from their homes due to military counterinsurgency tactics. In the state of Chiapas, Mexico, many native peoples continue to be harassed. Moreover, these groups in Mexico and elsewhere in Latin America continue to experience widespread undernutrition, resulting in retarded growth and poor health generally.

In the vast region of the Amazon River Basin, European and Euroamerican contact with native groups has been minimal until quite recently. Over the last twenty years, however, rapid development has resulted in social, economic, and environmental chaos.

As the frontiers of this enormous region are pushed back, colonization motivated by a variety of interests—including mining, ranching, and settlement—has resulted in the introduction of new diseases and deterioration of health for native peoples. First contact for the Waorani of Ecuador began in the late 1950s with the arrival of Christian missionaries. Within a decade, mortality from epidemic diseases resulted in numerous deaths. The Yanomami of Amazonian Venezuela and Brazil have experienced a similar pattern since the 1970s; many continue to die from recently introduced epidemic diseases. The discovery of gold in the 1980s opened up the "protected" Yanomami territories to invasion by some 40,000 miners. Along with malaria and environmental disruption, this invasion has introduced scrofula, a form of tuberculosis that was common in medieval Europe, and is seen only rarely in the developed world today.

In the study of the skeletons of native New World populations, a number of important lessons have been learned. In addition to the greater appreciation for the unprecedented stress levels and widespread death leading to the extinction of some groups, and decline for most of those that survived, I have become just as impressed with the remarkable survival and accommodation of new and biologically challenging circumstances by native New World peoples. The biological and cultural resilience of native groups, in the face of some extraordinary pressures, such as labor exploitation, displacement, disease, population crowding, and malnutrition, is impressive. This underscores the remarkable vibrancy and plasticity of humans, a story told time and again in the history of our genus.

When we think of colonial expansion and its impact on native populations, we usually think in terms of the impact on the populations being encountered by the colonists. In the next chapter, I look at the other side of the story, through the study of the health and activity in the colonists themselves. Although colonial expansion after 1492 involved millions of people, the movement of Europeans and later, Euroamericans, into marginal frontier regions usually touched on the lives of small groups of people. Thus, the skeletal record representing these early colonists is quite small.

For all of Spanish colonial Florida, I know of no European skeleton, Spaniard or otherwise, that has been found outside the city of St. Augustine. Inside the city walls, the remains of eleven Spaniards buried at a church cemetery were archaeologically excavated and minimally described. The study of these remains resulted in little information about their health status, except to say that most of the Spaniards displayed evidence of osteoarthritis, infection, dental caries, and tooth loss. This small bit of data does not allow a considered presentation of the bioarchaeology of the European side of Spanish colonialism.

In the last few years, a handful of bioarchaeologists have been studying the lifestyles and health of the first Europeans to arrive in the New World and later Euroamericans who colonized the western frontier of the growing United States. In the next chapter, we look at the health and lifestyle in the mid-Atlantic settled by British colonists in the seventeenth century and a setting in the American West—now known as the Midwest—in the first half of the nineteenth century. The bioarchaeological picture indicates an important aspect of stress and adaptation that has been largely ignored, except by historians.

NOTES

1. Five hundred fifty-seven individuals are represented in the combined skeletal samples of Santa Catalina from St. Catherines Island, Georgia, and Santa Catalina from Amelia Island, Florida. The skeletons from St. Catherines Island have been returned to the island for reinterment at the site of Santa Catalina. The skeletons from Amelia Island were reinterred near the site of the mission.

2. Dickinson 1699, p. 70.

3. The laboratory work involved in dental histology is technically demanding. First, the fragile enamel must be stabilized in embedding material and then cut into extremely thin slices or sections for the microscopic analysis. The defects are then identified using a standard laboratory light microscope. In order to determine the age at which the defect occurred in the growing tooth, the distance is measured between the defect and a standard reference located at the junction between the enamel and dentine. In order to identify the key structural features of the defective enamel identified via light microscopy, another thin section is prepared and examined under the scanning electron microscope at powers as high as 5,000x.

4. It is possible that body weight relative to height was systematically altered in the mission-period Indians. Mechanical demand on the lower limb—the femur—is related to stresses derived from a combination of both activity and body weight. Mechanical loading should be proportional to body weight, multiplied by a factor related to level of activity. In order to control for variability in body size in the different populations and between individuals within populations, we divided the cross-sectional geometric properties by length of the bone to the fourth power. By length-standardizing the cross-sectional geometric properties, Ruff determined that the properties could be affected by both activity level and body weight. Due to the increase in sedentism in this setting and the overall shift to a poorer-quality diet, it is possible to argue that the proportion of body weight to height actually increased in this setting. A greater dietary focus on carbohydrates in combination with an increase in sedentism and confinement of movement of native peoples living in the missions could have led to relative weight gain. If true, then this would have the effect of increasing the body weight to bone length ratio and, thus, the length-standardized cross-sectional properties. The implication, then, would be that weight gain played an important role in explaining the increase in second moments of area than activity per se. However, the increase in osteoarthritis argues against invoking weight gain as the sole cause for these changes in second moments of area. In reality, increased work demand and increased body weight probably acted simultaneously in increasing the second moments of area, I and J, in the historic-period Guale Indians.

5. Hann 1988, p. 158.

References

Alchon, S. A. (1991) *Native Society and Disease in Colonial Ecuador.* Cambridge: Cambridge University Press.

Baker, B. J., and Kealhofer, L., eds. (1996) *Bioarchaeology of Native American Adaptation in the Spanish Borderlands.* Gainesville: University Press of Florida.

Cohen, M. N., O'Connor, K., Danforth, M., Jacobi, K., and Armstrong, C. (1994) Health and death and Tipu. In C. S. Larsen and G. R. Milner, eds. *In the Wake of Contact: Biological Responses to Conquest.* New York: Wiley-Liss, pp. 121–133.

Danforth, M. E. (1997) Late Classic Maya health patterns: evidence from enamel microdefects. In S. L. Whittington and D. M. Reed, eds. *Bones of the Maya: Studies of Ancient Skeletons.* Washington, D. C.: Smithsonian Institution Press, pp. 127–137.

Dickinson, J. (1699) *Jonathan Dickinson's Journal, or God's Protecting Providence.* Port Salerno, Florida: Florida Classics Library.

Ezzo, J. A., Larsen, C. S., and Burton, J. H. (1995) Elemental signatures of human diets from the Georgia Bight. *American Journal of Physical Anthropology* 98:471–481.

Fackelmann, K. (1998) Tuberculosis outbreak: an ancient killer strikes a new population. *Science News* 153(5):73–75.

Hann, J. H. (1988) *Apalachee: The Land between the Rivers.* Gainesville: University Press of Florida.

Hemming, J. (1985) *Change in the Amazon Basin.* Manchester, England: Manchester University Press.

Hrdlička, A. (1908) *Physiological and Medical Observations among the Indians of the Southwestern United States and Northern Mexico.* Bureau of American Ethnology Bulletin, no. 34.

Hutchinson, D. L., Larsen, C. S., Schoeninger, M. J., and Norr, L. (1998) Regional variation in the pattern of maize adoption and use in Florida and Georgia. *American Antiquity* 63:397–416.

Kaplan, J. E., Larrick, J. W., and Yost, J. A. (1984) Workup on the Waorani. *Natural History* 93:68–75.

Knowler, W. C., Pettitt, D. J., Bennett, P. H., and Williams, R. C. (1983) Diabetes mellitus in the Pima Indians: genetic and evolutionary considerations. *American Journal of Physical Anthropology* 62:107–114.

Koch, J. K. (1983) Mortuary behavior patterning and physical anthropology in colonial St. Augustine. In K. Deagan, ed. *Spanish St. Augustine: The Archaeology of a Colonial Creole Community.* New York: Academic Press, pp. 187–227.

Larsen, C. S. (1994) In the wake of Columbus: native population biology in the postcontact Americas. *Yearbook of Physical Anthropology* 37:109–154.

———. (1997) *Bioarchaeology: Interpreting Behavior from the Human Skeleton.* Cambridge: Cambridge University Press.

Larsen, C. S., Crosby, A. W., Griffin, M. C., Hutchinson, D. L., Ruff, C. B., Russell, K. F., Schoeninger, M. J., Sering, L. E., Simpson, S. W., Takács, J. L., and Teaford, M. F. (n.d.) A biohistory of health and behavior in the Georgia Bight: the agricultural transition and the impact of European contact. In R. H. Steckel, J. C. Rose, and P. W. Sciulli, eds. *The Backbone of History: Health and Nutrition in the Western Hemisphere.* New York: Cambridge University Press, forthcoming.

Larsen, C. S., and Harn, D. E. (1994) Health in transition: disease and nutrition in the Georgia Bight. In K. D. Sobolik, ed. *Paleonutrition: The Diet and Health of Prehistoric Americans.* Southern Illinois University at Carbondale, Center for Archaeological Investigations, Occasional Paper, no. 22, pp. 222–234.

Larsen, C. S., and Hutchinson, D. L. (1992) Dental evidence for physiological disruption: biocultural interpretations from the eastern Spanish borderlands, U.S.A. In A. H. Goodman and L. L. Capasso, eds. *Recent Contribu-*

tions to the Study of Enamel Developmental Defects. Journal of Paleopathology, Monographic Publications, no. 2, pp. 151–169.

Larsen, C. S., and Milner, G. R., eds. (1994) *In the Wake of Contact: Biological Responses to Conquest.* New York: Wiley-Liss.

Larsen, C. S., and Ruff, C. B. (1994) The stresses of conquest in Spanish Florida: structural adaptation and change before and after contact. In C. S. Larsen and G. R. Milner, eds. *In the Wake of Contact: Biological Responses to Conquest.* New York: Wiley-Liss, pp. 21–34.

Larsen, C. S., Ruff, C. B., and Griffin, M. C. (1996) Implications of changing biomechanical and nutritional environments for activity and lifeway in the eastern Spanish borderlands. In B. J. Baker and L. L. Kealhofer, eds. *Bioarchaeology of Native American Adaptation in the Spanish Borderlands.* Gainesville: University Press of Florida, pp. 95–125.

Larsen, C. S., Ruff, C. B., Schoeninger, M. J., and Hutchinson D. L. (1992) Population decline and extinction in La Florida. In J. W. Verano and D. H. Ubelaker, eds. *Disease and Demography in the Americas.* Washington, D. C.: Smithsonian Institution Press, pp. 25–39.

Larsen, C. S., Schoeninger, M. J., van der Merwe, N. J., Moore, K. M., and Lee-Thorp, J. A. (1992) Carbon and nitrogen stable isotopic signatures of human dietary change in the Georgia Bight. *American Journal of Physical Anthropology* 89:197–214.

Larsen, C. S., and Sering, L. E. (1999) Inferring iron deficiency anemia from human skeletal remains: the case of the Georgia Bight. In P. M. Lambert, ed. *Bioarchaeological Studies in Life in the Age of Agriculture.* Tuscaloosa: University of Alabama Press.

Larsen, C. S., Shavit, R., and Griffin, M. C. (1991) Dental caries evidence for dietary change: an archaeological context. In M. A. Kelley and C. S. Larsen, eds. *Advances in Dental Anthropology.* New York: Wiley-Liss, pp. 179–202.

Lovell, W. G. (1988) Surviving conquest: the Maya of Guatemala in historical perspective. *Latin American Research Review* 23:25–57.

Miller, E. (1996) The effect of European contact on the health of indigenous populations in Texas. In B. J. Baker and L. Kealhofer, eds. *Bioarchaeology of Native American Adaptation in the Spanish Borderlands.* Gainesville: University Press of Florida, pp. 126–147.

Milner, G. A., Humpf, D. A., and Harpending, H. C. (1989) Pattern matching of age at death distributions in paleodemographic analysis. *American Journal of Physical Anthropology* 80:49–58.

Price, R. A., Charles, M. A., Petitt, D. J., and Knowler, W. C. (1993) Obesity in Pima Indians: large increases among post-World War II birth cohorts. *American Journal of Physical Anthropology* 92:473–479.

Reinhard, K. J., Tieszen, L., Sandness, K. L., Beiningen, L. M., Miller, E., Ghazi, A.M., Miewald, C. E., and Barnum, S. V. (1994) Trade, contact, and female health in northeast Nebraska. In C. S. Larsen and G. R. Milner, eds. *In the Wake of Contact: Biological Responses to Conquest*. New York: Wiley-Liss, pp. 63–74.

Reitz, E. J. (1990) Zooarchaeological evidence for subsistence at La Florida missions. In D. H. Thomas, ed. *Columbian Consequences, Volume 2: Archaeological and Historical Perspectives on the Spanish Borderlands East*. Washington, D. C.: Smithsonian Institution Press, pp. 543–554.

Ruff, C. B. (1987) Sexual dimorphism in human lower limb bone structure: relationship to subsistence strategy and sexual division of labor. *Journal of Human Evolution* 16:391–416.

Ruff, C. B., and Larsen, C. S. (1990) Postcranial biomechanical adaptations to subsistence changes on the Georgia coast. In C. S. Larsen, ed. *The Archaeology of Mission Santa Catalina de Guale: 2. Biocultural Interpretations of a Population in Transition*. Anthropological Papers of the American Museum of Natural History, no. 68, pp. 94–120.

———. (n.d.) The mechanical environment of La Florida. In C. S. Larsen, ed. *Bioarchaeology of La Florida*. Gainesville: University Press of Florida, forthcoming.

Santos, R. V. (1991) *Coping with Change in Native Amazonia: A Bioanthropological Study of the Gaviao, Surui, and Zoro, Tupi-Monde Speaking Societies from Brazil*. Ph.D. dissertation, Indiana University, Bloomington.

Schmink, M., and Wood, C. H. (1984) *Frontier Expansion in Amazonia*. Gainesville: University Press of Florida.

Schoeninger, M. J., van der Merwe, N. J., Moore, K. M., Lee-Thorp, J. A., and Larsen, C. S. (1990) Decrease in diet quality between the prehistoric and contact periods. In C. S. Larsen, ed. *The Archaeology of Mission Santa Catalina de Guale: 2. Biocultural Interpretations of a Population in Transition*. Anthropological Papers of the American Museum of Natural History, no. 68, pp. 78–93.

Schultz, M., and Larsen, C. S. (n.d.) Deficiency diseases and infection in La Florida: histopathological cranial evidence. In C. S. Larsen, ed. *Bioarchaeology of La Florida*. Gainesville: University Press of Florida, forthcoming.

Simpson, S. W. (n.d.) Patterns of growth perturbation in La Florida: evidence from enamel microstructure. In C. S. Larsen, ed. *Bioarchaeology of La Florida*. Gainesville: University Press of Florida, forthcoming.

Simpson, S. W., Hutchinson, D. L., and Larsen, C. S. (1990) Coping with stress: tooth size, dental defects, and age-at-death. In C. S. Larsen, ed. *The Archaeology of Mission Santa Catalina de Guale: 2. Biocultural Interpretations of a Population in Transition*. Anthropological Papers of the American Museum of Natural History, no. 68, pp. 66–77.

Storey, R. (1986) Diet and health comparisons between pre- and post-Columbian Native Americans in north Florida. Paper presented, American Association of Physical Anthropologists (abstract: *American Journal of Physical Anthropology* 69:268).

Szathmáry, E. J. E. (1994) Non-insulin dependent diabetes among aboriginal North Americans. *Annual Review of Anthropology* 23:457–482.

Teaford, M. F. (1991) Dental microwear: what can it tell us about diet and dental function? In M. A. Kelley and C. S. Larsen, eds. *Advances in Dental Anthropology*. New York: Wiley-Liss, pp. 342–356.

Verano, J. W., and Ubelaker, D. H., eds. (1992) *Disease and Demography in the Americas*. Washington, D. C.: Smithsonian Institution Press.

Worth, J. E. (1995) *The Struggle for the Georgia Coast: An Eighteenth-Century Spanish Retrospective on Guale and Mocama*. Anthropological Papers of the American Museum of Natural History, no. 75.

Wright, L. E. (1990) Stresses of conquest: a study of Wilson bands and enamel hypoplasias in the Maya of Lamanai, Belize. *American Journal of Human Biology* 2:25–35.

Sot-Weed to Sangamo:
Life and Death in
Frontier North America

WE NOW HAVE an emerging picture of the bioarchaeology of European colonization, from the perspective of American Indians. What about the other side of the story: What happened to the health and lifestyles of the *colonists*? In this chapter, we look at the bioarchaeology of a family cemetery dating to the mid-1600s in Chesapeake Bay, Maryland. Analysis of these mostly European-born colonists reveals a great deal of evidence of physiological stress and wear and tear on the skeletons. This study helps us to understand what happened to the lives and lifestyles of both the colonized and the colonizers.

Long before studying colonial-period Europeans or Euroamericans, I had developed some opinions about this matter from my many conversations with my maternal great-grandmother, Marie Brust Clough, while I was a child. Born in the early 1880s in rural central Illinois, she migrated as an infant with her parents to frontier southeastern Nebraska. For most of her juvenile years, her family lived a primitive existence on a remote farm. I was fascinated by her stories of life-threatening storms, the lack of electricity, no modern sanitation, extreme isolation, and the ever-present infectious diseases that claimed the lives and livelihoods of many of their friends, neighbors, and relatives. In the first decade of the twentieth century, she and her husband, Ralph Zachariah Clough, moved to western Nebraska, the last frontier in the state opened

A family and its home, or "soddie," on Nebraska prairie in the late 1800s. The European and Euroamerican settlers in most places of North America had a tough, demanding existence in the early days of colonization. From Nicoll 1967; reproduced with permission of the University of Nebraska Press.

to homesteading by the Kinkaid Act of 1904. As with most of the other "Kinkaiders," the going was rough for the Clough family. Severe drought, poor soils, economic depression, and the death of their infant daughter eventually caused them to abandon their farm and move back to the southeastern part of the state. Similarly, my paternal grandfather, Richard Larsen—the son of Danish emigrant parents and new arrivals to Nebraska—shared his accounts with me about the rigors of life for early settlers on the prairie in the late nineteenth century. His stories made an enormous impression on me—life for these people was tough, in sharp contrast to what I had experienced growing up in the same region of the country during the 1950s and 1960s.

Conditions for earlier emigrants arriving on the Atlantic coast of North America were worse than for my Nebraska forebears and others settling the West in the nineteenth century. For the British colonists arriving in the first wave of settlement in New England

and the mid-Atlantic in the early to middle 1600s, the health burden was excessive. Half of the settlers at Plymouth, Massachusetts, died—mostly from starvation and disease—before the end of the colony's first winter in 1620. By the end of the first year at the Jamestown, Virginia, colony, only 38 of the original 104 settlers were still alive; more than three-quarters of the population—4,800 of 6,000—who arrived at the colony between 1607 and 1625 were not alive after 1625. Starvation and contaminated water were the primary reasons for this staggering mortality, although violence among members of the colony resulted in additional deaths. The situation there was greatly exacerbated by the fact that they happened to have settled in the region during one of the most severe climatological disasters ever. Climate reconstruction based on tree rings and other evidence reveals that the settlement of Jamestown occurred during the driest stretch of time since A.D. 1185.

By any measure, including those stories conveyed to me by my grandparents and great-grandparents, colonization of the western frontier by individuals of Old World ancestry in the eighteenth and nineteenth centuries involved hardship. For the nineteenth century, one has only to visit the numerous pioneer cemeteries between Omaha and Sacramento to understand the hazards of the settling of western North America by Europeans, Euroamericans, African Americans, and Asian Americans. I had often thought that bioarchaeology could be highly informative about the stresses of colonization.

In the late fall of 1991, I got my chance to look at a side of colonization that was virtually unexplored by biological anthropologists. Archaeologist Joseph Craig phoned me to ask if I would consult on the bioarchaeology of a Euroamerican pioneer cemetery, the Cross cemetery, that he was about to excavate near Springfield, Illinois. Recognizing the potential insight that could be gained from a bioarchaeological study of colonization—especially from the point of view of Europeans and Euroamericans—I readily agreed to participate in the project.

In addition to providing a perspective on the health and biology of colonists, the study of the skeletons from this and other historic-era, non-native cemeteries from North America contributes to an ongoing dialogue among economists, historians, and anthropologists about the connection between economic growth and health. Beginning with primary school education, it is drilled into all of us that the United States is a nation of advancement, achievement, and progress, in all respects. We are taught that even before the founding of the republic, life for Americans including our health, longevity, and overall well-being, improved steadily. But, in fact, have health and well-being improved over the last several centuries in the United States, culminating in our present status? Surley, North Americans today are enjoying unprecedented levels of health—we are living longer, healthier lives. But, what do we know about the history of health in North America over the last several centuries, and how can bioarchaeology contribute to this important discussion? In some ways, key aspects of our health have actually declined; increased access to high-caloric food and improved technology are making us a fatter, more sedentary nation. What do we know about the history of activity in North America that might provide insight into labor and caloric expenditure? In other words, were appreciable numbers of our forebears inactive and overweight, like the current generation of Americans? More fundamentally, is it even important that we address these questions about health and activity in the first place?

Yes, it is important to know as much as possible about the record of health and activity of earlier Americans in order to understand our present. The European colonists arriving on the shores of the Atlantic coast of North America beginning in the seventeenth century set the stage for who we are today, at least from the perspective of health. The habits and lifestyles of our forebears have evolved into something wholly new and different today. But our current status was influenced in many ways by decisions and adaptations that developed long before the current generations of Americans were born. Health, then, is an integral component of economic development and overall well-being, and to understand its history is to understand ourselves in a more informed way.

Height and Health

One set of details for delineating past health trends in North America was recorded by various military organizations. Beginning in the middle 1700s, height was often entered into the record as part of a recruit's mustering process. These heights were used primarily for identification purposes, such as to identify deserters, to assess fighting capabilities, to make sure the correct pay was given to the correct soldier, and for later disbursement of pensions. Because the earliest recruits were born beginning in about 1710, we have a continuous record of heights for early eighteenth-century birth cohorts to the present.

Economic historians Dora Costa of the Massachusetts Institute of Technology and Richard Steckel of Ohio State University have analyzed this record of heights of military recruits, especially those who were born in North America. Comparisons of the heights of thousands of these individuals indicate that while health improved for some stretches of time, it declined for others. Costa and Steckel's important study reveals that for military recruits born between the years 1710 and 1830, there were steady increases in height by about an inch or so over the 120-year period. For the remainder of the nineteenth century, however, height dropped by nearly two inches, and then rebounded beginning in about 1900. By the middle of the twentieth century, height increased by about two-and-a-half inches.

The increase in heights of Americans in the twentieth century is due to the huge improvements in medicine, health care, delivery of public sanitation, diet, and all the factors that contribute to one's health. What is curious, though, is the decline in height—and, by inference, health—in the nineteenth century, a period of time when the economy of the United States dramatically improved. Taking into consideration all the factors that contribute to health, there are some good reasons why health declined over the course of much of the later 1800s. Key in this regard is the deterioration in sanitation and increased exposure to infectious diseases as Americans shifted residence from farms to large,

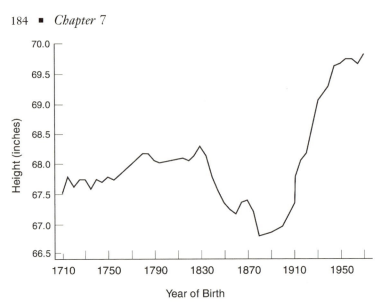

Average adult heights of European-descent, American-born males by birth cohort for the period of 1710 to 1970. Note the marked dip in height beginning after 1830 and continuing through the remainder of the nineteenth century. The decline in heights coincides with the movement of population from rural to urban settings. Unlike life on the farm, sanitation and health conditions in urban locations during the second half of the nineteenth century were poor. The increase in height after 1890 is due to improvements in public sanitation and improved health overall in the American population. Adapted from Costa and Steckel 1997; reproduced with permission of the authors and the University of Chicago Press.

crowded cities. Simply, the declining height of the adult population reflected the declining health of newly urbanized people across the United States.

Bioarchaeology of Colonists

Trends in height have revealed a great deal about the history of American health and well-being. From my perspective as a bioarchaeologist, however, there is much more to be learned about the history of health than from height alone. In doing the background reading for the study of the skeletons from the Illinois site, I learned that, although bioarchaeologists had been involved in the study of human remains from a variety of Euroamerican and other historic-era cemeteries in North America for quite some time, only a handful of the skeletal samples represented the earliest generations following initial colonization. Moreover, while offering important perspectives on health and disease in frontier settings, bioarchaeological studies tended not to follow the same research protocol that we developed for the Illinois cemetery, especially focusing on health, well-being, and physical activity. One important exception was an investigation undertaken by physical anthropologist Douglas Ubelaker, in collaboration with archaeologist Julia King, at the Patuxent Point site, a rural family cemetery from the Chesapeake Bay area of Maryland dating to the middle to late 1600s. Unlike the study of the Illinois skeletons discussed in the next chapter, their study did not include an analysis of stable isotopes of carbon and nitrogen for dietary reconstruction, but virtually all other skeletal parameters were analyzed using most of the same methods and techniques as in our Illinois research. Moreover, like the Illinois setting, an abundant historical and documentary record provides important context for understanding the skeletal biology of stress and adaptation in a frontier environment. Their study, then, offered a comparative context for our work on an Illinois pioneer family living a century and a half later.

This and the next chapter present a bioarchaeology of these two groups of skeletons, the earlier in Maryland and the later in Illinois, each representing the edges of the western American frontier as they stood in the seventeenth (the Atlantic coast) and nineteenth (the Midwest) centuries, respectively. For each setting, we take a look at the historical contexts, the circumstances for colonization, and the archaeological and biocultural contexts for the study of skeletons. We explore the various parameters of health (such as dietary reconstruction, height, iron deficiency, growth disruption, oral health, and infection) and activity (such as osteoarthritis and tooth use) in order to develop a biocultural profile of the people facing the challenges of life on the frontier. The samples of skeletons that I talk about in these chapters are small in comparison to those I have discussed up to this point. The original founding European or Euroamerican populations in these frontier

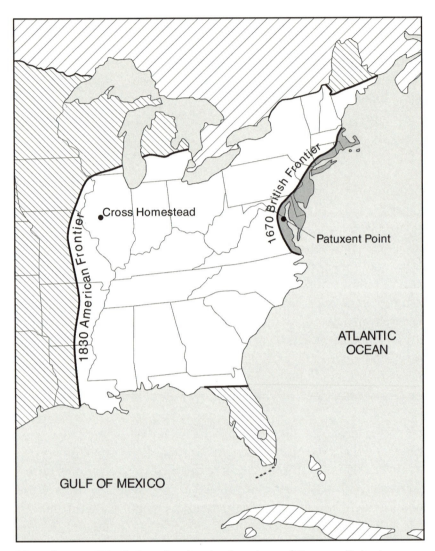

Map of eastern North America showing locations of Patuxent Point in the Chesapeake Bay, Maryland area, and Cross Homestead, Illinois. These settlements are located on the margins of the British and American frontiers as they stood in about 1670 and 1830, respectively.

settings were small, and thus, their numbers that we studied from cemetery contexts are also small. Despite this limitation to population study, we nevertheless stand to gain a lot by the study of these skeletons, especially in relation to the health and activity of individuals and their families.

PATUXENT POINT: SEVENTEENTH-CENTURY CHESAPEAKE BAY

The Historical Setting: Life on the Maryland Frontier

England's first, albeit modest, success in its colonization of North America came in 1607 with the settlement of Jamestown, Virginia, on the western side of Chesapeake Bay. Despite the heavy population losses in the first couple of decades, farms and villages were rapidly established around the shores of the bay in the Virginia and Maryland colonies. Chesapeake Bay, the core of the "tobacco coast" in the middle of the seventeenth century, was a remote frontier, overshadowed by its more successful sister colony to the north in Massachusetts Bay. Compared to the settlements in Boston, Cambridge, and elsewhere in Massachusetts, the Chesapeake Bay colony was a hardship case. Access to resources from England was more sporadic, the population was less literate, the economy was fueled more by family agriculture than by mercantilism, and the environment was less healthy in the Chesapeake Bay than in Massachusetts. In New England, many colonists were able to bring capital with them for construction of significant living quarters. Not so in the Chesapeake Bay area—Chesapeake Bay inhabitants lived in more primitive housing, thereby contributing to poorer health conditions than those of their counterparts in Massachusetts.

Archaeology of a number of colonial-period communities in the Chesapeake Bay region is adding a great deal to what we know about the lives and lifestyles of early European settlers. This record, along with historical documentation, presents a rather bleak picture for the seventeenth-century colonists—life was short and physically demanding. On the other hand, some evidence suggests that the diets of the Maryland colonists may have been better than that of their counterparts in England. Archaeologist Henry Miller has analyzed various colonial estate inventories and archaeological food remains from various places in the Chesapeake Bay region, finding that residents of colonial Maryland consumed large amounts of fish, fowl, and meat. Early in the seventeenth century, colonists depended mostly on locally available foods, such as wild game and native domesticated plants. By mid-century, Euroamericans had shifted their eating patterns to include the European domestic animals—cattle, pigs, and sheep. Food remains found in archaeological sites indicate an apparent diversity of animals eaten by the early colonists, both domestic and wild. Miller speculates that this diversity meant that the diet of colonists was more nutritionally sound than before when foods were more limited.

My reading of the record, however, suggests that the apparent dietary diversity of Marylanders in the 1600s was tempered by the daily focus on corn, which formed an essential foundation of the colonial nutrition. All kinds of foods were eaten, but the typical seventeenth-century family ate one-pot meals with corn as the primary ingredient. Corn was first beaten into flour, then sifted to remove the shell matter. Coarse grains and fine grains were separated. The coarse grains were boiled for more than eight hours into hominy or porridge, a soft mushy substance, and the fine grains were baked into bread, and consumed along with the hominy. As the archaeological evidence indicates, many other foods were eaten in addition to corn, but the importance of corn in the day-to-day diet suggests some significant health risks, including amino acid deficiencies (see chapter 3).

The regular eating of soft, corn-based mushes by the Maryland colonists would also have had negative consequences for oral health, such as promotion of dental caries, gum disease, and premature tooth loss. Processed sugar shipped in from the Caribbean was also available to some households, but this was a highly irregular event, and corn would have played a far more important role in the diet of Chesapeake Bay colonists.

Few people living in the Maryland colony escaped the heavy workloads that were typical of life on the farm. The economy was fueled by tobacco, known locally as "sot-weed," and planting, care, harvesting, and processing of the crop were tedious, back-breaking tasks. In most households, all members—men, women, children, and servants and slaves—shared in the labor that went into the production of tobacco, as well as food grown on the individual farmsteads.

Europeans arriving in Maryland in the early days of settlement were mostly male indentured servants from England. For every woman, there were at least three men in the colony. The lopsided sex ratio was very much influenced by the composition of the immigrant population during the seventeenth century. Planters preferred bringing to North America strong, able-bodied males who could toil for long hours in the tobacco fields. Owing to this disparity between numbers of adult men and women, it was difficult to begin a family; population size was maintained largely by immigration and not by births. A very small minority of colonists came from Africa or the Caribbean as enslaved, indentured, or freed persons. Even a constant flow of colonists to Maryland failed to keep population size up, at least in the beginning—for the period of 1634 to 1681, between 23,500 and 40,000 people came to the Maryland colony, but only about 19,000 were present in 1681.

Regardless of their ethnic or social origins, many colonists died during their first days or months in Maryland, and mortality may have been more than 35 percent to 40 percent in the period that became known as "the seasoning." Life expectancy—the number of years an individual can expect to live, on average—for a young adult male was only about forty to forty-five years, and probably shorter for a young adult female. Mortality for children born in the 1600s in Maryland was about 40 percent to 55 percent, and much of it was due to infantile diarrhea and myriad infectious diseases. In the pre-antibiotic era of seventeenth-century Maryland, recorded disease diagnoses were vague and impressionistic. The terms used to describe various diseases included "agues," "bloody flux," "burning fevers," and "swellings." The agues may represent malaria, and bloody flux or swellings could be dysentery. Colonial physicians frequently recorded a cyclical pattern of chills and fevers in their patients, which is consistent with malaria.

Certainly, the parasites responsible for the infection were abundant in this region. Dysentery and typhoid also affected many people. Although the diseases themselves are not necessarily fatal, the weakening of the immune system could have predisposed people to early death in the absence of a good diet and a healthy environment.

Patuxent Point Bioarchaeology

THE CEMETERY

The study of the skeletons from the Patuxent Point site allows bioarchaeologists to test hypotheses about the health and lifestyle of the early colonists, especially by matching what we learn about the people from their skeletons against the historical or documentary record. A 1987 archaeological survey of a former tobacco field in preparation for development of luxury condominiums on the Patuxent River near Solomons, Maryland, revealed surface evidence of a seventeenth-century farmstead. Follow-up excavation by the Jefferson Patterson Park and Museum, under the direction of Julia King, identified the posthole impressions for the foundation of a house, various habitation features, and a family cemetery containing eighteen graves. Douglas Ubelaker and his associates Erica Bubniak Jones and Abigail Turowski at the Smithsonian Institution studied the skeletal remains from these graves.

The written documentation of the people who lived and died at the Patuxent Point farmstead is sketchy. The few details that are available from land and other records indicate that the property was occupied mostly by families, first in the late 1650s by John Hodgins and his family, followed for a brief time by Captain John Odber, and finally, by an unknown family. The farm was abandoned in the 1680s. Archaeological evidence reveals that the households present during this thirty-year period were economically middling. The people living at the farmstead ate a predominantly British type of diet, consisting of beef, pork, and other staples, but foods native to the region were also consumed, including various wild game and corn.

Sixteen of the eighteen graves were found in two groups; the other two graves were isolated. One grave contained the remains of an adult female and a very young infant, perhaps a stillbirth, bringing the total number of people buried in the cemetery to nineteen. In keeping with the standard Christian practice of the time, the heads of most of the individuals were oriented toward the west. Four children, aged five to thirteen, were buried with their heads to the east, which may indicate some significant aspect of the death and burial of a child in colonial frontier society. Half of the individuals were buried in wooden coffins. Copper-alloy pins and pin fragments in the graves indicate that the deceased were buried in cloth shrouds. The only African-American found in the cemetery (see below), a fifteen- to seventeen-year-old male, had a single copper alloy button in the pelvic area (probably a clothing item) and a white clay tobacco pipe held in his hands. No other individual was buried with grave accompaniments.

ANCESTRY

Because both Europeans and Africans lived in the Chesapeake Bay region during the seventeenth century, Ubelaker and his team needed to determine the ancestry of the Patuxent Point skeletons. Forensic anthropologists have developed both visual and statistical means of determining ancestry of human skeletons. The skulls of Africans and individuals of African ancestry differ in subtle ways from the skulls of Europeans and individuals of European ancestry. In Africans and individuals of African ancestry, the distance between the left and right eye sockets is wider, the nasal aperture is wider and less sharply demarcated on its lower margin, and the projection of the lower face is somewhat greater than in Europeans and individuals of European ancestry. Visual examination and statistical analysis of the Patuxent Point skulls indicate that the fifteen to seventeen-year-old male buried with the clay tobacco pipe was probably the only African (or person of African ancestry), whereas all the others were of European ancestry.

There were no obvious indications that the individuals in the cemetery were drawn from the same gene pool, such as from a family. However, the presence of similar congenital abnormalities of the spine in ten individuals, such as spina bifida and unusually shaped neck vertebrae, indicate the presence of a common biological relationship and shared life experiences for the people buried in the cemetery.

DEMOGRAPHY

Eight juveniles (less than sixteen years of age) and eleven adults were identified by Ubelaker and his coworkers in their analysis of the Patuxent Point skeletons. The age and sex breakdown showed the following composition:

3 infants (≤ 2 years)
5 children (5–14 years)
1 adolescent/young adult male (15–17 years)
4 adult females (24–43 years)
5 adult males (27–45 years)
1 older adult female (55–60 years)

Contrary to the expectation that more adult males than adult females would be found in the cemetery, an equal proportion of adult men and women were identified (six and five, respectively). Excluding the African-American male, the youngest adults are three females in their mid- to late-twenties and early thirties. The average age at death for the entire series is 21.6 years. Adults died at an average age of 32.6 years; females lived about five years more than males (females = 35.6 years; males= 30.9 years).

As calculated from all of the ages at death in the Patuxent Point series, life expectancy was only 21.8 years, meaning that a newborn in this group could expect to live only about twenty-two years at the time of his or her birth. This value is well under what the life expectancy would have been for an upper-class male in England at the time, who could expect to live to about age thirty at the time of birth.

DIETARY RECONSTRUCTION AND NUTRITIONAL INFERENCE

Although stable isotope analysis was not undertaken for the Patuxent Point skeletons by Ubelaker and his team, the historical and archaeological records indicate that the Maryland colonists consumed a variety of wild and domestic game and plants. The historical information for how corn was prepared and its importance as a food strongly suggests that this plant figured prominently in colonial diets. The people living at the site likely had some access to sugar in the form of sugar cane, which was used as a sweetener. However, sugar did not become widely available in North America until the second half of the nineteenth century. Therefore, sugar was probably only infrequently present on the dinner table of these seventeenth-century families.

GROWTH STATUS: HEIGHT

Based on the adult long bone lengths, the average height for Patuxent Point women was 5 feet 3 inches, and the average height for men was 5 feet 7 inches. The female height is greater than that for Londoners for the same time period (5 feet 2 inches), but within the range for other colonial and later Americans. The male height is similar to those of contemporary Londoners and other colonial Americans.

NUTRITIONAL DEPRIVATION: BONE MASS

The long bones of six skeletons are abnormally light, and the foot and vertebral bones of several others are unusually porous. These characteristics are symptoms of osteoporosis, or possibly other circumstances associated with low bone mass. There are two chief causes for these light and porotic bones: nutritional deficiencies and inactivity. Since we know that Maryland colonists worked very hard during their lives—physical labor would tend to make the bones robust—poor nutrition was the likely cause of this low bone mass.

The leg bones of one adult female and an infant are abnormally bowed. The femurs of the female are severely bowed, in a manner that is much like the kind of deformation caused by rickets, a childhood disease caused by vitamin D deficiency. The femurs of the infant are slightly bowed, but the ultimate degree of deformation is unknown because the individual died at such a young age. Rickets, however, may have caused the bowing.

IRON STATUS

The presence of cribra orbitalia in four individuals whose ages range from eight to fourteen years suggests that at least some of the people living at the Patuxent Point farmstead suffered from iron deficiency anemia. The historical records of the region indicate that water was frequently contaminated. If so, the anemia may have been caused by parasitic infection. The lesions were well healed, suggesting that the anemia had occurred much earlier in the lives of these four people.

GROWTH DISRUPTION: ENAMEL DEFECTS

About 20 percent of Patuxent Point teeth display hypoplasias. Most of the teeth with hypoplasias are incisors and canines, which is a pattern that is typical for most humans studied by bioarchaeologists—for largely unknown reasons, front teeth seem to be more susceptible to growth disruption than back teeth. Most of the defects are found in adult women (29 percent) and children (20 percent); only 9 percent of adult males have enamel defects. The defective enamel is most prevalent in the regions of teeth forming at about age three or so. In many societies, young children are weaned from mother's milk at this age. Weaning can potentially introduce some new and unhealthy circumstances to the young child, such as the introduction of corn-based gruel (hominy), which lacks essential nutrients, potentially causing growth disruption.

Assuming that many of the Patuxent Point juveniles were born in North America and the adults were born in England, the high frequency of enamel defects in the children probably reflects the greater stress of living in the New World environments. The greater frequency of enamel defects in adult females than in adult males suggests behavioral and environmental differences between growing girls and boys in England, such as boys having better diets than girls.

DISEASE: DENTAL CARIES AND PERIODONTAL DISEASE

The Patuxent Point people have numerous decayed or otherwise diseased teeth—18 percent of the permanent teeth are carious and 9 percent are missing premortem. Although carious lesions are found on some chewing surfaces of teeth, most of the lesions are located on other surfaces or regions, such as at the base of the tooth crowns or on the tooth roots. Given that corn was such an important dietary staple in the Maryland colony, it seems reasonable to conclude that the poor dental health was due in large part to the consumption of this food, along with a lack of dental hygiene.

Adult females have far more numbers of carious teeth than adult males (30 percent in females versus 16 percent in males). This sex difference indicates that women ate more decay-causing foods—corn and other carbohydrates—than men. Women in colonial Maryland were responsible for all food preparation—they ground the corn into flour, cooked it, and prepared the bread. This strongly suggests that women had much greater access to corn than the men in the community, and hence, their oral health was considerably worse.

Some individuals display abscesses—holes in the bone supporting the teeth that are caused by infection. Most of these abscesses originated from infections that had spread to the bone from carious teeth. At least one adult male developed an abscess from extreme dental wear produced by habitual gripping of a clay pipe in his teeth. The wear was so extreme that it exposed the pulp chamber of a tooth, thereby leading to an infection that spread to the adjacent bone.

Calcified plaque—a substance dentists call calculus or tartar—is present on most teeth. Of 360 teeth observed by Ubelaker and his team of researchers, only six teeth lack calculus deposits.

DISEASE: NONSPECIFIC SKELETAL INFECTION

Only three individuals have bones with infections (periosteal reactions). Two adult males have lower leg bones with very minor swelling. These infections likely originated from minor cuts or abrasions on the lower legs. The third adult, also a male, had widespread infection involving different bones of his skeleton, indicating some kind of systemic disease. Except for this single person, infections that involve bone are a very minor part of the health profile for the Patuxent Point people.

ACTIVITY AND LIFESTYLE: OSTEOARTHRITIS

Most of the Patuxent Point adults have some kind of degenerative condition affecting the joints, especially the characteristic bone spicules on margins of joints that are symptomatic of osteoarthritis. The most severe expression of osteoarthritis is in the adult female in her late fifties. She has extensive lipping on most of her vertebrae and erosion of surfaces of many of her joints. The joint erosion is especially pronounced in that the surfaces are polished (eburnation) due to complete degeneration of cartilage, especially in the articular regions of her hand, wrist, and elbow joints. This pattern of joint disease suggests that her workload during life had been highly demanding, involving excessive use of her back, hands, and arms. Several adult males have Schmorls's nodes, which are pronounced indentations on the top and bottom surfaces of the vertebrae, especially in the lower vertebrae. These depressions develop when the cartilage discs separating the vertebrae rupture due to pressures on the back, such as from heavy lifting and carrying.

The African American male appears to have used his upper body and arms for very heavy work and activity. That is, the areas of the skeleton where primary muscles attach in the shoulder and upper arm are extremely well-developed. In particular, the attachments for the muscles that flex the arms, such as the deltoid muscles, are pronounced, especially on his right side. These features indicate habitual activity involving heavy work, probably over much of his lifetime.

In Ubelaker's extensive research on skeletal modifications associated with habitual activity in populations from throughout the Americas, he has identified an unusual extension on the articular surfaces of toe bones caused by prolonged kneeling. The type of kneeling associated with these features is caused when a person is grinding corn—the toes are bent backward for long periods of time. Close examination of the foot bones in the Patuxent Point skeletons revealed that an adult male and an adult female have these unusual features. Although it is not known what specific behavior caused these features, they do suggest that at least some members of this group engaged in activities involving a work-related habitual posture, for such work as grinding grain.

Overall, the muscle attachment sites on the skeletons of the Patuxent Point people are pronounced, indicating that they had substantial workloads during their lifetimes.

MASTICATORY AND EXTRAMASTICATORY USE OF THE JAWS AND TEETH

The chewing surfaces of the teeth of the Patuxent Point people are quite worn. For the typical adult, by the time he or she reached the mid- to late thirties, the enamel on the teeth is nearly worn through. The front teeth of many of the adults, especially males, are heavily worn. This kind of tooth wear is caused by a person's using his or her front teeth for noneating functions. For example, traditional Eskimos and northern-latitude people use their front teeth for gripping and pulling various kinds of materials and objects, such as animal hides for making clothing. The teeth in these people are worn nearly to the gums in older adults. The wear on the front teeth of the Patuxent Point males is, in fact, very much like the wear that bioarchaeologists see on the front teeth of traditional Eskimos. It is unknown what the colonial Marylanders did with their teeth, but perhaps they used their teeth to hold onto leather straps attached to draft animals during the plowing and tending of crops.

Two adults—one male and one female—display narrow grooves on the chewing surfaces of their front teeth, which could have been caused only by passing some kind of thin, hard material across their teeth. Ubelaker speculates that these grooves resulted from holding needles, pins, or thread with their front teeth. Some of the early settlers in the Maryland and Virginia colonies were motivated to come to North America because of a severe economic depression in England, which caused severe cutbacks in cloth production. These two adults may have been former textile workers forced to immigrate due to loss of employment, because tailors and leatherworkers were in demand in colonial Maryland.

Six of the eleven adults (two of the five females and four of the six males) and the thirteen-year-old display distinctive semicircular wear on the occlusal surfaces of the front teeth caused by habitual gripping of clay tobacco pipes. This kind of pipewear is commonplace in the teeth of colonial-period people living in North America.

SUMMARY OF PATUXENT POINT BIOARCHAEOLOGY

Ubelaker and his coworkers' study of skeletons from the Patuxent Point site adds an entirely new dimension to our understanding of the health and lifestyles of the early colonists living in the Chesapeake Bay region. The historical record indicates that the colonial population was composed of mostly male indentured servants from England, diet was adequate if not nutritious, disease was commonplace, life expectancy was low, and work was oriented around food production for support of the local community, along with tobacco production. The analysis of nineteen skeletons both confirms and contradicts different aspects of the historical

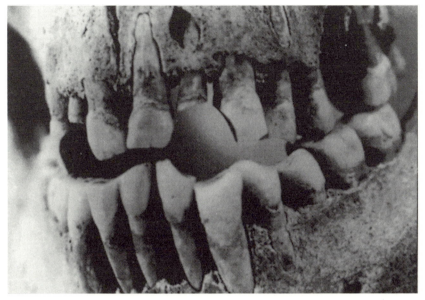

Adult dentition from Patuxent Point, Maryland, showing distinctive tooth wear caused by habitual smoking with clay pipe. The teeth have a semicircular indention in the upper and lower jaws, forming a circular hole when the teeth are in occlusion. The wear is caused by the presence of gritty material in the kaolin a clay used to make the pipe. From King and Ubelaker 1996; reproduced with permission of the authors and the Maryland Historical Trust Press.

record. The fact that the adult sex ratio is nearly even and that all ages are represented in this assemblage of skeletons strongly suggests that they are from a family or families. In some respects, their diet may have been adequate. At least in comparison with adult height in the late twentieth-century U. S. population (males average 5 feet 10 inches and females average 5 feet 5 inches), nutrition was not as good as it is today. Moreover, life expectancy was remarkably low—twenty-two years is considerably lower than in either the middle nineteenth century, when it was around forty years, or in the late twentieth century, when it approached eighty years.

The heavy dependence on corn, possibly in combination with periodic food shortages, may explain the presence of low bone mass and bone deformations due to deficiency diseases. The presence of cribra orbitalia in four of the individuals is significant, suggesting bouts with iron deficiency. Growth disruption is clearly indicated by the presence of enamel hypoplasias, severe enough to affect enamel development in one-fifth of the population. Although bone infection was not a problem for these colonists, their oral health was abysmal. A person today eating the foods eaten by colonial-era Marylanders would be struck by how gritty and rough-textured these foods were. Although the hominy was a soft mush, it likely contained abrasives, resulting in significant wear of teeth.

One of the most important findings to come out of the study of the Patuxent Point skeletons is the clear dichotomy in oral health (dental caries) and physiological disruption (enamel defects) between adult men and women. The difference in health may reflect different living conditions in women and men earlier in England and later in Maryland. Whatever the origin, the difference in the frequency of caries and enamel defects points to poorer health in women than in men in the colonial Chesapeake Bay area. Although women and men had some differences in health, both sexes experienced highly demanding work environments, as is indicated by the presence of osteoarthritis and degenerative joint disease in both sexes.

Both males and females and at least one juvenile living at Patuxent Point were habitual tobacco users, resulting in the characteristic pipewear on their front teeth. The presence of heavier wear on the front teeth of males but not females indicates that males used their teeth in some kind of extramasticatory, noneating function, probably related to the day-to-day work environment.

The bioarchaeology of some of the earliest Euroamerican colonists in North America makes clear that life for these people was demanding, in every possible way. In the next chapter, we will continue the story by looking at the bioarchaeology of colonization in later Euroamericans—the descendants of people who had earlier settled in places like Patuxent Point and were settling the American Midwest in the early and middle nineteenth century.

REFERENCES

Carr, L. G., Menard, R. R., and Walsh, L. S. (1991) *Robert Cole's World: Agriculture and Society in Early Maryland.* Chapel Hill: University of North Carolina Press.

Carr, L. G., Morgan, P. D., and Russo, J. B., eds. (1988) *Colonial Chesapeake Society.* Chapel Hill: University of North Carolina Press.

Costa, D. L., and Steckel, R. H. (1997) Long-term trends in health, welfare, and economic growth in the United States. In R. H. Steckel and R. Floud, eds. *Health and Welfare during Industrialization.* Chicago: University of Chicago Press, pp. 47–89.

Craig, J., and Larsen, C. S. (1993) *Life and Death on the Illinois Prairie: Archaeological and Osteological Investigations at the Cross Cemetery, Springfield, Illinois.* Springfield, Illinois: Hanson Engineers Inc.

Earle, C. V. (1979) Environment, disease, and mortality in early Virginia. In T. W. Tate and D. L. Ammerman, eds. *The Chesapeake in the Seventeenth Century: Essays on Anglo-American Society.* New York: W. W. Norton.

Faragher, J. M. (1986) *Sugar Creek: Life on the Illinois Prairie.* New Haven, Connecticut: Yale University Press.

Grauer, A. L., ed. (1995) *Bodies of Evidence: Reconstructing History through Skeletal Analysis.* New York: Wiley-Liss.

Hayflick, L. (1994) *How and Why We Age.* New York: Ballantine Books.

Hill, J. O., and Peters, J. C. (1998) Environmental contributions to the obesity epidemic. *Science* 280:1371–1374.

Jenkinson, B. L., Handler, A. B., and Lerner, W. (1949) *Historic Statistics of the United States, 1789–1945: A Supplement to the Statistical Abstract of the United States.* Washington, D. C.: U.S. Government Printing Office.

King, J. A., and Ubelaker, D. H. (1996) *Living and Dying on the 17th Century Patuxent Frontier.* Crownsville, Maryland: Maryland Historical Trust Press.

Komlos, J., ed. (1994) *Stature, Living Standards, and Economic Development: Essays in Anthropometric History.* Chicago: University of Chicago Press.

Larsen, C. S. (1997) *Bioarchaeology: Interpreting Behavior from the Human Skeleton.* Cambridge: Cambridge University Press.

Larsen, C. S., Craig, J., Sering, L. E., Schoeninger, M. J., Russell, K. F., Hutchinson, D. L., and Williamson, M. A. (1995) Cross homestead: life and death on the Midwestern frontier. In A. L. Grauer, ed. *Bodies of Evidence: Reconstructing History through Skeletal Analysis.* New York: Wiley-Liss, pp. 139–159.

Michaelsen, K. K. (1997) *Danes on the Prairie.* Odense, Denmark: Odense University Press.

Miller, H. M. (1988) An archaeological perspective on the evolution of diet in the colonial Chesapeake, 1620–1745. In L. G. Carr, P. D. Morgan, and J. B. Russo, eds. *Colonial Chesapeake Society.* Chapel Hill: University of North Carolina Press, pp. 176–199.

Murphy, C. (1998) Jamestown Revisited. *Preservation* 50(4):40–51.

National Center for Health Statistics (1992) Washington, D. C.

Stahle, D. W., Cleaveland, M. K., Blanton, D. B., Therrell, M. D., and Gay, D. A. (1998) The lost colony and Jamestown droughts. *Science* 280: 564–567.

Steegmann, A. T., Jr. (1986) Skeletal stature compared to archival stature in mid-eighteenth century America: Ft. William Henry. *American Journal of Physical Anthropology* 71:431–435.

———. (1991) Stature in an early mid-19th century poorhouse population: Highland Park, Rochester, New York. *American Journal of Physical Anthropology* 85:261–268.

On to Sangamo Country:
Colonizing the Midwest

THE PHENOMENAL expansion of Euroamericans from the Atlantic seaboard westward after the American Revolution, and especially in the nineteenth century, resulted in new life experiences for millions of people. In this chapter, we will look at lives and lifestyles of nineteenth century pioneers who settled in what would become the state of Illinois. The bioarchaeology of a group of skeletons representing the Cross family indicates that things did not get any easier during this expansion period of the United States.

CROSS HOMESTEAD: NINETEENTH-CENTURY ILLINOIS

The Historical Setting: Life on the Western Frontier

Soon after the War of 1812 ended, the American government proceeded apace with westward territorial expansion. As a result, Indians were forced to leave their homelands in the region of North America known then as the "Old Northwest." Some Indian groups stayed on the eastern side of the Mississippi River, but many others moved across the river and westward to the so-called protected lands in Iowa, Missouri, and elsewhere. The newly opened region for Euroamerican colonization, known today as the Midwest, covered a vast amount of terrain, including the present-day states of Ohio, Michigan, Indiana, and Illinois. Thousands of Americans began claiming agricultural land for settlement and cultivation. "Sangamo country" in central Illinois was such an area. Beginning in the early 1820s, settlers from Kentucky and Tennessee crossed the Ohio River into the region in droves. By mid-century, colonization was nearly complete—just about all available land was claimed by families seeking a better life and new economic opportunities.

These American settlers in the Illinois territory represented a diversity of economic, social, and political backgrounds. Despite having come from all manners of life experiences, the newcomers shared similar living circumstances once they arrived in the region. Historical records suggest that this period of colonization was not much different from the colonial period in the seventeenth and early eighteenth centuries. For example, most pre-1850 labor was still farm-based, and the farming technology and material culture were essentially the same as they were in the 1600s and 1700s on the Atlantic coast. Farmers and their families living in the early 1800s had to travel over long distances in order to seek goods and services not available in the immediate area, and they were exposed to a variety of hazardous conditions, such as food shortages, natural disasters, disease, and lack of health care. In other words, factors affecting health in rural Illinois in the early nineteenth century were remarkably similar to those discussed in the preceding chapter.

Like the Maryland setting, virtually all of our knowledge about the people colonizing central Illinois is based on historical and archival sources. These sources provide marvelous information about the health, lives, and lifestyles of early settlers in Illinois. However, bioarchaeology offers a new, fresh perspective about health and activity in the early nineteenth century. For most of the remainder of this chapter, we will look at what has been learned about the people who lived at the Cross homestead, an early nineteenth-century farm located in central Illinois.

In 1876, a detailed history of Sangamon County, the formal territory carved out of part of the original Sangamo country of central Illinois, was published by historian J. C. Power, based in part on his interviews with original settlers and their families, including members of the Cross family. This and other historical and archival sources were studied more than a century later by historian John Mack Faragher while writing his important history of Sugar Creek, an early nineteenth-century community located several miles from the Cross homestead. Both the Power and Faragher sources provide important environmental, social, and cultural contexts from which to interpret health and lifestyles based on our study of the skeletons from the Cross family cemetery.

Survival on the Illinois frontier in the early nineteenth century was made difficult by harsh climate, accidents, disease, starvation, and other negative environmental circumstances. Throughout the 1830s, weather was especially problematic, making agricultural pursuits and food production difficult. The decade opened with what early settlers called the "Winter of the Deep Snow," when three feet of snow fell beginning in December. Many family members died from the combined effects of poor diets and exposure. The simple homes of these early settlers offered little protection from severe storms, tornadoes, harsh cold, oppressive heat, hail, wind, and rain. Many descendants of the first Euroamericans in the area recounted trampling and destruction of fields by farm animals, prairie fires, insect infestation, drowning, disease, and general deprivation.

Childhood infectious diseases, including infantile diarrhea, pneumonia, tuberculosis, and intestinal disorders, caused most deaths in the first half of the nineteenth century. "Brain fever" (typhoid) was common in the summer and fall when flies, the chief carriers of the typhoid bacillus, thrived in pools of raw sewage common to every farmstead. Preston Breckenridge, a new arrival to Sangamo in 1834, observed pools of water and decaying vegetation following an especially wet summer. He remarked that "chills and bilious diseases prevailed to such an extent that in many cases there were not enough well persons to take care of the sick and bury the dead."[1] Breckenridge was probably describing symptoms of malaria and, indeed, endemic malaria was a major health concern, especially as low-lying areas of creek and river valleys were claimed for agricultural fields. These areas were conducive to the breeding of disease-bearing mosquitoes that served as the vector for the malarial parasites. Often referred to as the "pioneer shakes," the disease produced the typical pattern of chills and high cyclical fever. Mortality records for the 1850s indicate that 10 percent of childhood deaths were caused by malaria.

By the early 1830s, Asiatic cholera and its fatal symptoms of severe diarrhea and abdominal pain had struck many farmsteads in central Illinois. Two major outbreaks, the first in 1833–34 and the second in 1849–50, were especially horrific. Illness and death were so widespread during these epidemic years that most families refused to travel to population centers, such as at Springfield, in fear for their lives.

By all accounts, the winter of 1848–49 was one of the most severe on record. That winter, many farmsteads—including the Cross farmstead—experienced life-threatening illnesses. Dr. George Ambrose, a local physician, treated one of the Cross children on several occasions in December 1848. Several months later, Margaret Cross asked the doctor come to the farm to treat her ailing husband, Alvin Cross. The treatment was ineffectual; by March 1, the family patriarch was dead.

The Sangamon County health records for 1850 indicate that many deaths were due to infectious diseases, including cholera (5 percent), typhoid fever (10 percent), pneumonia (11 percent), and tuberculosis (11 percent). A century later, of these infectious diseases, only pneumonia was listed as a cause of death in Sangamon County.

Early settlers wrote in their letters home and in their diaries about the oppressive workloads they experienced during the first years of settlement. Faragher summed up the comments of early settlers: "The commitment of energy took its toll. Men's hands hardened from gripping plow handles, their legs bowed from tramping over the clods turned up by the plowshare; women's hands cracked, bled, and developed corns from the hard water of the family wash, their knees grew knobby from years of kneeling to grind corn or scrub puncheon floors."[2] Dennis Hanks, a cousin of Abraham Lincoln, remarked, "We had to work very hard clearing ground for to keep soul and body together."[3] Reminiscent of life in rural Maryland in the 1600s, all members of the typical rural family were required to put in long hours of hard physical labor.

In addition to bearing and caring for a large number of children, preparing meals, and completing household duties (such as cleaning, mending, and washing), women raised all of the garden produce, such as sweet corn, pumpkins, beans, and potatoes. Women also assisted in the fields. At one farm, for example, both husband and wife participated in plowing; he pushed the plow and she coaxed the oxen to move forward. Horseback riding, long-distance walking, field clearing, and other physically demanding tasks resulted in unrelenting physical labor.

Beginning in the middle of the nineteenth century, birth and death records were systematically recorded across much of the United States. For Sangamon County, birth and death schedules were available for the years 1850 and 1860. These records indicate that the early settlers had remarkably high fertility, combined with staggering levels—at least by today's standards—of maternal, fetal, and infant mortality. Unlike the demographic picture of colonial Maryland, population increased steadily in the early years of frontier Illinois from the combination of immigration and high fertility.

The important contribution of high fertility to population growth in frontier Illinois is underscored by Faragher's demographic analysis for Sangamon County for the year 1830. For the first generation of women living in Sugar Creek, only one in ten had fewer than five children, six in ten women had between six and nine children, and three in ten women raised more than ten children. Margaret Cross bore a total of eleven children; her first child was born in 1823 when she was twenty-one, and her last child was born in 1841 when she was thirty-nine. Her offspring included three sets of twins. Thus, very high mortality was offset by high fertility, leading to a population increase in the region.

The hardships of life on the Illinois frontier are indicated by a variation in age at death of adults according to where they were born. Women born elsewhere before 1800 and who settled and bore most of their children in Kentucky or Tennessee before coming to central Illinois died, on average, at age sixty-seven. In sharp contrast, younger women born between 1800 and 1840, and who spent their childbearing years on the Illinois frontier, died, on average, at age fifty. Similarly, life expectancy for adult males decreased from sixty-one years for those born elsewhere before 1800 to just forty-five years for those born after 1800 in Illinois. Infant mortality records were not kept with any degree of accuracy, but anecdotal evidence suggests that infants died at alarming rates. A local physician remarked in 1840 that "nearly one half of the children born die before reaching 5 years of age, and nearly one half of those deaths are from bowel troubles."[4] For 1850, death records indicate that 45 percent to 50 percent of deaths for Sangamon County were of children less than five years of age.

Cross Homestead Bioarchaeology

THE CEMETERY

During the fall of 1991, workers preparing an area of land for a housing development a few miles outside of Springfield, Illinois, encountered pieces of three gravestones, for Alvin Cross and his two daughters, Lavina Cross Williams and Mary Ann Cross Mitchel. The inscriptions on the gravestones indicated that the three family members had died in the years 1846 (Mary Ann) and 1849 (Lavina and Alvin). Soon after the discovery of the gravestones, archaeologist Joseph Craig of Hanson Engineers, a private contracting firm in Springfield, undertook a geophysical (magnetometer) survey and mechanical stripping of the ground surface in order to locate the graveshafts for the three burials. This work revealed that the markers had been moved from the original locations, and instead of three graves, Craig was now contemplating the excavation of twenty-nine separate interments scattered over about a four-hundred-square-foot area. Illinois law required archaeological investigation, and Craig and his archaeological crew excavated the cemetery in the winter of 1992.

Craig's excavation of the Cross family cemetery provides evidence that burial had taken place over a period of a couple of decades, corresponding with the period of American settlement of Sangamo country. The first owner of the farmstead was a nonresident, Polly Richardson, who leased the property to Alvin Cross, probably in 1829. Alvin Cross was born in 1799 in Kentucky, and migrated first to Tennessee and then to central Illinois, settling on the property in 1829. Most, if not all, of the individuals buried in the cemetery were members of his nuclear or extended family. The two headstones with the dates of 1849 represent the last burials in the Cross cemetery. In October of that year, the property was sold to Josephus Gatton, the Cross family moved from the property, and all surviving family members who died in the second half of the nineteenth century were buried in unknown places.

In all, the remains of eleven adults and eighteen juveniles were found in the cemetery. All adult graves contained partially to completely preserved skeletons; owing to poor preservation, six of the eighteen juvenile graves contained no skeletal remains. The juvenile status of graves without skeletal remains was determined on the basis of the diminutive horizontal dimensions—especially length—of the graveshafts.

As was characteristic of nineteenth-century burials in the United States, the original graveshafts were dug in two stages: First, a rectangular pit was excavated, and second, a secondary crypt fit to the size and shape of the coffin was carefully prepared at the bottom of the pit, with the head end of the coffin directed west. Once the coffin was lowered into the secondary crypt, the graveshaft was then backfilled. With the exception of the three stone markers, most graves were probably marked with simple wooden markers that had long since disappeared by the time the archaeological excavation by Craig's crews was undertaken. Thus, none of the skeletons could be positively identified in regard to assigning a name to a skeleton.

The remains of the coffins and other burial furniture indicate that the burials were extraordinarily simple affairs, which is typical of pre-1860s burial practices in rural North America. The coffins were constructed of locally available wood, and were held together by a minimum of wrought-iron nails; only three coffins had manufactured screws. No other hardware, such as handles, nameplates, or hinges, adorned the coffins. Three individuals—all less than six years of age at death—were not interred in coffins. The burial clothing was extremely simple. A number of individuals had copper alloy stains on some of their skeletal elements, indicating that at least some of the deceased were placed in shrouds prior to their burial. Two adults had trouser and shirt buttons, and an infant had nearly two hundred seed beads that had probably been attached to a burial garment at the time of burial. The very simple graves and the presence of only a few headstones indicate that the Cross family was from a very modest economic and social background, comparable in many ways to the families living at the Patuxent Point site a couple of centuries earlier.

ANCESTRY AND FAMILIAL ASSOCIATION

Our morphological and statistical analysis of the skulls from the Cross cemetery indicates that all individuals are of European ancestry. In particular, all of the adult skulls have flat faces, no lower facial projection, and narrow nasal apertures with sharp margins.

The flat bones of the human skull are separated by a special kind of articular joints called sutures, which are distinctive lines in childhood and early adulthood, but gradually become filled in with bone in later adulthood. These sutures are important, especially during the juvenile years, because they allow growth of the skull. The *metopic suture* separates the frontal bone (the bone forming the forehead) into right and left halves, but unlike the other sutures, this suture is completely gone by the second or third year of life. Thus, a one-year-old will have a well-defined metopic suture, but chances are that a ten-year-old from the same population will lack the suture altogether. The persistence of the metopic suture beyond two or three years is a hereditary trait found in less than 5 percent of people in most human populations around the world.

During the process of recording information from the bones of the Cross cemetery in my lab, my research assistant, Leslie Sering, and I found that one after another of the skulls had a persistent metopic suture. In total, nine skulls out of fourteen (64 percent)

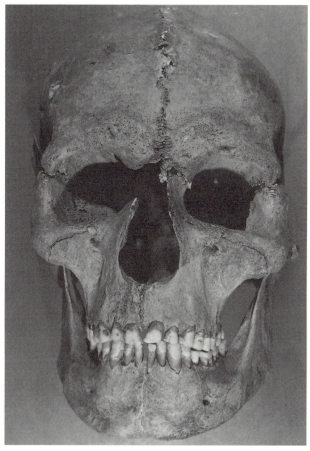

Adult male skull from the Cross cemetery showing the
metopic suture above the nasal opening. This feature is
rarely present in human populations. Its high frequency
in the Cross cemetery indicates a familial relationship for
the people buried there. From Craig and Larsen 1993.

that were complete enough for study have metopic sutures. This
very high frequency indicates a close biological association of the
Cross skeletons, as would be expected in a family group. This is
not to say that all families should necessarily have a high frequency
of metopism; rather, with respect to the Cross family, the gene (or
genes) for the trait was passed from one (or both) parents to their
children.

DEMOGRAPHY

Nearly two-thirds (62.1 percent) of the individuals in the Cross cemetery are juveniles (younger than sixteen years); the remaining individuals are six adult females and five adult males. Our study of the skeletons (and graveshaft dimensions where skeletons were not preserved) revealed the following age and sex composition:

10 infants (≤ 2 years)
7 children (5–14 years)
2 adolescent/young adults (one female and one unknown sex; 15–17 years)
3 young adult females (19–20 years)
2 adult females (both 38 years)
5 adult males (39–50+ years)

The infants make up more than one-third (34.5 percent) of the series, which is consistent with our expectations of very high infant and childhood mortality. The adults fall into two groups, a younger group of four individuals between the ages of sixteen and twenty years and an older group of seven individuals who are all older than thirty-seven years. There are no adults between the ages of twenty-one and thirty-four years. All of the younger adults are females, which may represent deaths due to childbirth. Only two of the older adults are females (both in their late thirties); all other older adults are males. The average age at death in the Cross family is just 14.8 years; the adult average age at death is 32.7 years. The average age for males is a staggering seventeen years greater than the average age for females (males = 42 years; females = 25 years).

Based on our calculations, life expectancy was only 18.4 years. This is extremely low in comparison with contemporary nineteenth-century Americans and later estimates for the twentieth century. The first reliable mortality schedules—for Massachusetts in 1850—indicate that life expectancy was 38.3 and 40.5 years for New England males and females, respectively. By 1900, when data were available for the United States as a whole, life expectancy at birth increased to 46.3 and 48.7 years for males and females. In 1997, the last year for which we have complete data for computing life expectancy, the figure stood at 74.3 years and 79.9 years for Euroamerican ("white") males and females.

Like any cemetery population, the composition of individuals that comprise a death assemblage is influenced by a number of factors, some that can be identified and some that cannot. Under-representation of adults in the Cross family cemetery has likely skewed the profile of death so as to exaggerate juvenile mortality. Although infant and juvenile mortality were likely quite high in this setting, they may not have been as high as would seem by study of these skeletons alone. In this regard, it is probable that most infants and children who died on the Cross farmstead were buried in the family cemetery. However, not all individuals who were reared on the Cross farmstead and who reached adulthood were buried there. In compiling the Sangamon County history, Power identified the fates of all eleven children born to Margaret and Alvin Cross. His interview of the Cross family revealed that only five children were likely to have been buried in the cemetery, including three unnamed infants and two daughters who died at ages twenty and twenty-one, Lavina and Mary Ann, respectively. Other offspring were either buried elsewhere—son Riley Cross, for example, died while serving in the Mexican War and was buried in the Rio Grande River valley in Texas—or were living elsewhere at the time the Sangamon County history was published in 1876.

Because the Cross cemetery was abandoned at the end of 1849, none of the Cross children living beyond that year would have been buried in the family cemetery. Moreover, the much greater average age at death for adult males than for females speaks to the fact that most males and relatively fewer females left the family farm on reaching adulthood. Thus, because the calculation of life expectancy at birth and average age at death is based on age at death for *all* twenty-nine individuals in the Cross cemetery, it is likely that the values of life expectancy and average age at death are artificially depressed, in large part because of the absence of adult offspring of Alvin and Margaret Cross. However, I hasten to point out that even taking into consideration the missing adults in the Cross family cemetery, infant mortality was very likely quite high in this setting.

DIETARY RECONSTRUCTION AND NUTRITIONAL
INFERENCE: ISOTOPE ANALYSIS

Accounts by early settlers indicate that they ate a variety of foods, including various native and domestic animals and plants. Because their accounts show that corn was a dominant food, we included an analysis of stable isotopes of carbon and nitrogen in our study of the Cross skeletons in order to identify just how important this C_4-based food was to the family's diet.

Nearly all Old World plant domesticates used by Euroamericans in North America have C_3 photosynthesis (wheat, barley, oats, and rye). If the Cross family ate corn on a regular basis, then their bone chemistry should reveal relatively high stable carbon isotope values (see chapter 3). In addition, stable isotope ratios of nitrogen provide an important perspective on the consumption of marine and riverine foods, with lower values reflecting terrestrial food consumption and higher values reflecting marine food consumption.

As we expected, the analysis of carbon and nitrogen isotope ratios from the Cross family skeletons at Margaret Schoeninger's lab at the University of Wisconsin revealed an average stable carbon isotope value that was quite high, well within the range for a population consuming C_4 resources (corn). The individual values and their average are similar to those of late prehistoric Indians who were intensive corn agriculturalists in central Illinois (e.g., Dickson Mounds, Schild, and Norris Farms). In addition, the individual values show little variation, as would be expected in a small group—such as a family—routinely eating the same foods, day in and day out, year after year.

The stable nitrogen isotope ratios are also tightly clustered, and they are higher than those usually seen in terrestrial populations from North America. Like fish caught in the ocean, Anne Katzenberg at the University of Calgary has found that freshwater fish in the diet produce high stable nitrogen isotope ratios. These high values at the Cross homestead suggest, then, that a major source of food for this family was freshwater fish. Likely sources of fish would have been streams such as Sugar Creek, located less than a mile from the Cross homestead.

By way of comparison, we took a look at isotope ratios for other contemporary Euroamerican pioneers, from the nineteenth-century Harvie pioneer family cemetery in southern Ontario. The Harvie cemetery is a family burial site, and is similar in size and age composition to the Cross cemetery. The Cross and Harvie families led very similar lifestyles—both were living in remote, rural nineteenth-century settings, with limited access to goods and services; most foods consumed were likely raised on the family farm. As analyzed by Katzenberg, the Harvie stable carbon isotope ratios are considerably lower than the Cross carbon values, indicating that the Harvie family consumed mostly C_3-based foods—wheat, barley, oats, and rye—and very little, if any, C_4-based foods. Corn, then, was completely absent (or nearly so) from the diets of the Harvie family. Katzenberg has also determined stable isotope ratios in the skeletons recovered from the church cemetery from the town of Belleville, Ontario, also dating to the mid-1800s. Her analysis also revealed low stable carbon isotope ratios in the Belleville skeletons, indicating that the people living in the town setting ate very little corn. The Harvie and Belleville carbon isotope values are very different from those of prehistoric Ontario Indians, who have high stable carbon isotope ratios. Unlike the later Euroamerican settlers, the prehistoric Indians had a diet rich in corn.

In contrast to the carbon values, the nitrogen values for the Cross and Harvie families are virtually indistinguishable. Clearly, then, both families ate fish on a regular basis.

The differences among the Cross, Harvie, and Belleville stable carbon isotope values represent contrasting food preferences in nineteenth-century North America—the Ontario diets were dominated by C_3 foods, and the Illinois diets were dominated by C_4 foods. In all likelihood, the Harvie family cultivated corn. Unlike contemporary Euroamericans living in Illinois, however, corn was used exclusively for feeding farm livestock; historical accounts indicate that corn in these British-descent populations was considered food for animals, and not fit for human consumption. The Cross family members, in contrast, were regular consumers of corn—apparently, the food taboos applying to frontier Ontario were not present in frontier Illinois. Probate records for the Cross family indicate that corn was grown for livestock feed; thus, corn consumers in the Illinois setting included both humans and the farm animals under their care. We might speculate that these regional differences in cuisine reflect a Canadian pattern versus an American pattern in the nineteenth century.

GROWTH STATUS: HEIGHT

From the lengths of their limb bones, we estimate the living heights of Cross family adults to be an average 5 feet 9 inches for the men and 5 feet 5 inches for the women. The Cross heights are similar to those of other nineteenth-century rural and urban Euroamerican populations, but are slightly taller than those of the seventeenth-century Maryland group, and somewhat below those of late twentieth-century Americans. By this single measure of relative health status, the Cross family was somewhat better off than the Patuxent Point group, but not as healthy as Americans living today.

NUTRITIONAL DEPRIVATION: BONE MASS

None of the Cross family bones are abnormally light or show any other evidence of low bone mass.

IRON STATUS

Cribra orbitalia is present in two adult females and in two older juveniles in the sample of fourteen skulls from the Cross cemetery. It appears that at least some of the Cross family members suffered from iron deficiency anemia.

GROWTH DISRUPTION: ENAMEL DEFECTS

Enamel hypoplasias are commonplace in the Cross teeth. Ten of the fifteen individuals (66 percent) with teeth have at least one enamel defect. The most commonly affected tooth is the maxillary right permanent canine (54 percent). This high prevalence indicates that a significant proportion of the Cross family experienced stress that was severe enough to produce disruption of enamel development. Because this is a nonspecific stress indicator, it is not possible to identify one cause for the physiological disruption. It is likely that various factors were involved, such as different infectious diseases or episodic malnutrition, or some combination of the two.

DISEASE: DENTAL CARIES AND PERIODONTITIS

The Cross family teeth display a very high frequency of carious lesions—21.7 percent of all permanent (adult) teeth and 19.6 percent of all teeth (permanent and deciduous combined) are decayed in some manner, ranging from tiny pits to complete destruction of entire tooth crowns, down to the tooth roots. Every Cross adult has at least one decayed tooth (two older adult males lost all of their teeth during their lives). Consistent with the high rates of dental caries, the Cross family suffered extensive tooth loss, which was probably due to gum disease (gingivitis and periodontitis); 26 percent of adult teeth were lost during life.

As with any archaeological skeletal series, I can only speculate about the cause of poor oral health in this frontier setting. However, diet was likely a factor—we have identified the heavy use of corn in the diets of the Cross family, which likely contributed to their poor oral health. Corn was probably prepared into hominy, which would have enhanced its cariogenic properties. The Cross family probably had access to refined sugar, but because of the cost of transport to the family farmstead, it was likely consumed on a very infrequent basis. Finally, the members of this family probably practiced little or no oral hygiene, thus contributing to dental disease and tooth loss.

Adult females and males have very different rates of dental caries—35.4 percent of female teeth are carious, whereas only 8.9 percent of male teeth are carious. This sex difference indicates gender variation in dietary practices between women and men, with women consuming more cariogenic foods, and probably on a more frequent basis, than men.

DISEASE: NONSPECIFIC INFECTION

Only three of the Cross adults have bone infections, including a slight periosteal reaction on a left tibia of an adult male and on a left fibula of an adult female. Individual 18, a forty-year-old male, has pronounced swelling of the right lower leg bones, the tibia and fibula. The swelling involving both bones suggests that an infection likely had originated in the soft tissue and spread to the bones of the lower leg. This adult had a difficult life—a number of ribs are fractured and he had extensive osteoarthritis affecting many of the joints of his skeleton (see below).

ACTIVITY AND LIFESTYLE: OSTEOARTHRITIS

The Cross family skeletons display an abundance of osteoarthritis; nearly three-quarters of the adults have some form of articular joint problem caused by heavy wear and tear. The aforementioned individual 18 must have led a demanding lifestyle involving a great deal of mechanical demands on his skeleton. He has arthritic lipping on the joint margins of all his lower back (thoracic and lumbar) vertebrae, the first rib articulation with the sternum (breastbone), and the right wrist/hand (end of the ulna). His right first metacarpal (the bone in the hand located at the base of the thumb) is swollen to twice its normal size, and there is a distinctive groove worn into the articular surface from excessive use of the thumb in some unknown activity. The distribution and severity of osteoarthritis indicate that this adult male did a considerable amount of heavy lifting and physical activity during his life.

Two adult males (including individual 18) have unusually shaped femur heads (the part of the femur that articulates with the pelvis). Normally, the femur head in humans has the shape of a nearly

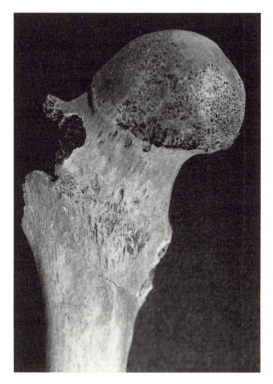

Femur head from an adult male from the Cross cemetery. Note the flat slope on the left side of the femur head. This feature probably reflects activity involving some manner of heavy agricultural labor by this adult male. From Craig and Larsen 1993.

perfect half-sphere. The surface of the half-sphere is smooth, and terminates abruptly where the head joins to the "neck" of the femur. For both individuals, the femur head articular surface continues onto the front of the femur neck. Physical anthropologist Lawrence Angel observed this unusual feature in ancient Greek and other archaeological skeletons, speculating that the articular extension was caused by an unusually large range of motion of the thigh, such as in running or walking downhill. The feature in the two Cross men was likely caused by some form of demanding and frequent activity, such as some kind of farm labor (e.g., plowing). It is unlikely, however, that the feature was caused by walking or running on steeply sloped surfaces, especially since the terrain in central Illinois is extraordinarily flat.

The widespread presence of osteoarthritis and well-developed muscle attachment sites in the skeletons of both adult men and women in the Cross series indicate that the heavy workload in frontier Illinois was shared equally by men and women. These characteristics argue that life in this frontier setting was physically demanding in all respects and for all persons.

MASTICATORY AND NONMASTICATORY USE OF THE JAWS AND TEETH

All of the older adults have very worn teeth. In contrast to the teeth of most living Americans, the presence of severe tooth wear indicates that the foods consumed by the Cross family were highly abrasive.

Distinctive sex differences in tooth wear indicate a variation in how teeth were used by adult women and men in this frontier setting. The front teeth, the incisors and canines, are more worn in males than in females. Moreover, unlike those of the females, the upper incisors and canines of the males tend to be more worn than the lower incisors and canines. This variation in tooth wear suggests that men used their front teeth as a kind of tool, for such tasks as gripping or pulling. There are no historical accounts regarding how early settlers, and men in particular, used their front teeth. My guess is that the tooth wear was caused by work-related activities, such as in gripping the reins of draft animals with the front teeth.

The front teeth of two older adult females and one older adult male are cracked and chipped, which was caused by some type of trauma, such as gripping or processing hard objects. It is possible that gripping a clay pipe between the upper and lower front teeth caused these fractures. However, none of the Cross teeth displays the distinctive semicircular wear pattern that is associated with smoking and the use of a clay pipe, which suggests that the tooth damage was caused by some other type of trauma involving the use of the front teeth in some type of extramasticatory function.

SUMMARY OF CROSS BIOARCHAEOLOGY

The historical record for central Illinois points time and again to the difficult and physically demanding nature of life in this remote nineteenth-century setting. The high frequency of metopism in the Cross skeletons indicates that most of the people shared strong biological (familial) relationships.

The results of our bioarchaeological analysis are fully consistent with the accounts given by early settlers that life on the Illinois frontier was unhealthy and physically demanding. Our analysis of the skeletons indicates that diet was oriented around corn, which contributed to poor oral health and, probably, iron deficiency anemia. By the first half of the nineteenth century, sugar was more readily available to Americans than it had been in previous years. However, sugar was not commonly available until after 1850 in North America, and especially given the remoteness of frontier Illinois, it is unlikely that sugar played any appreciable role in creating conditions conducive to tooth decay. The Cross adults were somewhat shorter than today's Americans, which suggests that their diets were probably not ideal.

Early settlers dealt with a variety of infectious diseases, iron deficiency, and shortened life expectancy. Although mortality was high, especially for infants and children, high fertility contributed to generally large families and population increase. Work was devoted mostly to meeting the immediate dietary needs of the family and to raising crops and livestock for market. Various indicators of mechanical stress reveal that the physical labor that went into crop production and work was arduous. Reflecting the primitive technology, adults in the family—especially men—used their front teeth as tools, probably in activities associated with raising crops and producing food.

Some Comparisons

The men, women, and children who lived and died in Maryland in the 1600s and in Illinois in the 1800s experienced far different lives and lifestyles than do people living in the late twentieth and early twenty-first centuries in mainstream American society. Despite the wide chasm of time separating the Maryland and Illinois groups, the two populations shared remarkably similar living conditions—during their lifetimes, individuals from both settings could expect to suffer trauma and disease, to work excessively hard, and to die young, usually after suffering from an infectious disease. Poor or otherwise marginal diets would have made people from both settings prone to various infectious diseases, thus contributing to a reduction in their lifespans.

In reading Ubelaker and King's compelling study of the skeletons from the Patuxent Point site and simultaneously completing the analysis of the remains from the Cross cemetery, I was struck by the strong similarity in the health and activity profiles of the two groups of skeletons and their living circumstances. This similarity can be summarized as follows: (1) both groups were from poor economic and social backgrounds; (2) both were heavily dependent on corn, used to feed themselves and their livestock; (3) adult heights of both were comparable to those of contemporary populations, but shorter than twentieth-century Americans; (4) both have significant presence of cribra orbitalia (iron deficiency), enamel defects (generalized physiological stress), and horrific oral health (dental caries and tooth loss) due to heavy reliance on cariogenic carbohydrates and living under poor conditions generally; (5) women from both groups have worse dental health than men; (6) both groups have relatively few individuals with skeletal lesions from localized bone infection; (7) both have osteoarthritis and pronounced muscle attachments sites on the bones, reflecting excessive work demands; and (8) males in both groups used their front teeth in extramasticatory functions that were probably related to their rural-based (agricultural) work.

One of the most profound lifestyle changes to occur in recent memory is the growing sedentism of late twentieth-century Americans, resulting in unprecedented levels of obesity. I draw the conclusion from the studies summarized in this chapter that the increasing sedentism and excessive weight gain was not nearly as prevalent in American society then as it is today. In fact, for these rural North Americans, excessive weight gain was likely nonexistent, or nearly so. That is, the physical hardships as reflected in osteoarthritis in the skeletons of the Patuxent Point and Cross families indicate that the high levels of physical activity in combination with a primitive technology simply would not have allowed the levels of weight gain that we see in Americans today. Clearly, the circumstances that promote overweight were not present for most of our nineteenth-century (and earlier) predecessors.

There are some important differences between the Maryland and Illinois skeletons. First, the heights of the Illinois settlers are somewhat greater than those of the Maryland settlers. Because the sample sizes are limited in both settings, I cannot draw firm conclusions regarding the significance of differences in heights between the two series. However, the adult male heights for the respective samples are squarely within the summary values presented by Costa and Steckel in their analysis of changes in heights of military recruits for the period of the early 1700s to the 1830s. Thus, their heights may be typical for the time they were living in.

Second, the Cross skeletons do not display the indications of bone loss and deformation—both of which are probably related to suboptimal nutrition—that Ubelaker and his collaborators identified in the earlier Patuxent Point skeletons. Thus, all else considered, nutritional deficiencies may have been worse in the Chesapeake Bay than later in central Illinois, which is also suggested by the shorter male and female heights in the earlier sample.

Third, the Patuxent Point skeletons lack the distinctive femur head articular extensions found in the Cross skeletons. This difference reflects the different regional cultures and behavioral patterns, especially with respect to specific activities that are associated with agricultural production. Unlike the Patuxent Point males, the Cross males were involved in some kind of habitual behavior resulting in distinctive skeletal morphological changes. Perhaps this difference is related to the fact that the Maryland people focused on tobacco production, and the Illinois people focused mostly on subsistence farming and grain production.

Finally, the Maryland colonists have a distinctive tooth wear caused by smoking clay pipes; this tooth wear pattern is absent in the later Illinois pioneers. This difference also reflects regional and local distinctions between cultures and their associated behaviors. Based on the bioarchaeological analysis of their teeth, it is unclear whether or not the Cross family smoked tobacco on a regular basis, but if so, they do not appear to have used clay pipes. This unusual wear pattern, however, indicates that members of the people who lived at the Patuxent Point farmstead certainly did so.

OTHER HISTORIC POPULATIONS

The health and activity patterns seen in the Maryland and Illinois skeletons are also present in other frontier Euroamerican skeletons, including those found in eighteenth-century Connecticut and nineteenth-century Ontario and Texas. Most of these samples express high juvenile mortality and elevated prevalence of enamel defects, caries, and osteoarthritis. Moreover, the demographic composition—especially in regard to the high number of juveniles—is similar between these other localities and the Maryland and Illinois groups. For example, like the Cross cemetery, the eighteenth-century Walton family cemetery near Griswold, Connecticut, contains a large number of juveniles (50 percent) and mature adults, individuals exceeding forty years (24 percent). Only a few of the Walton adults were between sixteen and forty years of age at the time of their deaths. In their study of the Walton skeletons, physical anthropologist Paul Sledzik and his collaborators suggested that the high frequency of juveniles reflects the "hardships of survival in colonial New England" and the low frequency of young and middle-aged adults "is probably a result of developed immunities and stronger resistance to disease."[5]

In light of the historical and bioarchaeological evidence presented in this chapter, I am inclined to agree with their assessment regarding the hardships of life—and negative consequences for lifespan—in colonial-era New England. However, my experience with the study of the Cross skeletons, especially in light of the fact that individuals surviving to maturity did not end up in the family cemetery when they died, suggests that factors limiting the presence of younger adults were similar in the Cross and Walton cemeteries. As with the Cross family, once an individual reached adulthood in the Walton household, he or she would have likely moved away from the natal residence, and, therefore, would not have been included in the family cemetery. It is certainly the case that health was less than optimal in the Connecticut setting. But rather than representing a situation in which the adults developed their immune systems, I believe that the underrepresentation of young adults in the Walton death assemblage—and presumably in many other cemeteries of this kind—is due to these individuals' having moved away from the family home once they reached adulthood.

The lopsided prevalence of dental caries in the adults, with men having far fewer carious lesions than women, is also present in the Walton series and in the Harvie and Belleville historic Euroamerican cemeteries in Ontario. These differences reflect the fact that women, the people responsible for food preparation, had greater access to cariogenic carbohydrates, and therefore, they had more diseased teeth.

In conclusion, the study of European and Euroamerican skeletons from frontier settings of North America has a tremendous potential for helping to build a comprehensive perspective of health and activity for the people directly involved in the colonization process and for contributing to the growing understanding of the relationship between economy and health. Before bioarchaeologists studied these skeletons, we knew that pre-twentieth-century Euroamericans lived demanding, unhealthy, and short lives, especially in comparison to what we enjoy today. However, the bioarchaeological record provides a new and arguably more biologically informed perspective on the lives of these people, setting the stage for a better understanding of (and appreciation for) American lives and lifestyles in the twentieth and twenty-first centuries.

NOTES

1. Power 1876, p. 137.
2. Faragher 1986, p. 99.
3. Id.
4. Rawlings 1927, p. 87.
5. Bellantoni et al. 1997, p. 140.

REFERENCES

Angel, J. L. (1964) The reaction area of the femoral neck. *Clinical Orthopaedics* 32:130–142.

Bellantoni, N. F., Sledzik, P. S., and Poirier, D. (1997) Rescue, research, and reburial: Walton family cemetery, Griswold, Connecticut. In D. A. Poirier and N. F. Bellantoni, eds. *In Remembrance: Archaeology and Death.* Westport, Connecticut: Bergin & Garvey, pp. 131–154.

Costa, D. L., and Steckel, R. H. (1997) Long-term trends in health, welfare, and economic growth in the United States. In R. H. Steckel and R. Floud, eds. *Health and Welfare during Industrialization.* Chicago: University of Chicago Press, pp. 47–89.

Craig, J., and Larsen, C. S. (1993) *Life and Death on the Illinois Prairie: Archaeological and Osteological Investigations at the Cross Cemetery, Springfield, Illinois.* Springfield, Illinois: Hanson Engineers Inc.

Faragher, J. M. (1986) *Sugar Creek: Life on the Illinois Prairie.* New Haven, Connecticut: Yale University Press.

Grauer, A. L., ed. (1995) *Bodies of Evidence: Reconstructing History through Skeletal Analysis.* New York: Wiley-Liss.

Hauser, G., and De Stefano, G. F. (1989) *Epigenetic Variants of the Human Skull.* Stuttgart, Germany: E. Schweizerbart'sche Verlagsbuchhandlung (Nägele u. Obermiller).

Hayflick, L. (1994) *How and Why We Age.* New York: Ballantine Books.

Hill, J. O., and Peters, J. C. (1998) Environmental contributions to the obesity epidemic. *Science* 280:1371–1374.

Jenkinson, B. L., Handler, A. B., and Lerner, W. (1949) *Historic Statistics of the United States, 1789–1945: A Supplement to the Statistical Abstract of the United States.* Washington, D. C.: U.S. Government Printing Office.

Katzenberg, M. A. (1991) Stable isotope analysis of remains from the Harvie family. In S. Saunders and R. Lazenby, eds. *The Links that Bind: The Harvie Family Nineteenth Century Burying Ground.* Occasional Papers in Northeastern Archaeology, No. 5. Dundas, Ontario: Copetown Press, pp. 65–69.

Keenleyside, A., and Clark-Wilson, E. (1991) Skeletal pathology. In S. Saunders and R. Lazenby, eds. *The Links that Bind: The Harvie Family Nineteenth Century Burying Ground.* Occasional Papers in Northeastern Archaeology, No. 5. Dundas, Ontario: Copetown Press, pp. 29–40.

King, J. A., and Ubelaker, D. H. (1996) *Living and Dying on the 17th Century Patuxent Frontier.* Crownsville, Maryland: Maryland Historical Trust Press.

Komlos, J., ed. (1994) *Stature, Living Standards, and Economic Development: Essays in Anthropometric History.* Chicago: University of Chicago Press.

Larsen, C. S. (1997) *Bioarchaeology: Interpreting Behavior from the Human Skeleton.* Cambridge: Cambridge University Press.

Larsen, C. S., Craig, J., Sering, L. E., Schoeninger, M. J., Russell, K. F., Hutchinson, D. L., and Williamson, M. A. (1995) Cross homestead: life and death on the Midwestern frontier. In A. L. Grauer, ed. *Bodies of Evidence:*

Reconstructing History through Skeletal Analysis. New York: Wiley-Liss, pp. 139–159.

Michaelsen, K. K. (1997) *Danes on the Prairie.* Odense, Denmark: Odense University Press.

National Center for Health Statistics (1992) Washington, D. C.

Nicoll, B. (1967) *Nebraska: A Pictorial History.* Lincoln: University of Nebraska Press.

Owsley, D. W. (1990) The skeletal biology of North American historical populations. In J. E. Buikstra, ed. *A Life in Science: Papers in Honor of J. Lawrence Angel.* Center for American Archeology, Scientific Papers, no. 6, pp. 171–190.

Power, J. C. (1876) *History of the Early Settlers of Sangamon County, Illinois.* Springfield, Illinois: E. A. Wilson and Company.

Rawlings, I. D. (1927) *The Rise and Fall of Disease in Illinois.* Springfield, Illinois: State Department of Public Health.

Saunders, S., and Lazenby, R. (1991) *The Links that Bind: The Harvie Family Nineteenth Century Burying Ground.* Occasional Papers in Northeastern Archaeology, no. 5. Dundas, Ontario: Copetown Press.

Saunders, S. R., De Vito, C., and Katzenberg, M. A. (1997) Dental caries in nineteenth century upper Canada. *American Journal of Physical Anthropology* 104:71–87.

Steegmann, A. T., Jr. (1986) Skeletal stature compared to archival stature in mid-eighteenth century America: Ft. William Henry. *American Journal of Physical Anthropology* 71:431–435.

———. (1991) Stature in an early mid-19th century poorhouse population: Highland Park, Rochester, New York. *American Journal of Physical Anthropology* 85:261–268.

Winchell, F., Rose, J. C., and Moir, R. W. (1995) Health and hard times: a case study from the middle to late nineteenth century in eastern Texas. In A. L. Grauer, ed. *Bodies of Evidence: Reconstructing History through Skeletal Analysis.* New York: Wiley-Liss, pp. 161–172.

Wood, J. W., Milner, G. R., Harpending, H. C., and Weiss, K. M. (1992) The osteological paradox: problems in inferring prehistoric health from skeletal samples. *Current Anthropology* 33:343–358.

Wright, R. O. (1997) *Life and Death in the United States: Statistics on Life Expectancies, Diseases and Death Rates for the Twentieth Century.* Jefferson, North Carolina: McFarland & Co.

Life's Transitions:
The Bioarchaeological Past

To MANY, ancient bones and teeth are dry, lifeless objects, suitable mainly as curiosities for exhibition in natural history museums. Ancient bones are indeed dry and lifeless. In life, the skeleton—its composition, size and form, and physical appearance—is influenced by a wide variety of environmental factors. Therefore, what makes old bones and teeth so important is the information they provide about the living person they represent, from the time well before the person was born through the years of adulthood. In this final chapter, we reflect back and take a look at what we have learned from the study of skeletons found in archaeological settings.

In the last ten thousand years, for many areas of our planet, human populations made a fundamental change in the foods they ate, going from a focus on exclusively wild plants and animals to domesticated plants and animals. The adoption of agriculture had an enormous impact on humans, especially on our quality of life and on workload and activity. The shift from foraging to farming occasioned a reduction in nutrition. Just about everywhere the transition occurred—and here, we are talking about vast tracts of Europe, Asia, Africa, and the Americas—the range of foods eaten decreased, going from a variety of wild plants and animals to a narrower range of domesticated foods. It would be inaccurate to say that this narrowing of dietary breadth characterized all human populations that made the change from foraging to farming, but it certainly was the case for many.

What is so bad about eating a narrow range of foods versus a wide range of foods? Any nutrition scientist will tell you that less variety can be harmful to one's health, especially if the foods eaten do not draw from the major food groups. Moreover, domesticated plants almost always have some negative characteristics, such as lacking key amino acids that the body requires for normal growth and development. As a result of declining nutritional quality, pre-historic populations show height reduction and other evidence of nutritional stress.

The adoption of farming almost always brought about a change in settlement and population size. As people made the shift to lifestyles involving the care of crops, they settled down into semi-permanent or permanent communities, they became less mobile, and their fertility increased, leading to population growth. In the long run, these conditions led to all manners of negative living circumstances, especially poor sanitation. Whenever and wherever people settle into one place, they live on top of their garbage and other waste. Imagine what life would be like in a major town or city if there were no sanitation or disposal of human waste: The smell would be unbearable, but more importantly, the pathogenic microorganisms bred in these settings would cause the rise and spread of chronic infections, like parasitism. Thus, it comes as no surprise that people in the past who lived in large, settled communities had more periosteal reactions than their ancestors did.

The change in diet had a significant impact on the shape and appearance of our skulls. As a result of eating softer, processed foods, skulls have become generally shorter and rounder. More importantly, the amount of bone in the area of the jaws that holds our teeth in place is reduced. Our chewing muscles have become smaller and smaller over the last ten thousand years. Consistent with Wolff's Law—which states that bone tissue is placed where it is needed and taken away where it is not—we see a reduction in the size of the bone supporting the teeth. With less room in the mouth for the teeth, our dentition has become maloccluded, impacted, and crowded. This change has important implications for our dental health. Not only is it more difficult to chew food when a person has crowded teeth, but it also creates places in the dentition where caries-causing bacteria accumulate.

The change from food collecting to food production had a major impact on our skeletal and body structures. For most areas of the globe where the biological indicators of physical activity and workload have been studied—either osteoarthritis or bone structure, or both—bioarchaeologists have been able to identify different levels and types of labor-associated behavior. Analysis of physical activity from ancient bones suggests that behavior (and its impression on the skeleton) is largely controlled by local factors. That is to say, in some settings, it is clear that workload increased, and in others, it declined. For example, Patricia Bridges showed that in one area of the American Southeast (Alabama), prehistoric farmers worked harder than did their foraging predecessors. This contrasts with the region of the Southeast that I have studied. In prehistoric people living on the Atlantic coast of Georgia and Florida, Chris Ruff and I found a decline in workload with the transition from a lifeway based on foraging to one based on farming. Based on our analysis of mobility from study of the cross sections of femurs, it appears that the mobility of people—and long-distance movement—decreased.

The general pattern of decrease in health globally with the shift from foraging to farming runs counter to the long-held perception that the Agricultural Revolution resulted in all things good for humanity. To most, "civilization" is synonymous with advancement, achievement, and progress of humanity. If increasing social complexity and technology are markers of advancement and progress, then we as a species are indeed further along than we were ten thousand years ago, before the invention of agriculture. However, the growing evidence based on bioarchaeology indicates that our health did not advance—quite the opposite.

Clearly, these transitions taking place in the last ten thousand years of human history have not (so far as we can tell, anyway) impinged on the ability of our species to reproduce. After all, human population size—an important measure of biological "success"—has increased enormously since the time that people first became dependent on agriculture. For much of our evolution, our planet's population size was under one million, and may have reached several millions by ten thousand years ago. Today, the population of our species is six *billion*.

As the human population increased and diet changed in such dramatic ways beginning in the early Holocene epoch, our genetic constitution has remained essentially the same as it was long before the transition from foraging to farming. Abundant evidence indicates that our bodies have simply not adapted to the focus on the grain diets that have become so prevalent around the world. The phenomenal increase in consumption of high-fat food in the present century in industrialized nations is especially problematic. Moreover, the environmental costs for increased population growth, especially in the major urban centers around the world, are large and growing larger. In the long run, the mismatch between our genetic constitution and dietary practices, along with the decline in the environment, cannot be beneficial for human beings. Yet, without agriculture, it is doubtful that humans would have developed the complex societies and technological innovations that we enjoy today. As characterized by nutritionist Loren Cordain, agriculture, and grain agriculture in particular, is "humanity's double-edged sword."[1]

If the transition from foraging to farming had so much negative baggage attached to it, why did humans make the shift and adopt this new lifeway? What are the factors that would have facilitated the transition from foraging to farming? Despite years of trying, archaeologists have been unable to provide a definitive answer as to why people became agriculturalists.[2] Some authorities take the viewpoint that perhaps early hunter-gatherers were somehow forced to change the manner in which food was acquired due to external pressures, such as population increases. With the increasing numbers of mouths to feed in the early Holocene, people simply may have had to figure out a way of producing more food; perhaps agriculture was the answer. Alternatively, agriculture may have been a "natural" outcome of changing climates after the Ice Age. People may have recognized the nutritional value of the wild ancestors of plants that thrived in the new climatic conditions—wheat and barley in the Middle East, rice in central China, and corn in North America—and with a bit of tinkering, humans developed the ability to control the lifecycles of these plants by planting the seeds and harvesting the crops.

It is becoming increasingly clear that these universal explanations for the origins and spread of plant and animal domestication are not especially good arguments, because they do not take into account all factors involved in all places and at all times. Domestication of one kind or another—mostly relating to plants—was independently invented in no fewer than seven places worldwide, and each of these settings is different in important ways. The domestication of rice in China, for example, involved very different environmental and cultural circumstances than the domestication of wheat and barley in the Middle East or corn in Mexico. Because of the differences in local circumstances and the realization that regional historical developments had a large role to play in the origins of domestication for each of these seven settings, archaeologists are beginning to focus on the factors unique to each region where the change occurred.

There are likely some factors common to different areas of the globe where agriculture was adopted, such as the availability of water; without ready access to water, there would be no agriculture. Moreover, agriculture provided a means for extracting more calories per unit area of ground than most forms of hunting and gathering.[3] It may be the case, then, that human population size in many of these settings simply increased to the point where humans needed some new way to feed more people. Moreover, the rapid adoption of a plant domesticate from somewhere else may be due to factors relating to population needs at a given point in history. For example, the adoption of corn by prehistoric people in the Georgia Bight may have been occasioned by the additional food needs of a growing population in the region.

Archaeologist Bruce Smith of the Smithsonian Institution argues that the underlying motivation that led people to domesticate plants and animals is part of a suite of behaviors employed by prehistoric foragers to increase the economic contribution and the overall reliability of wild species of plants and animals in areas of the world that were already relatively rich in natural resources.

The regions and their habitats where agriculture first arose were not marginal—they were relatively rich zones where the resource productivity could be introduced through manipulations eventually leading to domestication and full-blown farming.

Smith suggests that by increasing the reliability of the wild species through their domestication, the long-term risk of failure (increased numbers of deaths by starvation is one indication of failure) on the part of the humans eating these species is reduced. Thus, the invention of agriculture by some and the later adoption of it by others represent a kind of risk management strategy that has helped to promulgate our species over the last ten thousand years. The risk of death and population collapse may have been reduced by this wholly new adaptive strategy, but in this book I have argued that humans have paid a price for the change from hunting and gathering to agriculture, especially involving increased health burdens and, at least in some settings, more work.

The adoption of agriculture set the stage for important developments in world history, especially in laying the basic groundwork for modern patterns of health and disease. It also laid the economic foundation for the spread of people from Europe to far-off places around the globe. Europeans who colonized the New World were mostly agricultural, as were many of the people they encountered. Population size and demographic pressure are at the crux of why Europeans began to explore and colonize vast tracts of the Western Hemisphere. In the short run, European states were motivated by the economic advantages—real or perceived—of colonizing the New World. But, ultimately, the population increases and the terrific burdens placed on local and regional economies in premodern Europe provided the chief incentive for the movement of literally millions of Europeans from the Old World to the New World during the sixteenth, through the nineteenth, and into the twentieth centuries. One has only to look at the decline in the Mexican economy in the late twentieth century and the resulting migration of thousands to the United States to appreciate the picture unfolding in the last few centuries. New economic opportunities are a powerful driving force for migration, whatever the cost at the other end of the migration.

As Europeans arrived on the shores of the North American and South American Atlantic coasts, why didn't native groups simply flee the oncoming invasions? In fact, many did. And, if they didn't flee, they were physically forced to leave. This physical displacement was especially characteristic of British and American strategies for colonization, more so than the Spanish strategy. The British colonists, and later the Americans living in North America, wanted the land that was occupied by native populations, and the governments did all they could to claim these lands. Spain, however, viewed the Indians as their protective charges, and the mission systems in Florida, California, and other regions of New Spain clearly illustrate the strategy of colonization by direct exploitation, rather than displacement, of native people.

Bioarchaeology in Spanish Florida and elsewhere has greatly expanded our understanding of the biological impact of colonization on native peoples. The perspective on contact, and especially the biological consequences of European and Indian interactions, has shifted from the singular focus on reduction in population size and epidemic disease to a wider consideration of the context for change in native health and lifeways. Study of skeletal remains provides us with much-needed information about diet, settlement, disease, and lifestyles that are simply not available from historic written records. In Spanish Florida, for example, my bioarchaeological research team has documented evidence of increasing physiological stress, disease, iron deficiency, and other health changes that point to the complex array of factors that contributed to population decline. European-introduced epidemic disease wreaked havoc on the health of Native Americans, resulting in the deaths of many. However, equally important are the other factors that contributed to biological disruption.

The biology of the contact period is not simply a story of population decline and collapse. The biomechanical analysis of the long bones of pre- and postcontact skeletons shows that in some important ways, native peoples adapted to new and challenging circumstances. Historical records make clear that the Spanish practice of labor draft (*repartimiento*) was highly exploitive. The bioarchaeological record allows us to look at the physical manifestations of this practice—the skeletons of native peoples show the full impact of an increasing workload.

The colonists arriving in the New World faced new challenges and many health risks. Historical records tell us of the hundreds of colonists who died soon after arriving in places like Massachusetts Bay and Jamestown. Bioarchaeology of the skeletons of early colonists in the Middle Atlantic region shows, in clear detail, the health burden of colonization on the colonizers. Based on the findings by Doug Ubelaker and his team, the dental and general health of Europeans who first settled at Patuxent Point, Maryland, was grim. Our study of skeletons from central Illinois dating a couple of centuries later shows equally poor health. Basically, life on the frontier exacted a toll on Europeans and Euroamericans who lived in these settings, resulting from poor diets, poor health, and excessive workloads.

Why is it important to know that human health, activity, and quality of life changed over the last ten thousand years, beginning with the shift from foraging to farming, and later, colonial expansion? The reason is simple—an understanding of this past provides us with a context for understanding who we are as human beings and biological organisms in the late twentieth and early twenty-first centuries. Through bioarchaeology and study of ancient skeletons, and viewed in the cultural context and other factors that shape our biology, we stand to gain a more informed understanding of our life experiences and living conditions today. To understand our biology today, we have to understand how it came to be—the past is connected with the present. For example, the numerous dental problems that affect us now got their start back when people began producing food versus earlier times, when they hunted or collected it. Many of the chronic infectious diseases that we still experience today—such as some sexually transmitted diseases—got their start when people began settling down and living in permanent crowded communities and whose subsistence was drawn from domesticated plants and animals.

The bioarchaeological perspective on the human past gives us new understanding of our complex biology and factors that affect it, including the roles of environmental change, changes in land use, new habitats, new physical behaviors, and new foods. Human skeletons provide a unique perspective on the history of our species. We have much to learn about our past from ancient bones.

Notes

1. Cordain 1999, p. 42.

2. Some excellent overviews of the discussion in archaeology of the transition from foraging to farming are Cowan and Watson 1992, Price and Gebawer 1995, Redding 1988, and Smith 1995.

3. Cohen (1977).

References

Cohen, M. N. (1977) *The Food Crisis in Prehistory*. New Haven. Connecticut: Yale University Press.

Cordain, L. (1999) Cereal grains: humanity's double-edged sword. *World Review of Nutrition and Diet* 84:19–73.

Cowan, C. W., and Watson, P. J., eds. (1992) *The Origins of Agriculture: An International Perspective*. Washington, D. C.: Smithsonian Institution Press.

Eaton, S. B., Konner, M., and Shostak, M. (1988) Stone agers in the fast lane: chronic degenerative diseases in evolutionary perspective. *American Journal of Medicine* 84:739–749.

Hill, J. O., and Peters, J. C. (1998) Environmental contributions to the obesity epidemic. *Science* 280:1371–1374.

Price, T. D., and Gebauer, A. B., eds. (1995) *Last Hunters, First Farmers: New Perspectives on the Prehistoric Transition to Agriculture*. Sante Fe, New Mexico: School of American Research Press.

Redding, R.W. (1988) A general explanation of subsistence change: from hunting and gathering to food production. *Journal of Anthropological Archaeology* 7:56–97.

Smith, B. D. (1995) *The Emergence of Agriculture*. New York: Scientific American Library.

INDEX

Abu Hureyra (Syria), 107
active vs. sedentary lifestyle, 108; of
  Americans today, 182; and biomechanical analysis of bones, 48, 55,
  56, 58–59, 89, 108–9 (*see also* biome-
  chanical/beam analysis of bones); and
  carbohydrates/fats, 164–65; of Georgia
  coast people, 88–89, 90–91, 92, 230; of
  Great Basin people, 15, 21, 24, 58–59,
  60; of Hidden Cave populations, 21,
  47–48; and infection, 59, 91, 105–6;
  at lake margins, 15, 21; in later vs.
  earlier prehistoric people, 91; and
  obesity, 170, 171, 222–23; and osteoarthritis, 24, 46, 58, 88, 107, 115; of
  Stillwater people, 47, 55–56. *See also*
  workload
agricultural revolution. *See* farming, shift
  from foraging to
agriculture, 8, 70, 71, 73
AIR (ambient inhalable reservoir), 62n2
Alabama, 109–10
Amazon River Basin, 171–72
ambient inhalable reservoir (AIR), 62n2
Ambrose, George, 206
Amelia Island ossuary (La Florida), 131–
  34, 141
American Great Basin. *See* Great Basin
American oyster *(Crassostrea virginica)*, 74
Anasazi people, 59
Anderson, David, 148
Angel, Lawrence, 68, 219
animal domestication, 6–7, 146, 232
antelope *(Antilocapra americana)*, 36
anthropology, xiin1, 67
Apalachee people (Florida), 122 (illus),
  129, 130, 168

Armelagos, George, 68, 97, 106, 117–
  18n1
Asiatic cholera, 206
Atlantic coast, 65, 66 (illus), 67
Australopithecus, 71
Ayllón, Vásquez de, 128

Baker, Brenda, 106
barium, 149–50
barley, 37, 70, 102, 231–32
Barondess, David, 109, 169
Bass, William M., xi
Battle of Fort Caroline (St. Johns River,
  Florida; 1565), 128
beam theory, 48. *See also* biomechanical/
  beam analysis of bones
beans, 70, 98, 122–23
Belleville cemetery (Ontario), 215, 225
bighorn sheep *(Ovis canadensis nelsoni)*, 36
bioarchaeology, 3, 5, 11n1, 116–17, 126–
  27
biomechanical/beam analysis of bones:
  and activity/mobility, 48, 55, 56, 58–
  59, 89, 108–9; and size, 89; and
  strength, 49 (illus), 50–52, 51 (illus),
  53–54 (illus), 54–55; technology required for, 109
bipedal walking, 112
birth/death records, 207
birth rates. *See* fertility
birth weight, low, 43
blueback herring *(Alosa aestivalis)*, 74
bones: cortical bone, 100–101; damage to
  during excavation, 133; endosteal
  surfaces of, 51 (illus), 51–52, 100;
  environmental influences on, 228;
  facial, fragility of, 133; humerus, 53